THE
SINGLE MAN

The Authorized True Story of the Single Man's Approach to Life, Love and Everything in Between

John Paschal   Mark Louis

Writers Club Press

San Jose New York Lincoln Shanghai

The Single Man
The Authorized True Story of the Single Man's Approach
to Life, Love and Everything in Between

Writers Club Press
an imprint of iUniverse.com, Inc.

For information address:
iUniverse.com, Inc.
620 North 48th Street
Suite 201
Lincoln, NE 68504-3467
www.iuniverse.com

ISBN: 0-595-09939-4

Printed in the United States of America

To our mothers,
who are going to be upset when they read this book

CONTENTS

THE SINGLE MAN

The single man cannot be defined by a single description. To convey precise meaning, the dictionary picture adjoining "single man" would have to be a group photo. It takes all kinds. He may be single in name, but he is plural by definition.

What single men have in common is marital status. Each marks the box that says "not married." Reasons are many but the result is shared. The guy has no wife in his life. It's up to him how to handle it. It is for him to choose the nature of his bachelor lifestyle.

There are, in accordance with humankind's penchant for convenient stereotypes, three basic types of the unmarried man. In each lies elements of both fact and fiction:

1) The Single Man
2) The Single Schmo
3) Mr. Right

The Single Man is that bronzed hunk of manhood on Coors Light commercials, the buff-muffin with muscles like the Alps and shoulders like Kansas, the Chippendale fellow playing Olympic-level beach volleyball—"Nice dig"—with four swimwear models while simultaneously lowering his body-fat content to 1.2 percent. Not only that, he can do the New York Times Sunday Crossword in pen while speed-dialing the Red Cross to see if his donation arrived.

That, at least, is the Single Man archetype.

Cool, smart, funny, carefree but caring, the ideal Single Man is at once a man's man and a ladies man without trying to be either. He has a good job, good friends, a red convertible and a nice butt. He loves his mom and doesn't kick his dog. Sometimes he stays home to read a book.

Most of all, he is a stud. A babe magnet. A Romeo in Juliet. He looks equally good in an Armani suit or a terry-cloth towel, and women love him for it. Rugged but clean-cut, virile yet tender, he is a latter-day Casanova who, with ease and panache, can pitch effective woo to a variety of women. In bed he is strong yet sensitive—cold hard steel and rose petals—a man who knows just where to put it and for how long. Women crave him, and men…well, men would hate the bastard if he weren't so perfectly likable.

That, at least, is the archetype.

In reality there are several variations of the Single Man, none perfect, but each hewing to his own formula for love and sex in the modern world. Some are inclined to date women, others to chase women, others to love women, others to crave women. A common denominator among the various factions is, one could say, women.

Women in great plurality are generally preferred, yet some Single Men opt to go with a single solitary girlfriend. Indeed, some seek a Bondian sampling from the female spice rack, preferring sex and love in a consistent format of exciting premieres, lover after lover after lover. Others are one-woman kind of guys, preferring to know exactly whose toothbrush they're sharing while still remaining well outside the bonds of holy matrimony. And that's OK. In regard to matters of the heart, there is among Single Men a prevailing attitude of whatever floats your boat.

Whatever his modus operandi, the Single Man is—for now and for the foreseeable future—unapologetically single. The Single Man loves being single, hence the title. His bachelor status is a matter of choice, not necessity, for he prefers marriage only as a deferred option. He is not merely killing time until the Wedding March, the point at which life really begins, according to four of five women surveyed.

No, the Single Man is unabashedly and quite happily single, till marriage do him part.

Let it be said, however, that the everyday Single Man seldom measures up to the archetypical Single Man. For that matter, the archetype seldom measures up to the archetype. After commercial filming is finished, the Coors Light guy just might grab his Malibu Barbie doll and head for the hills to play house with a hairstylist named Rex. He might grab a pack of smokes, kick his dog and go steal his mother's Social Security check.

One never knows. Images are the purveyors of deceit, and so are Single Men sometimes. Thus the archetype is merely that: an archetype, a made-for-TV concoction designed to sell brewskis to workaday stiffs who want to be studs but aren't.

Likewise, ordinary Single Men routinely fall far short of the golden image. As run-of-the mill Single Men with imperfections ranging from male pattern baldness to male pattern love handles, we cannot hope to match the Single Man paradigm established by the Coors Light hunk. We cannot pitch woo or serve aces so effectively. In fact, whenever we play beach volleyball, we serve underhanded to women wearing oversized T-shirts. "Nice kill!"

But we play the game anyway, and we play it joyfully and well. We are— as the brochures might say—"singles enthusiasts." We are Single Men. And like that Coors Light buff-muffin, we remain single by choice—although our choices bear little resemblance to his choices. His choices have nicer legs.

Still we keep playing, one point at a time. We dig it.

The Single Schmo is part myth, part stereotype, part reality. Virtually every woman claims to have dated him, and virtually every man claims to have roomed with him. He is the embodiment of all of man's shortcomings. He goes through life joyfully oblivious to everything but the next few moments. He is, for all practical purposes, a Schmo.

That he exists is indisputable. That he alone represents all single men is ludicrous. But it must be said that there is a little Schmo inside us all, at least on the occasional Saturday morning in May. Dude, hand me the sports page and turn up the TV. I'm headin' to the throne.

A guy has to admit: It feels pretty good, if only for a Schmoment.

That said, citizens should remain posted: The Single Schmo is the prototype for men behaving badly. When they made the Schmo, they should have broke the mold. Instead they put the mold in his refrigerator. And there it grows: Schmold.

Pizza-fed and Budweiser-fueled, the Schmo is the real-world character most responsible for society's prevailing stereotype: the single guy as Neanderthal. Earthlings hear the term "single man," they envision a chubby guy watching two football games on separate TVs while wiping Cheez Whiz off his face with his flannel shirt sleeve. And again, the image is not entirely inaccurate, though it should not be applied indiscriminately to all unmarried men.

However odious he may be, the Schmo is out there. It is alive. This short but italicized statement is not based on vague reports of random Schmo sightings, strange dispatches from the kudzu-infested hinterlands of America: "Me and Elmo was sittin' there at the swamp, eatin' some Ding Dongs, when it came from outta nowhere. ...The Schmo."

No, the Schmo is not entirely myth, not at all. We have seen the Schmo. We have been the Schmo. And we will be him again, till bath (or job) do us part.

The Schmo's life is based solely on his own Schmotives. With an aversion to anything remotely productive, he exists on a steady routine of sloth with an occasional shot of torpor. For exercise, he turns his boxers inside out. After catching his breath, he puts them on again. To complete the Schmo Triathlon, he takes a leak. To celebrate, he turns the channel. Rinse and repeat.

The Schmo is a seeker of immediate gratification—as long as gratification is within arm's length. Guided by a warped sense of carpe diem, he is a consumer of easy earthly pleasures, primarily food and drink. It is more like carpe six-pack. His days are Cup-O-Fun, no effort required—just add

Schmo. His reading material consists primarily of a tip sheet and the December Playboy. He likes women, he likes them a lot. He dates them and sometimes has sex with them. He would prefer that they not block the TV.

The Schmo is the man most often referenced by women who hate men. They go out once with the Schmo and they think all men start their car with a screw driver. They think all men take a girl to dinner by driving around the block while the Wolf Brand Chili is reheating in the microwave.

Ding!"Well, here we are."

These women should be advised: We are not the Schmo. Koo-koo-koo-choo.

The Schmo does, however, represent the id of the everyday single man: He giddily follows his basic instinctual drive for all the stuff that makes him feel good—feel good now—even if it means he'll feel like hell tomorrow.

Carpe bean dip.

At some point in his life, virtually every single man has used a similar Shmolosophy to get his jollies. The difference is, the Schmo makes a habit of it.

Mr. Right is the Sasquatch of all single men, a mythic creature whose existence is often discussed but seldom if ever witnessed.

As much as single women seek him, single men loathe him. Why do men hate someone who scarcely exists? For exactly that reason. We, as ordinary single men, are constantly held up to a standard that simply isn't there. To compare us to Mr. Right is to compare us to the Buddha. We are not nearly so virtuous.

We hate Mr. Right. It's not like hating the Tooth Fairy or baa-hum-bugging the Easter Bunny. We hate Mr. Right for all the right reasons. He wreaks havoc on our tiny lives. As a dealer of misery, the man means business. He means mean business. Mr. Right does us wrong.

We're just a bunch of garden-variety bachelors, minding our own bach-elor business, yet somehow we're expected to perform in the likeness of

His Rightness. In all their high hopes, women expect us to follow the paint-by-numbers precedent established by the Reigning Ruler of Right. They expect us to buy flowers, lend a supportive ear, administer a full-body massage, rotate the tires, feed the dog and make love masterfully, all in one day.

In short, we're expected to Be Like Right. And to this we say, "Yeah, right," with all the appropriate sarcasm we can muster. For even on our best behavior, we do not measure up. We cannot measure up. We have not the ways or means to Be Like Right. We did not attend Mr. Right Camp. Nor did we get the instructional video series.

No, we are only ourselves, single men all. This is all we can manage. And evidently, that ain't good enough. Not that we're Mr. Rogers. Or even Mr. Ed.

We're just not Mr. Right. It says so on our birth certificate.

And it will say so on our death certificate, unless women have their way.

If women are right about Mr. Right, the Bible is all wrong: God did not make man in His own image, He made Mr. Right—which means God looks a lot like Brad Pitt, can play "Adagio un poco mosso" on piano, can build a nice fence and can rock an infant to sleep. In all likelihood, God also looks good in Dockers.

For a woman to expect Mr. Right is all wrong. Take it from us: The search for Mr. Right is the same as the search for Ms. Right: It is futile. It's like a man wanting a woman to cook like Julia Child and look like Julia Roberts.

Julia, fetch me some coq au vin, then come sit on my lappy-poo.

We want it, yes. We imagine it. But we do not expect it.

It is conceivable that women—conniving women with horns in their head—spawned the very image of Mr. Right. Just as members of the human race teamed up to create the image of Santa Claus, so might women have conjured a role model for the perfect man, a sort of idealized Stepford Guy. This image they could use as graft for good behavior, a small bribe for a certain tribe—in this case men—to act not naughty but nice. As the image of Kris Kringle creates good boys and good little girls, so does the image of Mr. Right create good little soldiers, men who seek a woman's acceptance by mimicking the ideal.

At least that's the idea. And to some degree it has worked. By creating a premium on chivalry, women have systematically manipulated men into acting nicer than they otherwise would. This is more evidence that, if they so desired, women could rule the planet. They would rule it with an ironed fist.

So in our calculated efforts to win a girl's hand, we do all the Right Things, or at least we try. We open her door, take her coat, pull out her chair, sniff the cork, order escargot and recite a lengthy French poem. We request more bread and summon the violinist to come hither. And for our gallantry we are rewarded with a long kiss goodnight—and, perhaps, an opportunity to do the Sir Walter Raleigh bit again next week. We bow politely, give thanks, and bid her adieu.

Meanwhile, all across America, 3 million other bachelor doofuses are doing the exact same thing, bowing politely and bidding adieu in an effort to make like Mr. Right. From outer space, we probably look very silly, all these Earth Men doing precisely the same thing to impress an Earth Woman. "When," Grog asks Mog, looking down upon the blue planet, "will those silly Earthlings learn?"

Ironically, Grog and Mog are right. This Mr. Right thing is a pox upon potential romance. In creating a template for perfect male behavior, women have screwed themselves. They have undermined the very essence of what makes a guy cool: his congenital gift for being himself. Indeed, it is our own custom-fitted faults and individual foibles that make each of us utterly unique and utterly human, so help us. And it is that imperfection that makes each guy the perfect choice for possible romance. In the words of a corny song, he is a man like no other. And that's why he has a coffee mug with his name on it.

But by extracting behavioral DNA from Mr. Right and creating 3 million nattering little clones, women have essentially sabotaged their one real shot at finding the real Mr. Right. In keeping with the status quo of Mr. Rightdom, a woman will find only reasonable facsimiles—a bunch of Boys From Brazil opening doors, ordering snails, sniffing corks and reciting poems in an effort to win her heart the Right Way.

But can only surmise that they are wrong, that only in forgetting Mr. Right will a woman find him.

These are several basic differences among the three types:

- Mr. Right knows what a woman is feeling without having to ask.
- The Single Man knows what she is feeling, provided she tells him.
- The Single Schmo doesn't give a rat's ass what she is feeling, unless she is feeling him, in which case he can stop feeling himself.
- Mr. Right irons his own shirt.
- The Single Man tosses his shirt in the drier to remove the wrinkles.
- The Single Schmo picks his shirt off the floor and sniffs it, but only at important times such as a wedding or funeral.
- Mr. Right calls his mom every day.
- The Single Man calls his mom. But not every day.
- The Single Schmo calls his mom once a month to ask if it's OK to eat the Hamburger Helper that's been in the refrigerator for the past three weeks.
- Mr. Right knows the number of the florist—by heart.
- The Single Man has been to the florist in the past six months—by golly.
- The Single Schmo remembers that there is a florist. He once spent $17.95 there on a blue-and-white mum, which he later tried to return for a refund—buy low.
- Mr. Right mows your lawn.
- The Single Man knows a kid who mows lawns.
- The Single Schmo mows his lawn when the city threatens action.
- Mr. Right wears starched khakis to the football game.

- The Single Man wears whatever's comfortable to the football game.
- The Single Schmo doesn't care what he wears to the football game, as long as it conceals the flask.
- Mr. Right can hang out with his girlfriend's best friend without making a move on her.
- The Single Man can hang out with a girlfriend's best friend, sometimes more often than the girlfriend might wish.
- The Single Schmo can't hang out with a girl's best friend without making a move on her. He is a Schmo. This is his purpose.
- Mr. Right is sure to call his girlfriend when he's out with the guys.
- The Single Man is sure to check his messages.
- The Single Schmo is sure to call his bookie.
- Mr. Right knows where her G-spot is.
- The Single Man knows where her G-spot is.
- The Single Schmo knows where her G-spot is. It's in her G-string.
- Mr. Right is looking for love in all the right places, which is probably wrong.
- The Single Man isn't looking for love, which is probably right.
- The Schmo thinks he might have left it under the couch, which is definitely Schmo.

The Whole Trinity of the Unmarried Man

The average unmarried man is a walking talking triad all three types, an intricate triumvir of unmarried-man influences. He is, in that sense, a sort of Unmarried Mongrel, a single creature bearing the perks and quirks of all three kinds. At different times of his day and life, the average unmarried man will exhibit signs of Schmoness, Mr. Rightness and Single Manliness.

He is, as they say, a complex person.

Mostly the unmarried man clings to a bachelor branch somewhere in the middle of Single Manliness. He doesn't spend all his time in bed with women, nor does he spend it on the couch alone. He spends it in ways he deems fit, even if those ways don't always fit properly. It's his life.

Mostly he remains unmarried for three very basic, very simple reasons:
1) He has not yet met the right woman
2) He enjoys his freedom
3) He enjoys his freedom much too much to actually search for the right woman

First and foremost, know this:

We, the single men, in order to form a more perfect lifestyle, are hip to freedom. Through the ages humans have fought for it, suffered for it and paid dearly for it. In olden days, people puked on wooden ships for it, spending 10 weeks at sea to reach the land of the free, where they could till dry dirt and worship the god of their choice—all for free. People have long died for the freedom to die for freedom.

In America, founding fathers based a nation's constitution on the concept of freedom. That kind of foresight is what allows modern-day bachelors the freedom to roam, the freedom to road-trip it to Lake Havasu. Hey, it's a free country.

In the spirit of freedom, single men base their own unofficial constitution on the concept—the freedom to choose, snooze or loose. The freedom to do whatever.

In particular, the single life is the single man's most basic—and most cherished—declaration of independence. It's not that we're incapable of love. It's not that we're incapable of marriage.

No, we're single only because this is the first—and for that matter, last—time in our lives when we are truly free. For now, we want to be Ricky without Lucy. Ozzie without Harriet. Fred without Wilma. We want to go to the Moose Lodge whenever we please, a man without restrictions.

It took us two decades to escape the bonds of authority. We had mothers who told us to take out the trash. Dads who told us, "Don't tell your mother." Coaches who told us to do another lap. Teachers who told us to solve for x. Vice principals who told us to grab our ankles. Professors who told us to please, share our little joke with the class.

We've been told what to do our whole lives. Now it's our turn. We want to tell ourselves what to do, even if it's nothing.

Basic Freedoms

Other than death by hanging, the last thing a single man wants is to be stripped of his sovereignty. He clings to his constitutional rights of life, liberty and the pursuit of whatever he damn well pleases.

If you think freedom isn't important to a single guy, watch Mel Gibson in Braveheart, when his character William Wallace—impaled by a pointy scabbard—shouts "Freeeeeedom!" to a lot of English people with dirty faces. Wallace then has his head freed from his body, but that's a different deal entirely.

We know how Wallace felt, and it doesn't take a scabbard to the backside to elicit a cry of freedom. "Freedom!" It is the mantra of single men. Where women often seek security and stability, single men more often seek the open road.

Single men yearn to be Easy Rider, cruising backroads in search of nothing more than tomorrow morning.

Webster's New Collegiate Dictionary defines freedom in several ways, maybe because it was first compiled by Noah Webster, who, according to definition, was a guy:

1.   The capacity to exercise choice; free will; ease or facility of movement

It is early Saturday morning. The cool earth warms to the rising sun. It is so nice outside that a really corny sentence pops into your head: "The cool earth warms to the rising sun."

You step onto the porch. The air smells of fresh flowers and a hot pot of joe. You sip your coffee, a smooth and rich blend. You feel so good you think you're in a FiberCon commercial.

You consider all your options for this fine day. A little golf. A little fishing. Your laptop at the beach. A long nap in the cool hammock.

Suddenly you remember that you are married. You have a wife.

You finish your coffee and get dressed for the Red Tag Sale.

The single man, on the other hand, can do the fabled Texas Triathlon: fishing in the morning, golf in the afternoon, cold beer at night.

In the Texas Triathlon, every man's a winner.

2.   Immunity from arbitrary exercise of authority

"Honey, you are not wearing that tie.

"But I like this tie."

"We're having dinner with my parents. You will wear the tie they bought you."

"But they bought it in 1972, and it's wider than the mouth of the Nile."

"You'll wear it and you'll like it."

"At the risk of sounding nosy, what makes you the boss?"

She gives him that look. He suddenly remembers what makes her the boss.

"I'll get the tie," he mutters.

Women wield executive privilege simply by virtue of their anatomy. If a man refuses to wear the tie, she refuses him access to the fun house.

But no one wields authority over a single man. If a single man doesn't want to wear the tie, he'll put on a Speed Racer T-shirt and go date somebody else.

3. Exemption from an unpleasant condition

This, too, is key to remaining single: a distinct aversion to a crappy relationship.

Some men fear commitment because they fear a repeat of abusive relationships they witnessed as children: "Mom. Dad. If you'd stop hugging each other in front of the TV, I could watch Archie ridicule Edith again."

We don't fear abdication of freedom, loss of Sunday golf privileges or relinquished dominion over the remote control as much as we fear getting stuck in the rut of a bad relationship that only gets worse. We fear Archie and Edith. We fear becoming them.

We have seen the couples who should be single: at restaurants, eating dinner without saying a word. At stoplights, arguing violently in the car next to us. At parties, drunk and disgusted with each other.

We know that people change with time. What if, with time, the woman we choose gets worse and worse? What if because of that woman, we get worse? What if over the years the haven in our home is not our wife's embrace but our favorite chair?

We fear Archie and Edith.

4. The right of enjoying all of the privileges of membership

Membership in the Clan of Single Men has one requirement: You must be single. You should also have a clean change of underwear. A flannel shirt would be nice, but it isn't necessary.

But that's it. Membership is easy, unless Liz Taylor has been tailing you with crosshairs fixed on a post-Fortensky appointment at the altar. With membership comes certain privileges: You can own one fork, one spoon, one knife, one plate, one bowl. You can vacuum only the exposed parts of the carpet. You can have a bottle of Robitussin that expired in October 1987. You can wear your favorite flannel shirt—all weekend.

Or you can do none of the above. The beauty of the bachelor lifestyle is the democratization of time and energy. A guy can toe the line on prototypical bachelor behavior, throwing his socks on the sofa and eating Twinkies over the sink. Or he can save the whales.

It doesn't matter. It is up to him. He is a Single Man.

There is but one stipulation. On the day of your wedding, a guy must relinquish all rights and privileges of the Clan of Single Men.

He might also have to change his underwear.

The Basic Ingredients of the Single Life

Whatever their particular motivations for remaining unmarried, single men have one thing in common: They genuinely love the single life. It's the best gig they have ever had. It's the only gig they have ever had.

This is not to say all single men are swingers. Single men do not remain single in order to service the retinue of bathing beauties outside their door. This is all '70s stuff—the Johnny Vegas guy with reel-to-reel Commodores tapes, mai tais and a leather couch, and the women who come and go and come again. No, that's not it at all—which is not to say it sounds entirely bad.

Contrary to the image of the predatory single guy, single men are not inherently afraid of commitment. Independence is not synonymous to Marriage Phobia. Single men are open to affairs of the heart—not just affairs of the pelvis, Elvis.

They are not afraid of growing old with someone. Nor are they afraid of growing old. The single man is not a Peter Pan desperately hanging on to his youth—he threw away his student I.D. years ago. Rather, he has created for himself a terrific life. Great friends. Interesting career. Exciting hobbies. He's a happy guy.

A single man isn't afraid of marriage at all. In fact, he views it with great expectation. He's just not diving headfirst into it. He won't abandon single life until he is certain—certain—that married life holds a greater reward, and he's not just talking about better meals. He will find a woman who not only makes his life better but who makes him a better person, or his name isn't so-and-so.

Meantime, he concentrates on mastering life its own self. He works hard, plays hard and, on occasion, stays hard. He conditions mind, body and spirit in the tradition of Plato, Hercules and Joseph of Arimithea.

A wife is not his primary objective in life. But if the right woman should happen to knock, he is free to have her, hold her, love her, squeeze her. He is free to marry her.

He is free. Period. End of sentence.

FRIENDSHIP: THE NEED FOR FRIENDS INDEED

Contrary to popular TV imagery, the single man is not 98 percent pre-occupied with women. Prevailing perception is that when he's not eating over the sink, the single man is chasing women, thinking of women, calling women or, in rare cases, actually bedding women.

In reality, the single man does not spend each waking nanosecond in pursuit of the tender gender. He does not spend his days looking for love, his nights looking for phone numbers and his happy hours winking at waitresses. He does pursue women, of course, but it is not his one calling. His interaction with the human race is not limited solely to meeting chicks. Rather, he spends time and effort building and maintaining friendships—not only with men, but women too. Great friendship, cultivated over time, is the cornerstone of the single man's existence. In fact, a quality single man needs to borrow fingers to count friends.

For a man, a night with friends is far preferable to a night with some dame who's trying to be a Charley Girl. Kinda hey, kinda wow! Even if he ends the night changing a flat tire in a dark lot, he knows the guy handing him the lug nuts will be a friend indeed.

His buddies expect nothing but the pleasure of his company, and maybe a key to the lakehouse. They accept him as he is and always will be They do not try to change him or rearrange him. This is good, because the single man clings to the Popeye Principle: "I yam who I yam, and I ain'ts no more."

Comrades in arms, friends at heart, his buddies ask nothing but that he share his joys and possibly his pizza.

His friends:

- don't whine that he doesn't dance.
- never say, "You're wearing that?"
- understand the romance of Wrigley Field.
- know immediately when he's quoting a line from Stripes.
- don't wish he had more hair, more money and more desire to marry.

To a single man, friends come first.

CAREER: BEING ALL THAT HE CAN BE

The single man doesn't pass his day in a bathrobe, eating Rice Chex and circling ads for menial jobs. Nor does he seek a trust-funded Trina to finance a lifestyle enjoyed primarily on the deck of a 40-foot yacht.

He works. He doesn't work system. He just works. He might be a CEO or a sandblaster, a lawyer or a landscaper, but the common denominator is that he works.

His chosen career is a lifelong endeavor, not just a temp job until marriage. Nor is life itself a temp job until the wedding bells ring. For now and the immediate future, the single man can climb the corporate ladder without worrying about getting to his child's Christmas pageant. He has no child, no wife, no pageant. Not yet. For now, his job is Job One.

The workplace is where he the single man makes his mark, and not just by scrawling his initials into the executive wash basin. No, it is in the workplace where he puts down stakes on his legacy. The workplace is not—repeat, not—an arena in which to scope a potential spouse, not necessarily.

Maybe she's in the next office, maybe she isn't. The single man doesn't sweat it. He's got work to do.

HOBBIES: ALL WORK AND NO PLAY

To the single man, golf is a hobby. Sculpting is a hobby. Stamp-collecting is a hobby—but a risky one. His pals might give him a wedgie for that one.

Lots of things are hobbies. A hobby is a way to have fun, expand the mind, lose weight, shed inches and maybe set a Guinness Book of World Records record—Greatest Number of Hobbies: 147.

For the single man, looking for Ms. Right is not one among the 147. Looking for Ms. Right is not a hobby.

The single man doesn't fret about finding the right woman. Women aren't going anywhere. He can go on a he-man camping weekend and when he gets back, women will be there, just as before.

For the single man, life comes first. Life—not wife.

Single Men: The Envy of Married Men

Married men envy single men. Single women envy married women.

This is a key difference in gender-based perspective. Married men envy the single man's independence. Single women envy the married woman's security.

Others envy David Hasselhoff.

No doubt about it: Some women marry not just for love but security. Many women live in primal fear of becoming dowdy spinsters, gray-haired old maids with a stack of TV Guides six feet high and a three-year stash of Swanson's Frozen Dinners. Marriage, they believe, is a convenient hedge against a dim future as an old biddy.

Men, on the other hand, don't marry for security unless they spent the last 18 months in drug rehab and just moved to Knots Landing, next door to the Widow Carrington. In fact, most men have less security in marriage than in bachelorhood—at least in the outlay of their own time and money. For better or worse, a single man gets to spend his disposable income on frivolous things, like fast women and fast cars, not proprietary things, like a wife and kids. Seldom does a single man sit with a State Farm agent to discuss policies and payment plans on life insurance. He might, however, sit with a State Farm agent behind home plate, third row, seats 3 and 4.

A single man can spend his time as he spends his dime: any damn way he chooses. He can spend them both stupidly and simultaneously in sunny Cancun or, if he is more fiscally or socially conservative, in sunny Cozumel. He can spend both until he has none of either—his time and his money rung up to the cashiers of great experience.

A single man probably doesn't realize it, but for this very reason, a married pal envies the bejeezus out of him. Shackled night and day to mortgage and meatloaf, the married guy is eight shades of green—he envies his single pal's freedom to roam, his wide berth around responsibilities, his license for spontaneity, his liberty to do as he pleases. Nor does the single man realize just how desperately his married friend needs "to get away," if only for a night.

For the single man, a free night is par for the course. For the married man, it's a double eagle. It rarely if ever happens, but when it does, he needs to take advantage of it in a big way.

Perhaps the fabled Ticket Scenario best illustrates a married man's desperate need for periodic shore-leave. The key difference between the single man and the married man rests squarely in their respective reactions to this simple situation:

Single Friend: "Hey, I've got a couple of tickets for tonight's game? Wanna go?"

You: "I'd love to, but I really need to get some work done tonight."

Single Friend: "Hey, no problem. We'll go another time."

The scenario changes dramatically when the friend is married:

Married Friend: "Hey, I've got a couple of tickets for tonight's game? Wanna go?"

You: "I'd love to, but I really need to get some work done tonight."

Married Friend: "Oh god, please don't do this to me. You have to go. If you don't go I'll have to take my wife. Please don't make me take my wife. I love my wife, I love my wife very much, but I'm with her day and night and I do not want to take her to the game. She'll let me drink just one beer—a medium beer—and I can't look at cheerleaders except out of the corner of my eye, and cheerleaders don't look as good that way. Plus, my wife always makes me leave early so she can watch Lotto."

Sometimes the message isn't even that subtle. Sometimes it's as simple as a married guy pulling his single friend aside and saying, "Stay single. It's so much easier."

In cases such as these, we are inclined to believe him.

Setting the Record Straight

1) Men Don't Necessarily Like to Hunt

The single man is forever included in the "Men Like To Hunt" theory—the concept of the male as Orion, mighty hunter, the stalker of prey.

In response to the theory, a single woman might portray herself as someone she isn't: an elusive babe so coveted, so mysterious, she is the human equivalent of a deer hunter's 16-point buck. For her elusiveness, the theory goes, the hunter male revels in the challenge of tracking, stalking and finally bagging the trophy prize.

Single men, say the theorists, love a challenge.

But in reality, single men don't necessarily love a challenge. Michael Jordan might love a challenge. George Custer obviously did. But a lot of single men don't—which, in many cases, is why single men are single, not married. If single men uniformly cherished a challenge, perhaps they'd all conquer the Rubik's Cube while simultaneously pursuing Michelle Pfieffer—or, more challenging still, attempt to tie the knot with a member of the opposite sex. Instead we flip it over to CNN to see what's up.

For the single man, a big challenge can be deciding which sock to put on first. Choices include right and left.

Consider, at the most basic level of male hormonal function: If all men loved a challenge, there would not exist the fabled "easy girl." Sure, she might have a genetic predisposition to easiness, but with no man could she be easy. Her promiscuity would go unfulfilled for lack of an agreeable playing partner. For what is an easy girl but a girl who provides the male everything but a challenge? She is, after all, easy. She is the Jiffy Lube of womanhood: She is open and available to every man, regardless of make or model.

If men really loved a challenge, the easy girl's telephone would not register so many 2 a.m. rings, nor her door so many 2 a.m. knocks. Nor would her name and number comprise a full 78 percent of men's room graffiti in the watering holes of America:

For a good time, call Tammy. 576-EASY

Soused on gin and wobbling toward that pay phone, they've got the number mem-o-rized. It's easy!

For all their good qualities—they can change a tire, they can cook a pig—men have a basic shortcoming: the lure of easy sex.

So when you say men like to hunt, first acknowledge that deer hunters use feeders, deer blinds and high-powered scopes.

Consider: If men loved a challenge, the world's oldest profession would be neither old nor a profession. Solicitation of prostitution clearly represents the average male's partiality toward easy pickin's. It's like rolling a shopping cart down the produce aisle, only this time the eggplant actually flags you down and jumps in your cart.

For a john on the make, the only real challenge is in avoiding arrest—and, perhaps, checking Eve for an Adam's apple.

Consider: If men loved a challenge, they would not go to bars to meet women. They would go to a gun and knife show. Or a Three Stooges convention. They'd go places where women ain't.

But men go to bars. And, fortunately, so do women.

No place on Earth matches a bar, nightclub, lounge, saloon, tavern, dance club or watering hole in expediting the boy-meets-girl scenario:

A) Women are dressed well, making themselves more attractive than usual;

B) Men are drinking, making women more attractive than usual;

C) It is dark, making everyone more attractive than usual;

D) Men and women gather at the bar itself, giving men the opportunity to slam a high-ball, rub female elbows, raise an eyebrow, purse his lips and say, "Hey gorgeous. Are you in the movies? Because if you aren't, you should be."

E) There is music, and they can dance to it.

F) The bar closes at 2 a.m., giving everyone a chance to walk together to the parking lot to exchange phone numbers and possibly saliva.

Consider: All the things that man created to facilitate his pursuit of women:

1) Musk oil
2) Red convertibles
3) A dozen roses
4) The waltz
5) Free weights
6) Cash money
7) Julio Iglesias
8) Fruity frozen drinks

9) More cash money
10) Tickets to the opera
11) Double-breasted suits
12) Trust funds
13) Picnic baskets
14) Brie
15) Words that rhyme

So, while men aren't exactly Nanook The Mighty Hunter, they don't want to marry Trixie the neighborhood tramp. Few men have ever looked down at the back of a woman's head and proposed marriage. If a man is looking for long-term commitment, he probably doesn't want a chick who answers to "Sweet Thang."

But men don't want to make a safari of it either.

TOO ELUSIVE: HERE'S A STORY OF A MAN NAMED BRADY

The woman who portrays herself as The Challenge Of The Century can act her Meryl-Streep-Masterpiece-Theater-self right out of a potentially meaningful relationship.

Consider the story of a man Brady. We know Brady, because he is us.

Soon after Brady began dating Sara, she began playing a game called Hard To Get. She didn't return Brady's calls. She ended dates early. She made it difficult for Brady to ask her out.

Sara was not a lovely lady. Or so it seemed.

Of course, Sara's elusiveness was merely a ploy, Act I in a dramatic interpretation of Hook The Hubby: Sara wanted Brady to think she was busy with three very lovely guys, that she was a babe in demand, and in response Brady just might hasten his commitment to a commitment.

Ah, what a tangled web we weave when first we practice to deceive.

After a few weeks of repeated defeat at the hands of the most noteworthy adversary Sara, Brady lost interest. Sara seemed to be ducking him like a doctor's appointment, so we—we mean he—assumed Sara never had any interest in him. We—we mean he—went his separate way.

And why wouldn't Brady do that? Brady felt like just another notation in her day planner. He felt like an occasional meal ticket, a periodic escort, a once-in-a-while ride to the picture show. He felt bad.

After an all-night bender of Bacchus proportions, Brady stumbled home one morning and told his buddies that Sara didn't like him. Brady said, "Fschtacy fshdoesn't ffffschlike mmmee." It was a shame, too, because Brady had liked Sara a lot—at least at first.

Que Sara Sara.

About three months later Brady ran into Sara at a local night spot. Sara gave him that look—the kind of look that says, "You done me wrong." Sara asked Brady why he never called her anymore. Knowing he had little to lose with full disclosure, Brady said, "Because you didn't like me."

"What gave you that idea?" Sara replied.

"Well, for one thing, you avoided me like an audit."

Sara stood there, speechless. It was a good look for her, one he hadn't seen before.

Finally Sara said, "I wasn't avoiding you. It's just that some good things are meant to be a challenge."

"A challenge?" Brady replied. "You weren't a challenge. You were an impossibility."

Sara stood there, speechless again.

Brady continued. "And the few times we did go out," he said, "you were so…elusive."

"You didn't like that?"

"Hell no!"

"You don't think a woman should be a little mysterious?"

"Yeah, if she's Nancy Drew."

"I'm sorry," Sara said. "I thought it made me appealing."

"No," Brady said. "It made you sort of wretched."

Brady is a fine, upstanding example of a single man who is not intrigued with a challenge. A small challenge, yeah, like getting a hole-in-one on the windmill hole at the Pine Valley Putt-Putt Hutt. But not a big challenge, like translating Sanskrit into Mandarin Chinese or dating a girl like Sara.

Well known is the clichÇd tale of the lonely prom queen. She sits at home eating Funyons every Saturday night because guys never ask her out. She is the ginchiest girl at Franklin High, the ultimate Teen Queen, yet her social calendar is empty. Why? Because guys think they have no chance. They think she's out of their league. So the junior miss sits at home watching reruns of The Love Boat while a dozen potential suitors do something else, like sit in their room and think about her.

It should serve as a lifetime lesson for both sexes. Some men do love challenges. That's why some men play golf. But when it comes to women, there is always another course to play.

2) Men Know Rejection

Men are born to a life of rejection. It's surprising that the delivery-room nurse, upon seeing our standard-issue genitals, doesn't direct us back to the womb with the admonition to bring flowers next time.

Birth is the last time in a guy's life when he doesn't face the sting of womanly rejection. To a man, rejection is like a slap in the face. Sometimes it is a slap in the face.

Rejection comes early for males. We first experience it in the 7th grade at the junior high fall dance, under the swirling strobes that bounce from the mirrored ball. Over the speaker system comes Lionel Richie's "Three Times A Lady." Inspired by thoughts of romance, we walk slowly across the gym floor to the girls' side of the gym, sidestepping 8th-graders in love. We approach the visitors bench to ask Susie to dance. Susie giggles. Susie says no. Susie turns us promptly away.

We must now endure the dreaded "Walk Of Shame"—the agonizing process of traversing slowly back across the half-court line to the boys' side of the gym, where we quickly learn a hard truth: We'll be getting no sympathy from our friends on this night—or in this lifetime. Instead, our pals will heap further ridicule upon us until we realize that for the average male, this is a life of frequent and painful rejection and subsequent ridicule.

"Hey, Johnny! Go dance with the ball rack! At least it won't say no!"

Our friends will administer this kind of pasting the rest of our lives. This is a quality exclusive to males—the ability to kick a friend when he's down. We suffer not only the embarrassment of rejection but also all the derision it inspires. And it's a lot of derision.

We'd better get used to it. The gymnasium scenario still happens to us, minus the Oxy-10 and the Earth Shoes: We notice the good-looking brunette at the bar. She's been staring at us for 10 minutes. We work up the courage to talk to her. We begin the slow march as our friends watch.

"I'm not one to be this forward," we tell her. "But I couldn't help noticing the eye contact we've been making."

"Eye contact?"

"Yeah, you know, eye contact. A smoldering kind of contact. With the eyes."

"Sweetie, I was looking at the guy behind you. My boyfriend. The bouncer. In fact, here he is now."

We begin the Walk Of Shame, with assistance from a large hand upon our shoulder.

Or we're at a party, a party whose purpose, it seems, is to introduce party goers to exotic cucumber hors d'oeuvres and to pit completely disparate people in that weird social arena of absurdly awkward conversation.

"So, you're an accountant."

"Yes."

"Have any good accounting stories?"

"No."

"Excuse me while I get another cucumber roll-up."

Amid the teeming discomfort we meet Meagan, a charming writer with a charming smile and a gift for mellifluous sentences. We talk for two hours that seem like 10 minutes, so quickly does the time pass as we're having fun. We have never gotten along so well, so soon, with any woman. In mid-roll-up we think, "My god, I could spend the rest of my life with this person." And we mean it.

Delighted but nervous in our sudden good fortune, we excuse ourselves, ostensibly to fetch two toddies but actually to devise strategy to ask the girl out. After brief deliberation we decide on the art-museum date. We know nothing of art, of course, but we know we can fake it by muttering the occasional "hmmmmm" at appropriate paintings. Plus, we heard about Picasso's "Blue Period" on Jeopardy.

Ready to resume the budding romance, we return to the couch. The only thing on the couch, we discover, is cushions.

Meagan is gone. Vanished. There's not even an indentation where her butt had been.

We try not to look panicked, try not to look sad, but we cannot conceal a battered heart. We stand there—a man alone with a drink in each hand—looking like we lost our puppy.

Alone and blue, we resort to the justifications of the jilted man: "Maybe there was an emergency," we think, nodding absently. "Maybe it's her grandmother."

On the thin wings of slim hope, we call her the next day, hoping against hope that her grandmother died a horrible death, may she rest in peace.

"Meagan, this is Mike."

"Mike?"

"Yeah, Mike. From the party? Remember? 'I like Mike'?"

"Mike."

She says "Mike" not like "Oh, Mike!" but like "What Mike?"

And suddenly it is clear.She does not remember us.

A conversation that to us had been dual Shakespearean sonnets was to her an exercise in passing time. What to us had been the start of something beautiful was to her a chance to take a load off.

We shrink to a height of 1-foot-8. We hang up the phone and join the circus.

Or we're at a concert with friends. Amid flashing lights and curling smoke we see Elise, a beautiful girl with raven hair and deep green eyes and a voice like smoldering fire.

We have often admired the fair Elise, usually from afar and away, but have never spoken to her, not once. For each time we muster the requisite courage to begin a conversation, something stops us—something called fear.

Fear—in its woman-induced form—strikes even the most eloquent of men with Tangled Tongue.

Under the influence of Tangled Tongue, a man's words sound fine when they leave his mind, but by the time they arrive at his tongue they have picked up several phonetic hitchhikers. What begins as the Gettysburg Address comes out like play-day at Penny Whistle Park:

"So, you tonight music good like band hear and beat goes on?"

We stand 10 feet but 100 miles from the lovely Elise, tethered by fear. Well, it's for the best, we think, rationalizing or own inadequacy for the 185th time this month. She is much too good for us. Much, much too good.

We content ourselves in the knowledge that words to Elise would constitute words wasted, a misappropriation of breath directed at a woman whose condescension we could not beg. We slug a beer and dive into the mosh pit.

A month later we see Elise's friend Jennifer. Jennifer tells us—in that I'm-going-to-make-you-feel-really-crappy way inherent to women— "Elise waited all night for you to talk to her, but you never said a word. She thinks you think you're too good for her."

We have committed the unpardonable sin. Instead of toeing boy-girl protocol and allowing the girl to reject us as per custom, we did the dirty work ourselves. We pulled our own plug.

We have committed romanticide.

The Availability Issue

It is this uncertainty regarding the availability of the fair sex that perplexes us so. Upon initial observation we don't know if a girl is available, unavailable, interested, not interested, married, divorced, gay, straight, dead or alive.

OK. We know she's alive by the way she keeps declining our invitation to join us in the Lambada.

But it's not like going to Kmart, where everything is labeled accordingly:

Dress socks—Aisle 9.

Power tools—Aisle 7.

Available women—Aisle Be Damned.

It's not like this: "Attention, Kmart shoppers. Take advantage of today's Blue Light Special on single women, ages 24 to 31, who enjoy French films and long walks on moonlit beaches."

Instead, we men must embark on an illogical mystery tour where a woman's status is anybody's guess. The ring thing doesn't help much. Most men can tell a wedding band from a cigar band, but after that it's advanced gemology. We can't tell an engagement ring from a mood ring. If she's wearing the Hope Diamond, yeah, OK, she's engaged, but otherwise it's just another piece of costume jewelry. It could mean anything.

What to do about all this ambiguity? Well, in a brave new world, we could require all women over age 19 to undergo color-coding: Green means she is available. Yellow means she might be available. Red means she is marrying a Russian powerlifter tomorrow.

As it is, we mistake red girls for green ones, and green for red, and risk serious damage to both our face and our ego each time we mistake one primary color for another.

In their earnest attempt to clear up any confusion, the Puritans hung a scarlet "A" on Hester Prynne, a symbol of her adultery. This made it hard for Hester to get a date. Yet have we not learned from history's lessons? Are we not enlightened by the error of our ancestors' ways and means? Are we not made smarter by the ignorance of our antecedents? Well?

It's only an idea, but perhaps we could help the latter-day woman land a date with a swell guy by placing on her a simple symbol, a basic code of availability. If a woman can wear a T-shirt that says "I'm With Stupid," then surely she can wear one that says:

- "I'm Available."
- "I'm Not Your Type."
- "Don't Even Think About It."
- "If You Don't Leave Me Alone Right Now, I'm Going To Call The Cops, You Sleazy Dirt Bag."
- "Call Me!"

ASK AND YE MIGHT NOT RECEIVE

Determination of availability solves just half the problem. Availability doesn't mean diddly if you don't get the goods. Put it this way: A great many of us single men are technically available for the NBA draft, but as yet the Knicks have not called with a contract offer.

Likewise, just because a girl is available does not mean she is available to us. It is a lesson we learned most painfully the moment Suzie giggled at the junior-high dance: We can't have any and every woman we desire. In fact, we can't have most women we desire.

It is a maxim we continue to live by: All men were not created equal. Some were created as Robert Redford and some were created as Danny DeVito.

Through process of elimination, we determine possible partners from the available talent pool. She's too smart...she's too fat...she's too cute...she's just right.

We pick them; they don't necessarily pick us. Unlike politicians, we do not have the benefit of an Iowa Caucus to determine the merit of our own candidacy. Where a caucus might tell us we don't have a chance in hell, we alone must ascertain our potential as a suitor.

Thus we risk painful defeat in the only poll that matters: the one-woman poll. In the fair electorate of a girl's own preference, we risk defeat by landslide. She might despise our platform—"Date Me, Don't Hate Me"—or she might simply prefer another candidate. She might prefer his position on premarital sex over our position, which is basically missionary. We just pray she doesn't choose Ross Perot over us. Ross might rub it in our faces: "That giant suckin' sound you hear? It's comin' from my bedroom!"

Still we forge onward, braving the possibility of rejection and risking a full belly of swallowed pride. We try, try again, hoping we might get it right.

Once we have zeroed in on a girl we like, we can choose any of several methods of date solicitation:

A) The Telephone Call: Dial "R" For Rejection

This is how a guy does it:

He picks up the phone and calls a girl, just like that. He sounds breezy, happy, busy, as if the phone call is merely another whim in a long lifetime sequence of happy-go-lucky spontaneity. Yep, he's just a happy carefree fellow on his way out the door when—hey, what do you know?—he just happened to think of the girl, right out of the blue.

"Hey, just headin' out the door to play Frisbee with my dog Brutus, and I thought I'd see what you're up to…"

This, of course, is a ruse. This is a Daytime Emmy.

In reality he's been pacing the carpet for two hours, alternately picking up the receiver and putting it down again, biting his nails practically to his elbows. For two hours he's been playing a mental game of Worst Case Scenario: Boy calls girl, boy says hi, girls says "who?", boy hangs up.

When finally he conquers his fear and calls the girl, he pretends it's just to say hey—even as he clutches a crib sheet for cues on interesting topics and witty remarks.

Interesting topics:
1) Roe vs. Wade
2) Plessy vs. Ferguson
3) Good vs. Evil
4) Godzilla vs. the Smog Monster

Witty remark:
1) There once was a man from Nantucket.

For a guy given the alternatives, a telephone call can work pretty well. He can engage a girl in a light 12-minute conversation that seems neither threatening nor obsessive. And he can pretend the joy of the conversation prompted his proposal of a date, when in fact it had been his plan from the get-go.

"It's been so fun talking to you," he can say, following the script, "why don't we do it over a drink sometime?"

Of course, he can barely hear her reply over the boom-boom-booming drumbeat of his own pulse.

Which brings us to the final point:

A phone call eliminates the embarrassment of a face-to face rejection. Should she say no or hell no, he can hang up the phone and bang his head against the wall in private anguish. Dissociative rejection is much easier to handle than refusal vis-a-vis.

He doesn't have to fake a conciliatory smile. He doesn't have to say, "Aw, that's all right. I was walking around with these two tickets to the ballet and hey, I just happened to follow you from the gym to the super-market to the library and I thought hey, maybe I'd ask you to go with me, and you said no, hell no, which is fine because, hey, I was going to ask someone else."

He doesn't have to say that at all.

B) The Wait-Till-You-See-Her-Out Query: Nice To Have Seen You

Each time you see Catrina—at a party, at the market—she is very nice to you, nicer than a car salesman. She makes you feel great. But you are unsure and insecure about Catrina's friendly treatment, which borders on Casper The Friendly Ghost.

"Maybe it's not me," you think. "Maybe she's nice to everybody"

And you might be right.

This is the problem with nice women. We are drawn to them because they are nice. Everyone is drawn to them because they are nice to everyone.

"Good morning, Mr. Ripper!"

"Please. Call me Jack."

A girl's blanket distribution of glad tidings can cause a guy some serious consternation. Given her all-inclusive approval system, we don't know where we rank with her. We could be that special someone or just one of the multitudes. When she smiles, we don't know whether to drop to a knee or merely smile back. We could just as easily be the Pope or Ozzy Osbourne.

Fearing an embarrassing misinterpretation of intent, we opt not to call her:

"I noticed you smiling at me and…."

"Yes?"

Sure, we know if the girl rejects us, she'll at least be nice about it: "I'm sure you're a wonderful guy…" and all that jazz, but it won't anesthetize us to the pain. It won't make us feel any better.

So we devise a plan, if it can be called that: We'll go out as often as possible—to the gym, the mall, the market, the bookstore, the coffeehouse, the park where she plays with her dog. We will go where she goes. Frequent exposure, we believe, will help us gauge her interest. We can see if she smiles at us or at everyone. We can also speculate that the frequency of our meetings might presage a destiny together.

"Amazing how we keep running into each other like this," we might say, sheepishly kicking the dirt as we stand next to her at the park.

"It sure is," she might respond. "Maybe we could end all the amazement by—"

"By going out?"

"No. By not running into each other like this."

This would mark the debut performance of her mean streak.

C) The Fishing-For-Clues Method: Trying To Land The Big One

The fishing-for-clues method goes back to the early days, when we first sought to measure a girl's interest by nonconfrontational means. We had not the courage to find out for ourselves (nor do we now), so we relied on spies, emissaries and printed information to determine potential amorÇ.

The trend began in the 7th grade, after a year of denial that we even liked girls. In retrospect, 7th grade was pretty easy—at least as far as procuring a possible mate. Girls were all over the place. Unless you lived in the Appalachian states, every girl was single and without child. Every girl was the right age. And every girl spent each school day in the confines of our tiny universe—the junior high school, a vast repository of kindling urges.

If we liked a girl, the junior high gave us easy access. We saw her in the halls, at lunch, at the assembly. It wasn't hard to get a fix on her location or her availability. If a girl liked us, we'd hear it from her friends immediately—within 12 minutes of the initial revelation. We might hear it by word of mouth, we might get an anonymous note in our locker. It was a great warm feeling, one of mystery and incipient passion.

Likewise, whenever we liked a girl, we purposely leaked the information to our friends, as if we were a mole on the inside. By 4th-period English, she knew all about it. By 5th-period math, we knew if she was interested.

"She said she likes you," our friends might report.

"She said you're a dork," they might say.

Many people describe the current era as the Information Age. Hardly.

The Information Age was age 12. It was 7th grade. If we didn't discover first-hand that a girl liked us, there were alternate methods: Graffiti on walls. Carvings in tree bark—Jenny + Jim = LUV 4EVER. Then there was the Slam Book.

The Slam Book was exclusive to junior high, a phenomenon not seen before or since. The Slam Book consisted of about 100 pieces of looseleaf paper strung together by colored yarn. It began as a blank notebook and for the next week it traveled hand-to-hand throughout the school. Kids would write whatever they wanted in the Slam Book. A favorite topic, of course, was on whom a kid had a crush. We boys wouldn't admit it, but finding our name in the Slam Book was one of life's great joys.

Nor would men admit it today, but we'd pay good money to use a Slam Book in adult circles. Have we really changed that much? Are we really more emotionally mature than in 7th grade? If somebody has a crush on us, wouldn't we like to know? If we have a crush on someone, wouldn't we like to offer clues to our identity? As it is, many potential relationships go unexplored because we lack accurate information.

Still today we send out feelers. Preliminary polling. Market research. We ask a friend to find out if a girl is dating anyone. We ask him to mention our name to see how she responds.

Then we wait. We wait like 7th graders.

For us single men, all the scheming and maneuvering culminates in one of two results: rejection or acceptance. Men live in the fear brought on by the polarity of the two answers. That may be why men drink more Budweiser than women.

It is a basic dynamic with complex ramifications, a romantic application of the Chaos Theory. From a single action might occur any of several reactions:

We ask a girl out. She rejects or accepts our proposal. If she rejects us, we tuck our tail and move on to the next girl. And we start all over again, embarking again on the perpetual-motion carousel of the dating game. 'Round and 'round we go.

If she accepts, we entertain her for an evening. We do all the right things. We give her warm fuzzies, buy her Junior Mints, refrain from shutting the car door on her skirt. If we think we entertained her, we ask her out again. And we begin the process anew. Will she accept or reject?

That's how it works—or doesn't work:

We call the girl. The girl calls the shots.

Sometimes those shots strike close to the heart.

LIVING WITH REJECTION

Our lifelong experience with women is one of frequent exposure to the old heave-ho. What is a wife but the only woman on the planet who ultimately did not reject the man? And still she has the power to demand exile to the sofa, till death do him have a crick in his neck.

But men deal well with rejection. We have become inured to its sting. It happens with such frequency that in the course of the continued physical evolution of homo sapiens, men are probably growing thicker skin.

Thick skin is necessary. There are no support groups for men rejected. There is no crisis hotline, like 1-800-SHE-LEFT. Men simply dust themselves off and try again.

Women deal with rejection differently. When a women is spurned by a man, she convenes with a friend to share her pain. They sit cross-legged on the carpet in their flannel pajamas, open a gallon of Rocky Road and participate in the equal distribution of anguish.

Men are different. Men don't eat Rocky Road. Men live it.

Too often, we men are issued the pink slip before we get a chance at romance. We ask a girl to dance and she says, "Go away"—which is a dance we haven't heard of. Is that like the Watusi?

We ask a girl to dinner, and she says she has to wash her hair, visit her sick grandmother, rebuild her carburetor and pick up her tux from the cleaners.

Then, instead of compassion from our friends, we get the standard barbs: "Nice job, Casanova. Will you be giving a seminar?"

"Yo, Romeo. Wherefore art thou? Alone in front of the TV, eating Mrs. Paul's Deluxe Fish Sticks?"

As men, we have suffered rejection and ridicule since the first days of puberty. Sure, it still bothers us. But we're veterans.

When you have done the Walk Of Shame, everything else is cake.

THE SINGLE MAN'S REALITY OF DATING AND RELATIONSHIPS

We envision the salty old man, still single after all these years. He is standing alone on his 12-foot dinghy, gazing out at a lonely sea, wondering what the heck happened to his life.

He's still pitching woo at 72-year-old retirees from White Plains, N.Y., still having the fleeting fun he had as a 20-year-old. But the fleeting fun has lasted the better part of five decades, and now it's more fleeting than ever. He'd like to get married and settle down, but first he has to find his teeth.

Generally, young single men love the single life, mainly due to the existence of young single women. But with the passing years, women aren't so young and single. For this reason, most men hope to be paired off by the time they're buying Dent-U-Cream and The Clapper.

At some point in their 20s, men begin to date. Usually they begin these endeavors with great trepidation, for they are fraught with hazards: rejection, dejection, bankruptcy. Whatever the inherent dangers, these casual couplings might someday lead to sex, love and/or the Wedding March.

In the beginning, however, one thing is clear: The date seems like a pretty dicey idea.

The Economics of Dating

Penny For Your Thoughts, $100 For Your Happiness

Women view dating as a chance to wear new earrings. Men view it as a chance to spend twice the money for half the fun.

While our friends are spending a total of $27 to meet flight attendants in several nightclubs, we're forking out $108.79 to spend an entire evening with a red-headed CPA who, it turns out, not only laughs like a horse with its head caught in a gate but is also considering becoming a nun.

This is but one of the perils of dating. It is a simple matter of economics: Will I be rewarded for my investment? Or would I be better off going out with my friends? Should I spend money on a woman I hardly know? Or should I go out with friends and spend money on several women I hardly know?

For a young man with little discretionary income, dating is a cumbersome expense. Often he must decide whether to spend his money on A) taking a girl out on Saturday night or B) paying the electric bill.

After all, a month of Saturday-night dates can cost upward of $500 (dessert included) unless, of course, a guy is taking his date to "DY-NO-MITE DOLLAR NIGHT!" at the local Southtown Cinema.

"Veronica, the Ishtar retrospective begins at 7 and Wendy's doesn't close until 10. My coupon for the Meal Deal Combo doesn't include drinks, so I've iced down a couple of Shastas."

This is a good way to save money. Not only are Shastas inexpensive when purchased in bulk, but it will be your last date with Veronica.

Money is the biggest variable in the dicey dating ritual. It's why lawyers date and day-laborers watch fat women dance naked at Candyland Express. A personal-injury lawyer can take a woman for dinner and drinks at La Mansion and come morning, she'll be making omelettes.

"Steve honey? Your Denver omelette is ready!"

"I'll be down in a minute, Veronica! I'm still naked and slathered in baby oil!"

While F. Lee Lawyer escorts the fair Veronica to La Mansion for $12 fuzzy navels, Joe Roy Roofer totes a 12-pack to Candyland Express. It's BYOB, and the featured entreÇ is a 12-oz. bag of Hot n' Spicy Pork Rinds. Not that Joe Roy is missing his chance at romance. He'll meet a woman later and, if all goes well, she will not be a craftily dressed member of the vice squad.

"Wayne?"

"It's Dwayne."

"Wayne, Dwayne, whatever. You owe me 10 bucks. And I ain't doin' jack with that Spackle."

Men are reluctant to spend money on a date because there's no guaranteed dividend. It is not a normal transaction of goods and/or services rendered for payment. A man spends $100 at Sears, he get a fishing rod. He spends $100 on a date, well, at least he still has the fishing rod. He might not get much else. He might get a hardy hi-ho Silver.

What the single man needs is an incentive plan, a hierarchy of rewards:

- A $50 expenditure guarantees the man a few laughs, plus dibs on the last fried mushroom.
- A $75 expenditure guarantees that the woman doesn't pronounce it "supposubly," that she understands a majority of our improvisational humor, and that she has a working familiarity with college football rankings.
- A $100 expenditure guarantees that she has sexy lips and sips her drink through a straw.
- A $150 expenditure guarantees that she hates Kenny G, loves Robert Earl Keen, tolerates The Three Stooges, makes fun of women who do yoga, and that she once rushed the stage, quite drunk, at a Willie Nelson concert in Luckenbach, Texas.

- Finally, a $200 expenditure guarantees that she looks good in an old Harvard sweatshirt, that she can explain the infield fly rule and that she never uses the phrase "I'm the kind of person who...."
We're the kind of person who doesn't like that.

A single man needs some kind of good-faith guarantee for the investment, a covenant of you'll-get-yours. It would be nice to know it early, so we can make an informed decision regarding this particular futures market. Contrary to popular belief, the reward does not have to be sex. It can be sex, but it doesn't have to be. It's just that men don't want to be used as a free ticket. Men have feelings too.

WOMEN AND MONEY: A LOVE STORY

Women are lying. They love money. Love it. Most women would date a dead president if he left photos of himself around the apartment—green rectangular photos with numerals on them.

"Andrew Jackson, now that I am dating you, may I keep this wallet-sized photo of you that I found in your underwear drawer?"

"Yes. Just don't tell George. He's a little sensitive about his situation."

Money doesn't buy happiness, but it's a great down payment on a great time. Women know this. So spare us the "sensitivity and kindness" stuff. How often does a beautiful babe hang on the arm of a Peace Corps volunteer? We do not believe that gorgeous blondes hang out with skinny rock stars because these men are clinically proven to be very nice guys. We think it's because rock stars have a lot of money and several backstage passes.

A woman likes a guy to spend money on her because it makes her feel special. Women are into this "feeling special" feeling. Men are content to feel like there's some picante sauce left in the refrigerator. But women want to "feel like a princess."

It all began with stories like "Cinderella," in which a wealthy and handsome man in an expensive carriage tracks down the woman of his dreams and—against all odds—they live happily ever after.

News flash: This is a FAIRY TALE.

In real life, the guy would be denounced as a spoiled rogue with a foot fetish who had nothing better to do but scour the countryside for his next 17-year-old conquest. They would not live happily ever after because Cinderella would obtain a restraining order against him.

We have a theory: A woman tries to determine exactly how much of a guy's money she can waste before he begins to notice. Thus she ascertains not only his wealth but his commitment to her. It's the old Oh-Jimmy-Buy-Me-A-Stuffed-Animal routine.

ALL THE BEST PLACES

The theory goes that all the best women love to be seen at ALL THE BEST PLACES. The opera. The ballet. The Mint Julep Jamboree.

Most single guys won't go to an opera unless it's the rock opera "Tommy." Or unless it has the words "Grand Ol'" in front of it. Or unless his date isn't wearing underwear. A single guy will go anywhere if his date isn't wearing underwear.

To a lot of guys, a night out at ALL THE BEST PLACES is not an issue of being seen but of not being seen. If the single guy attends the ballet with a date, he usually skulks the dark corners while fetching her a chardonnay, careful to stay out of sight. Usually this clandestine maneuvering is to no avail, because his pals have well-heeled spies in attendance.

The next day he shows up for Frisbee golf, and he hears this: "Hey, Nuryev! How was 'The Nutcracker?'"

Oooooh. A Single-Guy Demerit.

But the single man will risk the good-natured contempt of his peers to spend an evening with a woman he likes. He'll gladly take the demerit if it means a night with Ms. She-Might-Be-Right.

Finding Someone to Date

The first step in dating is, of course, finding someone to date. Many women like to further complete the task by insisting that they be asked out four days in advance.

There is a simple reason that men wait until mid-week to ask a woman on a date: There might be something better to do.

Let's say Bob calls Sue at 7:30 p.m. Tuesday to ask for a date on Saturday.

At 7:31 Sue says what the hell.

At 7:31.02 Bob's friend Steve calls Bob with two box seats to the Orioles-Yankees game on Saturday night.

At 7:31.10 Bob says convincingly, "Dammit."

At 7:31.15 Steve tells Bob that the adjacent seats are usually occupied by members of the Flight Attendants Union Local 406.

At 7:31.18 Bob says convincingly, "Crap."

At 7:32 Bob calls Sue. "Listen, Sue. Something came up. My grandmother died again."

Bob goes to the game. He meets the flight attendants. He asks three of them out, but each is dating a pilot in order to join the Mile-High Club.

Lonely, Bob calls Sue. Sue says, "Bob, I have to wash my hair. Again."

Bob has no one to date.

Finding Someone to Date Part 2

For a guy, a night with his pals often outshines a night with a girl—unless it is the whole night with a girl.

Here's the deal with single men. Usually we do a comparative analysis of Saturday-night options: Dates are fun. But guys en masse are a blast.

It is an unimpeachable fact. Nothing could be finer that 10 guys in a diner. Or a bar or a car. With 10 guys together, even a barn-raising is fun. In fact, that's how Amish guys party.

No offense to women, but history's great expeditions were seldom co-ed. Marco Polo? All guys. Eric the Red? Lewis and Clark? Columbus? All guys. Last year's road trip to the beach? All guys. At least for a while.

Moses led what essentially was a huge mixer through the Red Sea, but several years later the participants began having sex with each other, and you see where that got them. Forty years doing laps in the desert.

A night with the guys causes considerable less anxiety than a night with a girl. We don't have to think about everything we say. In fact, we don't have to think about anything we say. We can say, "Dog juice book down in the train yard," and all is well and cool as far as our friends go.

We don't have to worry that a well-meaning comment about the rain forest might upset the girl. How were we to know that last summer a tree she was hugging sexually harassed her?

A night with the guys is easy. Our discussions are unabridged and uncensored. Sentences flow freely without the gatekeepers of forethought and tact.

- We don't have to ask our friends if they'd like a salad.
- We don't have to pretend that, yes, we hate deer hunting too.
- We don't have to compliment our friends on their clothes. To a guy, the phrase "Nice shirt" is inherently sarcastic.
- We can play sports trivia without having to explain that Cy Young is not the president of the Hair Club For Men.
- We can recite every single line of dialog from the movies in the Men's Movie Pantheon: Caddyshack, The Holy Grail and Blazing Saddles. Women do not appreciate or even tolerate our ability to say, "It's twue! It's twue!"

One more good thing about going out with the guys: We don't have to see if they "get in safely." If they are locked out of the house, tough biscuits. They were Boy Scouts. They can survive a night in the bushes. Eat your holly and shut up.

Finding Someone to Date Part 3

We hope our mothers don't read this, but here it is. The single man groups desirable single women into two categories: those he'd like to date and those he'd like to do.

There are many women who we'd like to do and date: Cindy Crawford, Pamela Anderson, Courtney Cox, the women of Melrose Place. Cokie Roberts is a woman we don't want to do or date, but we'd like to drink beer with her. Marge Schott is a woman we'd like to gag, and Janet Reno is a woman we'd like to engage in a friendly joust, or perhaps a match of Greco-Roman wrestling.

As single men, we review the great gallery of eligible bachelorettes on a weekly basis. We see them at bars, at parties, at the coffeehouse. We promptly categorize them as "do's," "don't's," or "dates." Circumstance dictates their availability.

Meeting women is not difficult. Women are everywhere. They are either everywhere or they are at aerobics.

But meeting quality women is more challenging.

We could meet women at church, but we're afraid we'd have to wait until marriage to have sex with them, and what if they weren't any good at it?

We could meet women at the coffeehouse, if they'd ever look up from their manuscript, but we're afraid they'd be smarter than we are.

We could meet women at the art museum, but we're afraid they'd be from France.

Or we could meet women at a bar.

So let's reexamine a night at the bar:

We walk in the door and do the requisite reconnaissance. It's like a live version of the old TV show The Dating Game, with bachelorettes 1, 2 and 3 sitting at the bar with their legs crossed in a stunning display of black hosiery.

Bachelorette No. 1 tells us that she is attending South Wampus Junior College "right now." We know this line. We have heard it before. It is meant to convey that she is attending South Wampus "right now" because "right now" she is caring for her ill grandmother, but that she'll be attending Yale next semester. We're thinking, "Yale what? Yale School of Hair n' Cosmetology?"

Bachelorette No. 2 is cool. She's smart and funny. She can't explain the infield fly rule, but she has heard of it. We buy her another Frozen Fruity Taste Concoction. We like her. She likes us—until a BETTER-LOOK-ING GUY walks in. We spend the next three minutes talking to a woman who is peering directly over our left shoulder at somebody else. This is a serious ego-ectomy. We excuse ourselves to go to the bathroom, where we put our hands on the sink counter, stare into the mirror and mutter, "What's wrong with me?"

Bachelorette No. 3 is gorgeous. But she's bitter. We soon discover that her boyfriend just left her for another man. She stares at us like we have horns coming out of our head. She will use everything we say as evidence that we are indeed a man, which is an indictable offense punishable by loathing. She will probably go knock over our mailbox later. We excuse ourselves so that she may drown alone in her own bile.

So we stand in the corner with our buddies, drinking beer and talking baseball. Later we look for Bachelorette No. 1, but she left with Bachelorette No. 2's BETTER-LOOKING GUY.

Finding Someone to Date Part 4

Desperate times call for desperate want ads. People have become marketable commodities, and we have the personal ads to prove it. Others resort to dating services that separate single people as if they were cans of Campbell's Soup on Aisle 5. There are dating services for :

- Busy executives
- Christian singles
- People who have a spare $5,000 for a membership fee
- People who like people of the same sex

A single man approaches these endeavors with a healthy dose of skepticism. We learned at an early age that advertising is not always a forum for the truth. Usually we discovered this after wasting $5.99 (plus postage and handling) on a pair of X-ray glasses from the back pages of Boys Life.

We'll pass on these modern methods of date acquisition. We'd just as soon order a pair of polyester slacks from Parade magazine than we would rifle through the personal ads in hopes of finding our soul mate.

Finding Someone to Date Part 5

The supermarket is rumored to be a good place to meet women, especially women who eat food. But the timing has to be exactly right, or you will be labeled a stalker. Not a celery stalker but a vile, evil, contemptible stalker who prays on women who eat food.

The thing is, you'd better anticipate her next move, and you'd better make it look like you belong on Aisle 5 and pray it's not the cosmetics aisle, or she'll know you're tailing her. If you nonchalantly cross paths in benign places like the Soup Aisle or the Crouton Aisle, you might make it work. You might be able to say something to her—"Nice soup"—without being wrestled to the floor by supermarket security.

The bookstore is a good place to meet women. But it requires the subtle maneuver of tearing a woman away from the paragraph she's reading. This is dicey. It's not like you can say, "Is that a good paragraph?" Or, "Can I read that paragraph when you're finished?" You can't ask her to read it aloud.

So you stand there, waiting for her to look up, when suddenly you realize you're in the Menopause section. You dash over to the Photography section and blindly pick out a book. You hold it up just as a beautiful woman passes. She smiles. You smile. It is only then that you realize that you are holding a collection of homoerotic photographs by Robert Mapplethorpe.

Typically, it's luck when a guy meets a girl who eventually agrees to a date. Usually she's a friend of a friend of a friend, and she just happens to sit next to us at the football game. Or she's new in town, and she hasn't had time to confirm all the rumors.

Joe Namath: The Original Anti-Dater

Some guys don't waste time dating. They are anti-daters. Anti-daters follow in the hallowed footsteps of their patron saint, Joe Namath.

In 1969, Namath added some snap and crackle to the world of sports—and solidified his position atop the pantheon of single men.

His New York Jets were heavy underdogs to the Baltimore Colts in Super Bowl III. Namath, the Jets' quarterback, boldly predicted a New York victory. Everybody thought Joe was nuts.

But by the morning after the Jets' 16-7 victory, Joe Namath had become a household name—mostly in the households of women. Suddenly, Broadway Joe was the toast of Gotham. He knew who buttered the toast. Women buttered his toast.

With hep sideburns and a cool demeanor, Namath cruised the scene as New York's No. 1 stud. He will forever be known among single men for one phrase:

"I don't date women. I just kind of run into them"

Namath didn't call women on Wednesday for a Saturday night date. He didn't call them at all. Women went where he went. He cruised the Big Apple's great night spots, and he seldom sat unattended.

We kneel to His Joeness. He taught us that good girls come to guys who wait.

Today's anti-daters hate the formality of dating—the planning, the nervous anticipation, the shaving. They'd rather meet a woman at a back-yard shindig where neither is concerned about broccoli between the teeth. A relationship can begin—or end—unencumbered by the artificial constraints of a date. They don't feel obligated to stay until the bananas Foster arrive.

The "anti-date" provides several advantages over the conventional date:

- the woman doesn't have to wear control-top panty-hose
- the man doesn't have to wear socks
- the woman doesn't have to eat like a bird
- the man can drink too much
- the woman can wear her sweater around her waist
- the man can pee in the bushes

Men and Women:
We All Want What We Can't Have

We know we're not Joe Namath. We know we can't have any girl we want. We want to go to Spago with Cindy Crawford. We know we can't have it.

We want Cindy hanging on our every word, laughing at our little jokes, shaking her head in amazement as we recite "The Iliad" in Latin. We can't have it.

We want an endless supply of supermodels, an endless supply of money.

We can't have it. And we know we can't have it. Unless we play for the Dallas Cowboys.

A woman's ultimate fantasy is—or was—John F. Kennedy Jr., perennially the country's most eligible bachelor, according to such authorities as People magazine. So coveted was John-John, some women just wanted to marry his hair.

Other women wanted all of John-John. Their longing was a long-shot, yes, but not completely unrealistic. After all, it came true for one woman. One woman crossed the threshold of the new Camelot.

The difference in the two fantasies: Men know their fantasy will never happen. Men do not spend their time writing Tyra Banks' first name with their last name. "Tyra Baumgardner. It's perfect." It doesn't happen.

According to social custom, men are authorized to ask women out. We know just how far this power will take us. Realistically, it will not take us to Tyra Banks' house.

And according to custom, women must wait for the man to come knocking. Though many people believe this unwritten rule is outdated, most still abide by it. This allows women to fantasize that someday the name "Denzel Washington" will pop up on their caller I.D.

Or that George Clooney will send a charming note.

Or that at the office the secretary will announce, "Stephanie, a Mr. Brad Pitt on Line 1."

Conjuring a glorious romance is part of life's experience. We lie in bed at night, imagining a romantic slow-motion montage like the ones in bad '70s love-story movies: We chase Tyra through the park as brittle leaves crunch underfoot; we tumble across the grass locked in love's embrace; we steal away to a small cave as cool rain pours. We kiss.

But when reality sets in, men realize they'll never get Tyra's phone number, much less have the courage to call. Mostly we just look at the pictures. We don't really think the supermodel might someday be ours.

The Duties of Dating

A woman's duty in dating is twofold: saying "Yes" or "No" to the date and "No" or "Not a chance" to any future advances the male might explore. Once she says yes—and this is one of life's great ironies—all responsibilities fall to the male.

Say what?

Most men can't decide on a breakfast cereal, yet we're expected to effectively captain an entire date from beginning to end? Shouldn't there be a rush chairman or a den mother available for consultation?

No. We are expected to assume the role of Date Dictator and hand down the evening's agenda as if we received it via divine guidance upon Mount Sinai.

"Thou shalt take her fine self to dinner and a movie."

This is fine if you're a member of a Utah survivalist commune whose women are all named "Naomi" and make their own butter. It's fine, too, if you're a Japanese businessman whose conversation with females consists solely of the sentence, "Bring me more sakÇ."

But for a normal American single guy whose lineage does not include the Hussein family, being a Date Dictator is no great thing. For 18 years our moms told us to take out the trash, and suddenly we're telling a woman the movie starts at 7:30?

In dictating the date, the man must first determine what the female wants to do without actually bothering to ask her. She might be allergic to theater seats, but that doesn't matter. She might have an aversion to solid foods, but so what?

One reason that single men are single is because we have a difficult time making decisions that affect our own lives. If we can't decide between sausage and pepperoni, how can we decide the manner in which two people spend an evening?

It's like, "I'm not sure what I'm going to do, but I know what you're going to do."

The woman can make the man's task more difficult by asking questions that would otherwise be considered legitimate, if in fact they weren't asked of a single male. Questions such as, "What time are you picking me up?"

DECIDING WHAT TO DO

And so it falls to the male to choose the night's agenda. If we choose something too exotic, she'll think we're a swami or a loon. A visit to the psychic fair is out (we assume the psychics will know we're not coming). War games might be considered odd.

If, on the other hand, we go light on originality, she'll think we lack spark and pizzazz. While enjoyable, the dinner-and-movie date isn't exactly what Buddhists call "original spontaneity." News flash: Other people have done it. Isn't it odd that you're on a dinner-and-movie date, and thousands of other couples are experiencing the exact same thing?

Mmmmmmoooooooooooooo.

We should approach other dinner-and-movie couples and inquire about their experience:

"How is your dinner and movie?"

"Delicious and dramatic, with just a hint of whimsy. And yours?"

"Two thumbs up!"

The Dating Game:

THE FIRST DATE

Some things you don't do on a first date. A funeral, for example.

"Jenny, this is my mother. She's not shy. She's dead."

A seance is a bad idea. Group sex is a bad idea. Dinner with Meemaw at the nursing home is a poor choice.

"Go ahead and scoop the soup off Meemaw's chin, Jenny. Thaaaaat's it. Meemaw loves it."

Another thing you don't do on a first date is go out for barbecued ribs, or anything else that requires you to rip flesh from bone with your teeth. You both look like Fred Flintstone tearing into a stack of Stegasaurus ribs, and for the rest of the night you have cow stuck between your teeth.

Other bad first-date dates:
- Bingo Night at the K of C
- A quilting bee at the community center
- $10 Table-Dance Night at Candyland Express
- A Klan rally
- An all-male revue at Oil Can Harry's
- A squirrel hunt
- Deep-sea fishing on a small wooden boat
- A stage production of "Caligula"
- A lecture on metallurgy
- Football practice

DYNAMICS OF THE FIRST DATE

The first date is hard for a guy, mostly because he has to cut short his game of flag football in order to get there on time. But seriously.

A guy really does want to do and say the right things. But he doesn't want to do and say the things that EVERY OTHER GUY does and says. So he chooses between extremes of cliche and original thought:

- "You sure look nice tonight."

Safe, but no style points. It's the verbal equivalent of a brown suit.

- "You make my toes curl up and my eyes roll back in my head. Join me fireside for a game of Twister?"

Style points, but risky. She might think you enjoy an extensive video library of mildly erotic films.

- "Given the feeble tools of the English language I cannot adequately describe the warm sensation I am currently feeling upon the sight of you answering your door in a tight red dress and shiny high-heeled shoes."

Several style points. But as soon as she opens the door in that tight red dress, she will probably close the door in that tight red dress. And she will not open it again. You are officially guilty of "coming on a bit too strong."

The problem is, as men, we are never really sure what a girl wants us to say. We suffer under a barrage of conflicting messages:

- Female wants to be respected for her mind. Female wears WonderBra.
- Female wants serious commitment. Female dates 18 men.
- Female says sensitivity is more important than a man's appearance. Female can't talk now about the orphanage fund-raiser right now, female is watching a Mel Gibson movie marathon.

When it comes to women, men wallow in a murky netherworld of uncertainty. What we need is a starter kit, a woman with training wheels. If a VCR comes with instructions, then why not a woman? Is someone telling us that a VCR is more complicated than a woman?

FIRST-DATE PAIN AND SUFFERING

For the female, the first date begins in the morning when she begins preparing for the evening: hair, nails, pores, follicles and other stuff that guys don't ever notice.

For the guy it begins that afternoon, when he looks at his watch.

"Whoa, guys! Gotta go! I have a date in 48 minutes!"

"Dude! It's fourth-and-goal from the eight!"

"All right. But if the game goes into overtime, I can't stay. Unless you need me."

Don't get us wrong. Men do think about the date—we think about it in the shower or when we are drying off.

It's not that we don't worry. It's just that we don't worry about worrying until it's time to start worrying. Then we worry.

And when we like a girl a lot, we worry a lot. Unlike those charming leading men in the movies, our lines aren't provided by a team of gifted Jewish writers. We have to think them up all by ourselves. Usually our lines just spill out in stupid first-date questions:

"So, you've always been a woman?"

The inquisition usually begins in the car, after we pick up our date. We ask about her hometown, her school, her job, all while desperately hoping we didn't miss a spot when we shaved the right side of our face.

The drive is chaos in slow-motion, turmoil in molasses. We feel like Jim Lovell on Apollo 13, handling a hundred things at once as our world burns around us. "Houston, we have a problem. We missed a spot."

We watch... traffic...street signs...our face in the mirror for rogue nose hairs.

We listen...as our date says she once joined the Peace Corps...and came home because the Peace Corps wasn't air-conditioned.

We think...of what to say...and what to say next...we're always two steps ahead...so when she asks where we're from...we say, "I started out as a history major."

First dates in general are troubling because neither participant is paying attention to the date itself. The date is little more than a five-hour prelude to the end of the date, when the real drama begins. Will they go out again? Will they kiss? Will it end at the doorstep?

They talk religion and politics, but they're silently mulling their impending actions at date's end:

"If the Democrats regain control of Congress, we can look for cuts in Medicare."

- Should I ask her out again?

"Goodwill toward man is a central tenet to all the great religions."

- Should I kiss him good night?

"The Gramm-Rudman Bill is a vital component of the Alan Parsons Project."

- I wonder if she'll ask me up for coffee, like they do in the movies.

"Religion was created to help people explain the unexplainable, and as such was a forerunner to the Psychic Friends Network."

- I hope he likes French Vanilla.

"In politics as in life, it helps to get a good night's sleep."

Should I ask for a massage?

"Michael rowed the boat ashore, hallelujah."

- If he makes any slick moves, he's gone.

"If God is a merciful God, why did he create mimes?"

- I have GOT to use the restroom.

Probably the best thing a guy can do on a first date is end it. Euthanize it. This way he can move on to the less-awkward second date or just plain move on.

FIRST-DATE DO'S AND DON'TS

Do: Open the door for her
Don't: Open the door of the ladies room for her
Do: Pull out her chair

Don't: Pull out her chair and give it to someone else
Do: Compliment her on her dress
Don't: Compliment her on her breasts (unless she just bought them)
Do: Bring her flowers
Don't: Bring her shrubbery
Do: Look your best
Don't: Look better than her
Do: Tell her you love puppies
Don't: Tell her you love kittens and other little furry animals
Do: Pay for the date
Don't: Pay for the date with wheat pennies or wooden beads

THE FIRST-AND-LAST DATE

We know about the First Date. It is aptly named. Sometimes you have a First Date that doesn't lead to a second date. It isn't a terrible date—no one died—but it isn't sufficiently enjoyable to warrant a sequel.

The First-And-Last Date is much different. This is a date that is so bad from the outset that it can't end quickly enough. You actually hear the Sands Of Time dropping grain by grain through the hourglass. It's like you're having a date on a treadmill.

The First-And-Last Date occurs for several reasons:

It often occurs exactly one week after a guy meets a girl in dimly lit nightclub. The nightclub is smoky and chaotic. Lights are flashing. The beat goes chooka-chooka-chooka! The guy has consumed many cold beers. These factors combine to produce a hypnotic effect, which renders him unaware that the girl has a hair lip and wears a toupee.

He asks her out. She says yes.

His friends warn him all week that she isn't exactly Miss Snap-On Tool, but he thinks they're kidding. He thinks they're jealous.

He arrives at her apartment. A plumber answers the door. He asks the plumber to please tell Amanda that her date has arrived.

"I am Amanda," the plumber says, a thick strand of black hair jutting from a large mole on her third chin. "Wait here while I go put on my other overalls."

There is one trick the guy can use:

"Amanda, I suddenly remembered that I am gay."

Otherwise, he spends the rest of the evening waiting for the check.

A First-And-Last Date can also occur when a guy and girl—and this is for lack of a better term—hate each other. Mutual loathing doesn't happen immediately. As in all rancorous relationships, it builds slowly as each party begins to realize the other party sucks.

Montagues and Capulets. Hatfields and McCoys. Sonny and Cher. Given the opportunity, each would turn the other's cheek and start slapping anew.

Likewise, what begins as a date can end in jihad. Initial mutual attraction can quickly dissolve into shared repugnance.

That dimple he thought was so cute? Fairway divot.

That curly black hair she found adorable? Burnt noodles.

Her independent streak now borders on militance. "Who are you," he asks, "Joan of freaking Arc?"

What she had deemed sensitivity now seems like plain wimpiness. "You do Cosmo questionnaires to get in touch with your feminine side?" she asks. "God, you're a sissy."

By the time dessert arrives, they're like one of those couples on The Love Connection who had a date that DIDN'T WORK OUT.

THE DATE FROM HELL

Possible True Story: One night a guy who worked for the phone company went out with this girl. The next day he invented Caller I.D.

He also installed a burglar bars on his windows and a peep hole in his door.

The girl is not normal. Somehow, during dinner, she mistook the shrimp fork for an engagement ring. He asked her to pass the melba toast and she said, "I love you too."

Twenty-one times she has called him—21 times today. It says so on his Caller I.D. She will not leave him alone. He told her he wasn't interested, but she thinks he's playing hard to get.

"No," he said. "Not hard to get—impossible to get."

Still she stalks him. He goes to malls, nightclubs and the steam room at the Y, and there she is. His only refuge is the mens' room—and still he checks under the stall door. She might be standing on the pot, waiting to make her move.

THE PHONE DATE

Important lesson for the single man: A nice voice is a nice voice, and that's all it is.

Never assume that just because a woman sounds good on the phone that she looks good in person. This is why phone-sex operators are phone-sex operators and not Las Vegas showgirls.

Yet still it happens. We call the bank to check on our balance. We talk to Camille, and somehow Camille makes it seem kind of funny that we just bounced three checks. She is witty and smart. And she has the smoothest, sexiest voice since this side of Natalie Merchant.

We ask Camille if she'd like to meet us for coffee and dessert, and later a movie. She says she sure would.

We get to Sweet Dreams Dessertery eight minutes late. And there Camille sits, in her entirety, working on her fourth Crème Brule. We wonder how she'll fit in the theater seat.

THE BLIND DATE

The blind date is another of the great ironies. Single men spend many years and much deliberation seeking a woman to have and hold, and suddenly a co-worker's sister's friend's brother's girlfriend decides she knows exactly the girl for us?

Please. Save it for the Psychic Friends Network.

It happens all the time. The co-worker's sister's friend's brother's girlfriend calls us because her boyfriend told her that we have a job and hair. We listen as she describes her friend. It is up to us to decipher fact from fiction, reality from euphemism.

- "She just broke up with her boyfriend."

Her boyfriend just broke up with her because of her addiction to the Home Shopping Channel.

- "She is an account executive."

She sells toilet paper to high schools.

- "She went to the University of Chicago."

To pick up a friend.

- "She loves the outdoors."

Because she has to go through the outdoors to get to the donut shop.

- "She's very athletic."

Back when she was slim, she could juggle several men at once.

We must admit, however, to a fondness for the twisted intrigue of the blind date. It's exciting to wait for our date to open the door. Surely it's the excitement Let's Make A Deal contestants felt just before Door No. 3 opened. A rose or a thorn?—the answer is behind the door.

The blind date appeals to man's basic optimism, the same instinct that compels us to open the envelope from Ed McMahon and the Publisher's Clearinghouse Sweepstakes. We might get a winner.

We knock on her door. We hear footsteps grow louder across the hardwood floor. We strain to hear if the footsteps resemble those of a strongside linebacker or a Chinese ballerina.

We hear a clicking sound as she unlocks the deadbolt…a clicking sound as she unfastens the chain lock…a clicking sound as she undoes the doorknob lock. Enough with the clicking sounds!

The door opens slowly, creaking as if Bela Lugosi were at the controls. The mystery of the moment is too much to bear! On the other side could be Cindy Crawford or that fat woman from Hee Haw.

The door is open. Our blind date stands just across the threshold.

"You must be Jennifer," we say.

We are pleased or we pretend that we are pleased.

THE DOUBLE DATE

This is how a double date originates:

"Dude."

"What."

"I need you to double with me."

"I'm busy that night."

"I haven't told you what night."

"I'm busy that night."

"What night?"

"That night."

"C'mon. Judy has this friend, Veronica. Last time Veronica went out, some guy took her to Wendy's for a Meal Deal Combo."

"Jeez. That doesn't even include drinks."

"Exactly. She just needs somebody to go out with. Judy says she'll withhold favors from me unless somebody takes Veronica out. Dude, my boys are turning a mild shade of azure already."

"Is she a dog?"

"No, she's cute. She looks like Jennifer Aniston."

"Is she Jennifer Aniston?"

"Uhhhh…no. But she has a lot of friends."

There's trouble with the double: For some bizarre quirk of human nature, men are invariably attracted to the other guy's date. We devise ways to steal glances at her: We angle our spoon to see her reflection, convex though it may be. We ask her to pass the butter, the salt, the pepper six times each. We say strategic things to sabotage her date.

"Jim, how are those weekly visits to the psychiatrist?"

"Jim, how's it been since you moved back in with your mother?"

"Jim, do you still need to borrow $20 to pay for dinner?"

She captivates us not only because she is beautiful, but because she is unattainable. Put it this way: It would be rude to attain her. She is on a date.

We admire her from the safe haven of circumstance, secure in the knowledge that our relative positions make rejection impossible. If she acts uninterested in us, it is only because she must. She knows that any outward sign of affection would hurt her date's feelings. So she passes the butter, the salt, the pepper each time without actually looking at us. But we know, we know.

Her compassion toward her date and suppression of her true feelings reveals a sensitivity that makes her even more appealing. We buuuuurn for her.

We turn to our date and ask, "So how's your steak?"

Bad Dates, Life Lessons

Given the freedom of choice that single men enjoy, it usually it takes a bad date to teach us a hard lesson: that not all girls are custom-made for us.

We don't imply adherence to classism. This isn't India, where a member of the Brahmin caste can't take a member of the Untouchables caste out for yak milk. This isn't even a college fraternity, where a Kappa Sig won't date a girl outside the Panhellenic system for fear of meeting a dame who works for a living.

But for most of us, there are no restrictions. We can date whoever we please. Unfortunately, we're not always pleased with whoever we date.

The Up-with-People Person

You pick up Mimsy at her place. Its walls are decorated with aphorisms printed in bold red lettering: "If you can dream it, you can do it!"

At this point you think, "Then maybe I should call Tyra Banks."

In the 28 seconds it takes her to skip merrily to your car, she has called out encouragement to each of her neighbors. "If you can rake it, you can bag it, Mrs. Peters!"

For the next five hours you will be Up-With-Peopled up to here.

You put on your seat belt. Mimsy straps herself in, lest she injure herself. She sings along to a song on the radio: "I'm walkin' on sunshine—yeah-yeah! And it makes me feel good!"

You turn down the volume. You ask, "So, were you a cheerleader?"

"Go 'Huskers!"

You sit down to dinner. You have to get a new waiter because she just convinced your first waiter to go back and finish his master's.

"If you want it bad enough," she tells you, "you can achieve it."

"Well then," you say. "I think I'll achieve a cheeseburger."

The Go-Getter

You haven't been able to reach Alexis on the phone since you met her. This, you discover, is because for the past three weeks she has been trekking barefoot across Nepal.

You finally reach her on the phone. She is out of breath because she just ran the 10 miles home from tae-kwan-do lessons.

"I didn't know you were taking tae-kwan-do lessons," you say.

"I'm not," she says. "I'm giving them."

You ask her out, maybe dinner and a movie. She suggests that together you scale Mt. Whitney. You inform her that you are not afraid of heights so much as you are the ground below it.

You agree to go mountain biking. She shows up at 6 the next morning with some bananas and fruit bars. "Ready?" she asks, peeling a Chiquita. "It's a golden day!"

"It isn't golden," you say, "because the sun isn't up."

After an hour of cycling, Alexis agrees to your plan: Every 20 minutes, she will stop and wait for you.

That night you drop her off at her hillside home. "I'd walk you to your door," you say, "but I'm too sore to walk."

She says to take two aspirin and don't call her in the morning.

THE MILITANT CHICK

She wears black horned-rim glasses and a dress made of paper. It is "Organic Night" at the local coffeehouse, and Sher seeks to symbolize the destiny of a tree.

Sher is the most serious person this side of the Henry Rollins Band. And you are very attracted to her. She's no prom queen. If she was ever inside a sorority house it was probably to kick some Tri-Delt's ass for using too much toilet paper.

"Two squares!" Sher might have screamed, dragging Tiffany by the hair toward the ladies room. "Fold one square over another and it's more than enough!"

You sip Crème Latte with her at the coffeehouse and wonder if she's ever watched a sitcom, or skipped a rock. She tells you about all the things she's done: boycotts, demonstrations, vigils. She once convinced city council to turn a landfill into a city park.

You ask her out. She says she doesn't have time for men, unless she's boycotting them.

You opt for a compromise: You'll join her at her next demonstration.

By 10 the next morning you are handcuffed to a tree. This wasn't what you had in mind when you visualized a girl handcuffing you to something.

With 15 granola-heads you are chained to an oak at a city park that, ironically, is set to become a landfill.

The granola-heads are chanting:

"One, two, three, four!"

"We'll dump trash on your front door!"

"Five, six, seven, eight!"

"Until you have to fumigate!"

To symbolize the bulldozing, Sher has painted faux tire tracks across her chest. To represent the death of plant life, she is crucified to the trunk of a large oak. "You will choke on the refuse of your own imperialist ways!" she shouts at city leaders who aren't listening. "To kill this tree, you go through me!"

You stare at Sher in awe. She is Joan of Oak.

Two days later you sit at home, rubbing triple antibiotic ointment on your handcuff wounds. You see Sher on the local TV newscast, handcuffed to a nuclear reactor. Handcuffed with her is the Henry Rollins Band.

THE FLIGHTY NEUROTIC

The day you met Sara, she was standing on her head to see what things would look like if a person were to stand on her head. She said, "You look upside down."

You said, "So do you."

You liked her immediately. You were attracted by her spontaneity, her indifference to approval, her seeming incongruity with life on planet Earth. She was different, odd. She recited poetry that was actually pretty good. She had ideas derivative of nothing specific. She walked her dog backward.

Mostly you were attracted to her because she didn't do the really bizarre things that incongruous women do, like jump from moving vehicles or curl up in the fetal position in inappropriate places, such as crowded restaurants that serve good food to nice people. She just did the slightly bizarre things, like feed squirrels.

Friday night, you pick up Sara at her treehouse. She gets in the car and lights up a smoke. Halfway through her cigarette she runs her hand through her thick brown hair and says, "Mind if I smoke?" She sighs and stares out the window.

"Funny how street people never commit suicide," she says as you pass a panhandler. "I mean, not right on the spot. They live in this weird purgatory between life and death, but they still live, you know, they're out there smoking and drinking, and meanwhile CEOs toss themselves from 10th-story balconies because they don't have the money to pay for their ex-wife's therapist."

Sara asks you to stop the car. She gets out before you come to a full stop. She tumbles across the sidewalk, stopping when she hits a pole. She limps toward a homeless man, gives him a cigarette, lights it for him. "My name is Sara," she tells him. "I am lighting your cigarette."

She gets back in the car. "Life," she says from the floorboard, "is a series of moments." For the next few moments Sara warbles Celtic rhythms.

You arrive at the restaurant. Sara orders a hamburger with no meat. She says her meatless burger reminds her of childhood. Sara curls up in a fetal position on the floor next to the table. You look at her, then at her half-eaten meatless burger. You really can't think of anything to say except, "Are you going to finish that?"

THE PLAYER

You talk to Courtney's smart-aleck roommate much more often than you talk to Courtney.

"Courtney's not here," says roommate Jen. "She's on a date."

Courtney, you surmise, spends a majority of her life having car doors opened for her. Courtney is on a date—to quote from the movie Roger & Me—on Monday, and Tuesday, and Wednesday, and Thursday, and Friday, and Saturday, and Sunday.

She hasn't paid for her own entertainment since a rainy day in 1990, when she went to Wendy's and got herself a medium Frosty.

Jen says she can pencil you in for Saturday the 12th, beginning at 7 p.m. You are instructed to be there promptly or Courtney will assume you're not coming and proceed to her standard back-up date.

You show up at 7. Jen opens the door with a grin on her face that says, "Heh—heh, another sucker." Jen takes your flowers and puts them in…ah, the blue vase. Jen says Courtney will be ready in a minute. She offers you a Molson Golden. She adds that this is the only Molson Golden you will receive. It is part of the package.

You sit on the couch, drinking your Molson Golden. Courtney strides into the room. She is beautiful indeed. She is wearing a tight black dress that is probably made by some kind of designer.

"Well, hello," Courtney says in a breathy voice that you would pay to hear. Jen, her baseball cap on backwards, rolls her eyes.

"I've looked forward to this night for a very long time," Courtney coos. You think, "Press 'Play.'"

As you leave you look back at Jen. She looks kind of cute in that ball cap.

We wade the waters of single women, wondering where the good ones have gone. We enjoy elements of each woman, but we'd like to blend those elements into the perfect chick. She'd be funny and smart. Kind and happy. She'd let us hit the snooze.

As it is, we keep going and going, thinking maybe she'll show up.

Meeting the Right One, Maybe:

SERIOUS DATING

Temporarily tired of the singles grind, we begin dating as if dating were a demonstration sport in the next Summer Olympics. We go all out. We date Girl A, Girl B, and if not A or B then C. We pull out our "A material" on each girl. We send in the first string.

Problem is, after three weeks of obsessive-compulsive dating, patterns develop.

We begin telling the same stories. We preface comments with the question, "Have I told you this?" For 10 minutes we tell her all about our family. Finally she says, "I met your family. Remember?"

We get in real trouble later: We say, "Do that thing you do."

She says, "I don't do that thing."

There goes Girl C.

CHOOSING JUST ONE

The dating process is a weird thing. We go out with a woman, it's like an introductory offer:

"If after 90 days you are not completely satisfied, return the woman for a full refund."

Single guys periodically go off the market by getting a full-time girlfriend. They do any of several reasons:

1) They want to snuggle, eat takee-outee and rent two movies.
2) They want hassle-free sex.
3) They like her.
4) They want to marry her.

The strange thing about singlehood vs. girlfriendhood is that it's often greener on the other side. From here, there looks great.

Even the biggest cad in town occasionally craves a girlfriend, someone to hug at night and hold in the morning. Sex is easy, but a hug is earned.

He goes out with his friends on Saturday night. The singles smorgasbord is well-stocked. But he sees a guy and girl in the back booth, touching and giggling. He wonders what it's like to feel so strongly about a woman. To share joys and pains. To hold hands. To split the last quesadilla. Then he snaps from his reverie and turns his attention back to Miss Covington County.

Meanwhile, the guy in the back booth takes a break from nose-nuzzling. He looks at the cad hitting on Miss Covington County and remembers when. Remembers how fun it used to be. Sure, he has feelings for his girl, but man! Look at that! Girls are everywhere!

"Wouldn't it be great," he thinks, "to dive into the scrum just one more time?"

That's the way it is. You don't have a girl, you want one. You have a girl, you don't.

It is a phenomenon of the male existence: A guy gets tired of going full-bore single. Tired of seeing the same girls night after night.

So he gets a girlfriend. He goes out with her one night, and man!—it's like the new shipment just came in! Like this year's models just arrived on the showroom floor! Gorgeous girls are all over the place! Where were they a month ago? It's like they were hibernating, lying in wait for him to leave! And now they're all are staring at him! One is playing mouth games with her straw!

The guy tries to pay attention to his girlfriend, but he keeps getting up to go to the bathroom. He's doing a cursory mingle for old time's sake.

The Girlfriend

The most common reason a single guy gets a girlfriend is No. 3—he likes her.

He meets a girl, and it just happens. He wants to hang out with her.

It's auto-pilot fun. There are greater good times and fewer bad. It is not the sometimes manic existence of the single guy—the highs of big fun, the lows of Ramen Soup.

A major concern, however, is when the guy can feel comfortable doing guy things around his girl. When does the moratorium on guy behavior end? When can he walk around in his boxers? When can he read the sports page in her bathroom?

Throughout his life, a man follows the credo of "to each his own"—but now there's a her-own involved.

In any relationship, the initial enamel of glamour wears thin. It's weird. A good relationship has almost an inverted construction. We meet a girl we like. We're witty, charming and smart from the start. We're at our best because she brings it out in us.

Strange, but it can only get worse. We can never be quite as impressive as we were at first. We shot our personality wad at the get-go. We gave her all our big ideas on religion and the meaning of life.

Now we're getting Pop-Tarts out of the toaster.

But that's what a good relationship is. Just sharing Pop-Tarts.

AT THE CROSSROADS: THE RELATIONSHIP

Even a Pop-Tart relationship answers to greater concerns. The relationship endures or succumbs at the common breaking points, when our imperfections emerge from the shiny veneer of a new union. We begin making body-function noises. She plays with her hair. We ignore her when we're reading. She forgets to call.

At a restaurant one night, we happen to look at another woman. In retaliation, she brings up an old boyfriend. Over the bitter taste of jealousy and insecurity, we fail to taste the coq au vin.

All the imperfections we'd overlooked now bear closer scrutiny. At first, we didn't care that she followed the teachings of L. Ron Hubbard. Suddenly we do. We think her Dianetics is mumbo-jumbo.

She didn't care that we bet on football games. In fact, she thought it was cool. Now she's had it. She complains that every Sunday, we're on the phone saying, 'Gimme two dimes on the over." She says we ignore her the rest of the day. We say, "Wanna bet?"

She doesn't appreciate the snide humor. We sit on the couch, staring at each other in silence. She is still beautiful—just not as beautiful. Finally she says, "We're going to have to work at this relationship."

"If a relationship needs work," we reply, "maybe it's not worth working for. This isn't a job."

THE BREAKUP

Even in a sissy voice, Neil Sedaka said it right: "Breaking up is hard to do."

It's hard to end a good gig. One week we're cooking pasta al dente together, the next week she's asking whether the Jon Secada CD is ours or hers (It's hers). In one fell swoop, we go from a pair to two one-of-a-kinds.

When a relationship is ending, it's probably best that it end outright. We have to yank off the Band-Aid. We can't ease out of it. We can't keep hanging out together to slowly ease the pain of withdrawal.

And that's what sucks. It's not like we hate her. We just don't love her. Now we can't play with her anymore.

Sometimes we date a girl even though we know we won't marry her. Why is that? We like her but don't love her. We know it. So why bother dating her?

Well, we're not going to marry our best friend either. But that doesn't mean we tell him to take a hike.

And that's why it hurts to break up. We lose a friend.

BECOMING "A COUPLE"

It's the Dan-and-Jan Syndrome. If a relationship endures the breaking point, two individuals become A COUPLE. We are no longer Dan; she is no longer Jan. We are Dan-and-Jan. Like Adam-and-Eve. Lois-and-Clark. Romeo-and-Juliet.

Suddenly, as single men, our lives change:

Our friends have to knock—they can't just walk into our apartment.

Our friends have to call for a golf game—they can't just show up with the clubs.

Our friends can't set us up with flight attendants.

We start hanging out with other COUPLES. We play Scruples, Balderdash and charades. We eat cheese dip and those little sausage balls on toothpicks. It's fun. Just a different kind of fun.

One night we go to a bar as Dan-and-Jan. Our friends see us there. "Dude!" And then, "Oh. Hey, Jan."

There is an awkward silence. They start looking around the room. They say, "Well…" They excuse themselves to embark on another reconnaissance mission. They have a higher calling.

It is a sad but true divestiture of loyalty, a necessary but subtle parting of the ways.

We sit at a table, Dan-and-Jan. We forget about our friends and think only of each other. It occurs to us that this is very weird.

SINGLE-MAN DEMERITS

Sometimes the single man starts acting decidedly un-single. This behavior consists primarily of being way too sweet, way too soon, with a woman he just met.

It is then that his single friends issue him a demerit for the following infractions:

- Clipping out that "Love is…" comic strip
- Wearing matching shirts to the mall
- Feeding her cat after the second date.
- Giving her his beeper number after the third date
- Phoning her during his night out with the guys—a Single Man Felony
- Putting a note on her windshield
- Laying his head on her lap while his friends are in the room
- Telling her "I need you"—especially if his friends are in the room
- Holding her purse while she's trying on a blouse at The Limited
- Turning off a game in the last two minutes because dinner is ready
- Putting peach potpourri in his bathroom
- Telling his friends to make sure the lid is down
- Buying a Michael Bolton CD
- Listening to a Michael Bolton CD
- Owning a frilly pillow with hearts on it
- Reading Men Are From Mars, Women Are From Venus
- Putting on her bridesmaid dress so she can fix the hem

Holidays and the Single Man

A basic law of physics says that for every action, there is an opposite and equal reaction. Likewise, a basic law of the single man says that for every holiday, there is a distinct reaction—an attitude of gratitude or a hint of discontent that he has or has not a girlfriend. Each holiday offers a specific advantage or disadvantage for going steady or going stag.

Some men use a similar chart to choose optimum times to break up or make up with their girl. Other men simply wing it.

It should be stated that this chart reflects the attitudes of the everyday single guy—not the sensitive, sonnet-writing, kitten-stroking, weeping-at-the-end-of-Terms of Endearment single guy. Normal single men have two separate identities—the girlfriend side and the bachelor side—each magnified by the holiday's particular characteristics in accordance with the guy's single status.

The Single Man's Holiday Primer: When It's Good or Bad to Have a Girlfriend

New Year's Eve—Good

It's Dec. 31, 11:59 p.m. The room is filled with loving couples eager to start the New Year by exchanging saliva with the person they love.

You, on the other hand, are standing there with a dumb pointy hat atop your head and a noisemaker dangling limp from your lips. You are surrounded by five friends, none of them female, all equally drunk and equally lonely.

Clever you. You thought you'd go stag and then leave the party with a New Year's doe—start the New Year with a bang. But all the girls are paired off. They're tipsy on bubbly and purring in the ear of men who, unlike you, planned ahead.

You look at your friend Dave. He is doing the same thing you are: searching desperately around the room for some woman—any woman—who in the next 60 seconds he can meet, engage in witty repartee and soul kiss deep into the New Year.

You watch the seconds tick away. Cheers erupt. Horns blow. Men and women kiss. You stand alone, tooting your own horn.

You ring in the New Year exactly as you wrung out the old: alone.

New Year's Day—Bad

It's Jan. 1, 11:59 a.m. The theme of the day is "the hair of the dog." Last night's residual hangover has been replaced by today's breakfast buzz.

This is the sort of manly, beer-in-the-Cheerios behavior with which single men love to ignite the New Year. It is a portent of things to come: namely, weight gain and oversleeping important meetings.

The Rose Bowl is about to begin. You look around the room. Your buddies are wondering what will come first, kickoff or the eight large pizzas. The two most important things in their lives are, in no particular order, kickoff and the eight large pizzas. Perhaps that is nine important things.

You are having a whale of a time, doing what men do. You and your pals point at foxy TV models and say, "I wouldn't kick her out." You get to urinate loudly without closing the bathroom door. You get to spit snuff in a glass. You leave it there like some private reserve until someone kicks it over, thus testing the absorbency of '70s shag rug.

What a day! New Year's Day. Buddies, beer, football, pizza, body noises—all the accouterments in man's pursuit of New Year's happiness. You remember when New Year's Day wasn't so great—a year ago today. You had a girlfriend that day.

You missed every bowl game on TV, even the weenie games such as the Charmin Squeezably Soft Bowl. As a dutiful boyfriend, you escorted your girlfriend to the New Year's Day chamber orchestra concert at the outdoor ice rink.

While your buddies watched Florida nip Florida State with a last-second TD, you watched your girlfriend do triple toe loops to the strains of Mozart's "Serenata Notturna." As your chums quaffed additional Coors, you skidded painfully into a flautist.

You remember it well, noting with great relief that this year you broke from the gates as a single man. In celebration of your stagdom, you ask your friend to throw you a brewski. He throws and misses, striking a lamp. You survey the damage. There is no damage—the beer is unharmed.

You find it interesting that the next 364 days won't be quite this good.

Valentine's Day—Bad

Being without a girlfriend on Valentine's Day is like being in school without homework. No pressure. A free pass. Go directly home and collect phone messages.

Having a girlfriend on V-Day is more complicated. You do things you normally don't do, like give it some thought.

A lot of guys couldn't care less about Valentine's Day. They are the same guys who get birthday cards from Grandma and simply remove the $5 bill without reading the card, which probably says, "Help. I'm dying." These are not your sentimental types.

Other guys are a tad more sensitive. For them, Valentine's Day creates a lot of pressure. The day becomes less an expression of love than a wild stab at skillful consumerism. It's ironic: To express the one thing in life that is free—love—a guy is expected to purchase something.

That's where it gets sticky. The fact is, a guy may have a girlfriend but he's still a guy. And a guy doesn't know what to buy. That's one reason he has a girlfriend—so she can help him buy stuff, such as a shirt that does not make dogs bark and gay men cringe.

So here's the weird part: On Valentine's, a guy has to go buy something without the help of the woman whose help he needs in buying a gift for the woman who always helps him buy stuff.

If, on the other hand, a guy does not have a girlfriend on Valentine's, he operates free of pressure. It's just another day, like Tuesday or Wednesday. If Valentine's was a really important day for men, beer companies would sponsor something. You'd see those big inflatable beer bottles all over the place.

But for a guy with a girl, Valentine's is important. It's important to her, and by association, it's important to him. It is the mid-term exam, a one-day test of devotion to the subject. Expectations are high.

To a guy, Valentine's generosity is less an act of love than ceremony. It's something he has to do. And when he has to, he might be less inclined to want to.

Presidents Day—Good

Presidents Day is a great day for a couple. If you both work for the Federal Government, you can slack off as usual, only not at the office. Together you can hold presidents in memoriam by spending the day defending the Constitutional freedoms of life, liberty and the pursuit of napping.

The only thing better than lying around is lying around with someone you love—especially when everybody else is at work.

St. Patrick's Day—Bad

Any holiday where the primary activity is consumption of mass quantities of alcohol is a bad day to have a girlfriend. Unless she is driving.

Interestingly, this is also the reason it's a great day to find a girlfriend. At least for that one particular day. What's really cool is that the more you drink, the more candidates there are. In that regard, St. Paddy's Day is like the early stages of a presidential primary—candidates are all over the place. By midnight any number of girls would make for a good and proper girlfriend. Come morning, of course, it's a different story.

Generally, a huge party atmosphere is not exactly suitable for couples. In fact, a guy should never take his girl to a big outdoor bacchanal—unless their favorite activity together is a heated argument.

It's scientific. Whenever a couple goes to a big bash, one of two things happen: a) they get soused and have hot sweaty sex in the car, or b) they get soused, argue about something they won't remember tomorrow, then refuse to go home with each other. The girl calls friends to pick her up; the guy hitches a ride with a group of Marines he just met.

The principle applies to all huge celebrations. For example, a girl-friend/boyfriend should never go to Mardi Gras. It's the kiss of death. Amid drunken chants of "Show your tits!", the guy will look at alien breasts and the girl will respond by displaying her own. Both will get mad. One will return to the hotel, alone. The other will end up at a strip club with a group of Marines he just met.

A guy should take his girl to dinner and a play, not Sodom and Gomorrah. It's like a guy taking his girl to Spring Break. He might as well call it Spring Breakup because the relationship won't last past the first wet T-shirt contest.

Guys are genetically engineered to look at other women. At outdoor bashes there are tons of other women. Thus a guy's penchant for visual infidelity coupled with his girl's need to wait in long Port-A-Potty lines can spawn a messy breakup. By the time she gets back from that big blue canister, he's making like a judge at a beauty pageant. Later he will join those Marines.

As for St. Paddy's Day, consider this reworking of the old Irish slogan Erin go bragh.

"Aaron, go stag."

Your Birthday—Good

Too bad a birthday comes just once a year. It's the one day a year when a guy gets treated better than he should. If he has a girlfriend.

For a birthday boy, a girlfriend is the greatest gift of all.

Friends are fine, of course. Friends will take a guy out to the ballgame. Buy him some peanuts and Cracker Jack. Pick up the tab for parking.

But a girlfriend—she'll rock his world. She'll make him King For A Day. She'll do that thing she does.

It's a Today-Only deal. Carpe diem, birthday boy.

A birthday is the one day when a guy gets to get treated like the Sultan of Brunei, minus the 12 wives. He gets breakfast in bed. Breakfast includes coffee, juice, French toast and a hickey. He gets to go wherever he wants, even the Auto-Rama.

He gets to see his girl in that Valentine's negligee he bought her. Well, it's not the exact negligee. She returned that negligee for one that didn't have rhinestone studs. He gets to lie in bed and hear that sweet annual directive, "Now, you just lie still and let me do the work."

He can act like his normal selfish self. For 24 hours he can do nothing and like it.

Just one thing. Women have a memory. They also have a birthday.

Her Birthday—Bad

We were in 3rd grade when Mom doled out this bit of maternal counsel: "Just buy them something you would like."

The advice was based on a number of factors: We were boys, we had $5, we were going to little Jimmy Dugan's birthday party, and we all liked the same things: Hot Wheels, Lincoln Logs and little plastic Army men. We gave the kid stuff he already had, only this stuff was newer.

The advice worked well in adolescence, but it doesn't do diddly for the man with a girlfriend—unless she likes power tools and football phones. It's the same quandary we face on Valentine's: buying a gift for the woman whose help we need but can't have.

Today, as a girlfriend's birthday approaches, we're dazed and confused. We wish she'd tell us exactly what she wants, and how and where to obtain it. Instead she drops hints. We, in turn, fumble them. We can't remember if she said "hoop earrings" or "hoop skirt."

We go to Neiman Marcus, hoping that a lovely garment will jump right off the rack straight into our hands. We consult the sales clerk.

"What size is she?" she asks.

"I'm not sure," we say. "She's, you know…a good-looking size."

"Size 5? Size 6?"

"Uhhhhh, well…her butt is like yay-big," we say, holding our hands a width apart.

The problem cuts straight to a difference between men and women. Women shop; men buy. Women enter a mall with a vague notion of what they want and proceed to whittle their quarry by comparison shopping and deductive reasoning. Men shop with surgical precision. They know what they want, they go in, they buy it. Then they go home and use it.

That's just it: We know what we want but not what she wants. After a fruitless search at Neiman's, we buy her a rod and reel at Sears, thinking she might be interested in a new outdoor hobby. She is. It's called "walking out of the house in a huff."

A girl's birthday is her day, just like a guy's is his. A difference between men and women is that women feel it's their right to be treated right. Men feel it must be some sort of mistake. Women expect to be coddled. Men are pleasantly surprised by it.

What comes around goes around. At least it's supposed to. She brought him breakfast in bed? She's thinking, "Ditto." She rocked his world? Quid pro quo. Whip out Master Card, Johnny. Or else you'll be staring at the coldest of shoulders.

Men should keep this in mind on an annual basis.

For men, it's enough to get a hickey and quickie. Woman want Dooney & Burke. It will hold them for another year.

Arbor Day—Good

When planting a tree, it's good to have someone who can hand you a sandwich.

Fourth of July—Bad

Consider the first Fourth of July. The signing of the Declaration of Independence. It was an all-guy affair.

We acknowledge that Thomas Jefferson wrote a pretty mean position paper, but he didn't throw a very good party. In fact, a gathering of several men in white wigs seems kind of…you know…funny.

Today we like to celebrate Jefferson's work by having a beach blowout with a pleasant mix of both sexes. The whole point is to see how many wine coolers we can open for how many women.

When we attend a Fourth of July bash as a couple, we undermine the very concept of freedom. Only by going stag can we make a true declaration of independence.

Labor Day—Bad
(After Labor Day—Good)

Labor Day marks a shift in a single man's seasonal perspective on relationships. It is an important portal from summer to fall philosophy.

In summer, the single man is in constant reconnaissance mode. He is always on the lookout. Women are toned, tanned and in such abundance, to choose just one is a crime against manliness. To limit summer love to one summer lover is to eat vanilla at Baskin-Robbins.

Summer is the season of heat and fire—when the boys of summer want to meet the girls of summer. Girls plural.

From the summer solstice to nearly the vernal equinox, the stag man resists any relationship that could be classified as "lasting." He bypasses any palpitations of the heart. He opts instead for the manual application of SPF 15 on as many women as possible.

He is steadfastly single. To fall in love or have a girlfriend would miss the whole point.

Autumn, however, is when lust gives way to love. Or at least the possibility of it. Women begin wearing those cute oversized sweatshirts. Bikinis are dashed in lieu of blue jeans. Emphasis moves from butts to brains as school sessions begin and work loads kick in. Events—from football games to county fairs—become more couples-oriented.

To use a skating-rink analogy, summer is "all-skate" and autumn is "couples only."

And so Labor Day is a favored day—the end of endless summer and the rise of fall. It's a symbolic time. Women still are tall and tan and lean and lovely, but they are suddenly more than summer decor. More than a potential target for our predation. Conversation turns from "surf's up" to matters more worldly, politics and religion.

We discover again that they are women, great women, and we've been nothing more than schmucks all summer. Well-tanned schmucks, but schmucks nonetheless.

It is Labor Day. Time to go to work—work on getting a girlfriend.

Halloween—Good

For a man, Halloween would be very scary if this happened:

His girlfriend walks in the room. He looks at her and says, "Oh, you're dressing up as a witch this year."

And she replies, "I'm not dressed yet."

Otherwise, Halloween is the perfect time for a guy to introduce to his girlfriend the idea of role play. It can broaden any relationship. Halloween is the one day all year when it's cool for a girl to appear publicly as any of the following characters:

1) French maid
2) Prehistoric cave girl
3) Betty Boop
4) Jessica Rabbit
5) Josie of Josie and the Pussycats
6) Jeannie of I Dream of Jeannie
7) Candy Stripe nurse
8) UCLA cheerleader
9) Belly dancer
10) Catwoman
11) Miss Kitty
12) Malibu Barbie
13) Xena
14) Seka
15) Elizabeth Dole

If the girlfriend dresses as any of the above, the boyfriend will be dressed as one thing: a happy camper.

Thanksgiving—Good and Bad

If a guy is still playing the "look how much I can eat" game, then to have a girlfriend on Thanksgiving is truly a blessing. He gets to eat at both houses.

It is the Noah's Ark of dining experiences: Everything comes in pairs—take the turkey and multiply by two. Double the dressing and do dessert on the double. That's right: The pie are squared.

But a two-part Turkey Day can also have dire consequences beyond serious heartburn. Thanksgiving often marks a man's first encounter with the Two-Family Challenge. The one pressure-free holiday is now a test of his diplomatic skills. With his family, all he has to do wipe his mouth. With her family, he has to watch his mouth.

If he's polite as a Pilgrim, he'll get a good meal and perhaps a "midnight snack." But if he laughs when Gramps passes gas, he might not get dessert.

At Thanksgiving, a guy must mind his peas and Q's. He needs to please the keys to future ease: His girlfriend and his girlfriend's mom.

Christmas—Good

As winter approaches, many women go desperately seeking a boyfriend. Men are not averse to this idea.

Winter is the worst time to go stag. It's cold. It's dark. People mingle less and stay indoors more. It's the cold and flu season. People are at home in bed, half-addicted to Thera-Flu and The Maury Povich Show. Men and women are pale, plump and congested—it snot exactly the dating game out there.

Winter relationships are good. Seasonal monogamy is logical. It's eight degrees outside. Vegetation has been stripped from the Earth. Icicles are killing people. It's best just to stay inside and get cozy. Winter is the snuggle season, time to rent a movie and assume the spoon position. Oh what fun it is to ride.

For a man, winter sex with one woman beats playing Nanook Of The North, getting all bundled up for a night on the town. It's hard to act suave when you're wearing earmuffs.

Christmas itself is the worst time to go mateless. It is not the time to play solitaire. In fact, a single guy alone at Christmas gets not only blue but green—green with envy. Christmas is the one time all year when the single man envies the married man. While the married man gathers 'round the hearth with his loving family, the single man sits lamely at home watching the Perry Como Christmas Special while eating canned cranberry mold.

Depressed and lonely, he grabs his little black book and makes a few calls. Nobody's home. Every girl he knows is out buying stocking stuffers for her seasonal beau.

If the single guy is lucky enough to have a Yuletide gal, he drops the bachelor machismo and does those cute dorky winter things: goes caroling; hangs mistletoe; rubs his socked feet on the carpet and playfully shocks her with static.

The other good thing about a Christmas girlfriend: The guy receives a gift other than the six-pack—make that five-pack—of dark beer from his best friend.

A Christmas gift from a Christmas girl is cool. It doesn't have to be gold, frankincense or myrrh. It just has to be from her to him. It's proof that at Christmas, guys with girls are the real wise men.

HANDY REFERENCE CHART

clip and save

New Year's Eve	Good
New Year's Day	Bad
Valentine's Day	Bad
Presidents Day	Good
St. Patrick's Day	Bad
Your Birthday	Good
Her Birthday	Bad
Arbor Day	Good
Fourth Of July	Bad
Labor Day	Bad
Halloween	Good
Thanksgiving	Good and Bad
Christmas	Good

DATING THE SINGLE MOM:
A SINGULAR CHALLENGE

To date a single mom is, in most cases, to hit a moving target.

In general, a single mom has more to do than make goo-goo eyes at her lover while sharing a Cherry Coke with two straws. For her, romance comes in the abridged version. Any relationship is in Reader's Digest format. She edits out the superfluous stuff—long walks in the park, feeding the ducks—and gets right to the heart of it. Leisurely love is for people in French films. She has to get the kid to soccer practice.

Typically, the single mom is so busy that sex and love are like a McDonald's drive-thru: "I need a warm fuzzy feeling and an orgasm to go, please." It is love on the fly.

The dating game itself is Pin The Tail On The Bachelor. She wants to find a man and make him stick—no time to mess around with men who mess around. It'd be nice to get a husband and father out of the deal. Still, she makes it clear that a man qualifies only for the bronze—he is only the third-most important person in her life.

Thus for the single mom, the risks and rewards of romance are equally great. With an initial investment of the heart, she can qualify for a potential husband/father or just another guy who got scared away.

Indeed, it's one thing for a man and a woman to date, but quite another when a child is involved. A child can put the quick kibosh on the affair en fuego. A single mom puts her child's toothache above her own heartache. A night of sensual massage takes a back seat to helping the boy with his homework.

Worse is that after all the juggling, all the struggling, love can't always carry the affair to the altar. Even the deepest passion is feeble medicine for the wound opened by boyfriend-child conflict. Whatever the cause, that conflict can drive a serious wedge into plans for the Wedding March. If it comes to a choice, she'll choose the child. Blood is thicker than altar. And it's back to square one.

For a man, the risks are less daunting but nonetheless unique. Issues of love and companionship are the same as in any relationship. The warm glow doesn't discriminate—falling in love is falling in love. Theoretically, a single guy could fall in love with The Old Woman In The Shoe. But he can't ignore one fact regarding life with the single mom: She will always give him her divided attention. He'll be spending a lot of time on the back burner.

Many men shy away from dating a single mom. The thought of becoming Insta-Dad is often enough to curb any romantic notions. The notion of part-time attention repels them.

Other men are drawn to the single mom. To them, there's no one sexier than a mom in her morning bathrobe, combing her daughter's hair.

There are several distinct varieties of the single mom. Each presents a unique set of challenges to a man who dates her. Forthwith, a few scenarios:

The Over-Appreciated Date

—You've met a wonderful woman who, in an effort to raise award-winning children, has little time for earthly frills such as sleep.

She would love to join you for dinner if dinner doesn't interfere with her son's soccer practice, book report or Cub Scout project, or the monthly reports she prepares at home while folding clothes. The last time she practiced self-indulgence was a Friday night in April when she let the dishes wait until morning so she could floss.

Finally she agrees to an evening of dinner and—if the sitter doesn't mind—perhaps a movie. At the restaurant, she tells you how nice it is to discuss something other than last night's PTA debate on school vouchers. Twice before the salad plates are cleared, she excuses herself to phone home "just to see if everything is all right." She orders snapper and jokingly asks the waiter if it is served in the form of a fish stick. Later, without thinking, she reaches over to cut your steak into fun-sized pieces.

As you lean to kiss her goodnight, she tells you, "Tonight was the most fun I've had since last year's soccer banquet. All the parents sang 'We Are The Champions' to the boys. They came in eighth place but they won the Sportsmanship Award."

She kisses you on the cheek. "Thank you so much," she says.

Suddenly you realize you are her social savior, a recreational messiah to grant her furlough from laundry night and offer an abbreviated taste of the good life. You realize that a dream date for her might be a quiet game of Scrabble at the local coffeehouse. In its simple departure from child-rearing responsibilities, a game of Scrabble would constitute an orgy of guilty pleasure.

You ask her out again. Her eyes light up. She says yes, yes, she'd love to go out again—sometime in July, after her son goes off to Computer Camp.

You like this woman very much. It would help if you could see her more than twice a semester.

The Audition

—A single mom often rates a man on his potential as a papa. Not a biological papa, but a stand-in papa—a sort of stunt dad, a daddy double.

So when she asks if you'd be more comfortable driving her minivan, you quickly recognize her agenda. It's only your first date. The Audition has begun.

She hands you her keychain. It contains 87 keys, an emergency whistle and a photo of Junior. You sit behind the wheel of her maroon Ford Windstar. You pop in a cassette; it's a collection of Dr. Suess classics as read by Anthony Hopkins. You start to protest but rethink your objection when you get popped upside the head by Blue Power Ranger.

You turn to look at your date in the passenger seat. She is poised to judge your reaction to the Power Ranger assault, perpetrated by Junior, who sits menacingly in the back seat. You smile at her, then at Junior.

"Blue rules," you say, plumbing the lexicon of youth to sound as cool as you possibly can. You give him a thumbs-up, plus an exaggerated wink.

Your response—devoid of anger and with a hint of whimsy—earns you a score of five Papa Points, the highest possible rating on her scale of Potential Papahood. The Audition is in full swing. For now, you like this woman enough to continue The Audition. Who knows? You might make a good husband and stepfather.

She insists on dining at Chuck E. Cheese. There she gives you a handful of game tokens. You start to play the only game that you have ever seen in your life—SkeeBall. You quickly reconsider. By joining Junior in a game of Mortal Kombat, you score two more Papa Points for unselfish devotion to a child (although by playing SkeeBall you could have earned 68,000 game coupons redeemable for a Jolly Rancher).

Over a large cheese pizza, the conversation runs the gamut from tee-ball to Indian Guide camp outs. She believes these activities are good for child development. You agree. "I believe the children are our future," you say, racking up additional points. After four more dates—a family picnic, a piano recital, a birthday party at McDonald's and a trip to Discovery Zone—you realize the two of you have never talked above the fourth-grade level, except the day she inquired about your benefits package. Over a

Happy Meal you realize the entire relationship is Rated G. If the time should ever come, you'll probably have to use a Cat In The Hat condom.

It's like each date comes with fries and a medium Coke. Adult entertainment consists of sitting real close to her on the Ferris wheel. You haven't peed in an adult-sized urinal in three weeks. You have Gummi Bears stuck to your Dockers.

All you want is one night—just one night—when the kid doesn't ask for a piggy-back ride; one night when you can watch The World At War instead of Honey, I Shrunk The Kids; one night when you can spend the night—with her.

You come to a conclusion: You've never known her as a woman but only as a mom. You've never gotten to act like an adult with her. You've always wanted a wife and mother, not just a mother.

You read Junior one last bedtime story and then you say, "The End."

The High-Security Affair: Access Denied

—You respect the woman's decision: She doesn't want you to meet her boy. She doesn't want you getting cozy with the little moppet if you're just passing through.

That's cool. She's just protecting the child. If you turn out to be Mr. Gone instead of Mr. Right, the kid won't suffer the loss of another father figure. He's already had one dad subtracted and doesn't need another. His mom does not subscribe to the better-to-have-loved-and-lost theory as applied to a juvenile.

But after three months in the relationship, you still haven't met the boy, and you're starting to wonder if NASA uses a similar screening process for its astronauts. You don't know whether to feel flattered you've made it this far or upset you haven't been granted an audience with the boy king.

The kid is a mystery of milk-carton proportions. It's like you're in some Wes Craven movie, and the poor boy is locked in the basement, playing with bugs. You know this isn't the case. She loves the child very much—but maybe too much. The situation is getting extreme and unfair. You're not some pre-redemption Boo Radley. You are not Grindle the child-eating monster. You like kids.

You start dropping hints at how much you like them. Sitting with her on the sofa at night, you read your old Boy Scout Handbook while practicing square knots—"just in case we go camping." You tune to the Disney Channel and laugh aloud at any movie starring Dean Jones or Fred McMurray. You build a Lincoln Log fort reminiscent of the French-Indian War. You make Jell-O into funny shapes. You hum the melody to "I Lost My Poor Meatball."

Your hints are purposely over-the-top in hopes that you're levity will loosen the reins. Still she denies you any involvement in her child's life. You want to tell her there's no leash law governing children. It's OK to expose the boy to life itself. Yet the relationship is fast becoming two-thirds complete. There's a family portrait developing that says: "Not pictured—the boy."

Her overprotectiveness appears chronic. Her fear seems permanent. She is so afraid you'll leave the relationship that, ultimately, you leave the relationship.

The Endless Party

—Be it a response to a bad marriage or a do-over on lost youth, the woman is something of an uber-cruiser. The only evidence she has a son is the empty child seat in the back of her Camaro. She also has a pacifier dangling from her rear-view mirror. It is partially obscured by the graduation tassel.

With amazing regularity, her phone calls go like this: "Hey! My mom's coming to pick up Junior tonight! Let's hit the town!" Her son gets passed around like Aunt Velma's Christmas fruit cake, going from one relative to another with stunning frequency. The kid lives in a perpetual state of foster childhood, bouncing from one bosom to another, all to facilitate his mother's party agenda.

The kid is less a kid than an inconvenience, an everlasting asterisk on Mom's social calendar: "I have two tickets to the Loverboy Reunion Concert," she tells you one night. "But I have to do something with Junior."

Like luggage, the kid must be carried or stored.

You give her the benefit of the doubt. Maybe it's just a phase. Maybe she'll go maternal after experiencing what she missed during marriage. She skipped her early 20s and she wants them back.

She has a good heart, you're sure of it. You just need to chisel away a thick sedimentary layer of Ladies Night to discover the actual lady. You're sure of it.

You take her out to an early movie. Instead she suggests going to J.J. McGee's FunDrinkery for happy hour. She proceeds to get more happy than you, and for more than an hour.

She sees several friends. They squeal in unison, then engage in post-squeal hugs. Her friends have all the markings of women involved in a similar youth-reclamation project: thick makeup and black roots. They sip fruity drinks through pink straws. They check out your butt when you walk to the men's room. You hear additional squealing. "You go, girl!" They must be drunk.

The date doesn't end until a club employee, carrying a broom, asks you to please lift your feet as well as your date off the floor.

You appreciate her joie de vivre but feel her vivre should include less joie and more motherhood. Still, you welcome the week she goes to Daytona Beach with her gal pals. When she returns, she has a nice tan and a souvenir shot glass. She is surprised to see that Junior is older and bigger.

There is one upside to the relationship: She's going triple-strength on birth control. Junior is enough luggage. Ultimately, however, the most effective birth control is her dubious character. You wouldn't touch her with somebody else's.

What Single Men Dread

The Matchmaker

In the film Fiddler on the Roof, the young girl sings "Matchmaker, Matchmaker, make me a match...." Despite attempts by modern meddlers to replace her, the old Matchmaker is extinct.

The old Matchmaker existed in a time before bookstores, bars, fraternity mixers, dating services and 1-800 numbers. The dowdy old woman lived in a small village of small homes with thatched roofs. She knew everyone and the horse he rode in on. She knew mothers, fathers, grandparents. She knew family trees and coats of arms. She knew family secrets. She made it her business to know. Armed with this information she played village Cupid, carefully matching single young maidens with virgin young men.

Often she made a match made otherwise in Heaven, pairing two people perfectly suited to each other. The couple got along so famously, they probably gave her a pig or a chicken for services rendered.

At other times the Matchmaker made a serious mismatch. For this she likely suffered the angry couple's enduring wrath, for the angry couple had to live together under the same thatched roof for a pretty good while. For disservice rendered, the angry couple probably stole a chicken or pig or sabotaged the Matchmaker's chamber pot. Matchmaking could be dangerous work.

Today's matchmakers operate free of such accountability. When the modern matchmaker makes a match, the participating couple need only meet for a gin and tonic, not a marriage.

That's what makes modern-day matchmakers so dangerous. Their motives are unclear. Do they want us to marry each other, or just get drunk together? Do they see love on the horizon, or do they just want their friend to stop whining? Do they see two people with something in common, or do they see two people who might be fun to double-date with?

Whatever the motive, the modern matchmaker comes in two types: The Corporate Headhunter and the Big-Game Hunter.

The Corporate Headhunter

She has a good life with good things: a better home and garden, two lovely children and a Volvo. Like all her married friends, she is a valued member of the Junior League. Together they volunteer at the balloon booth during AprilFest.

Her husband is a good provider. He enjoys his job at the firm. His wife doesn't know exactly what he does for a living, but she enjoys his paycheck and his retirement plan, and she enjoys him too. She likes having a husband. She thinks every woman should get one.

Just one thing is wrong with her otherwise perfect life. Her friend Cheryl—bull-headed Cheryl—is still single. She is the last unmarried Chi-O.

Every Tuesday when the gang gathers for lunch and hairdo compliments at Soups 'N Salads 'R Us, Cheryl is there too. While the gang discusses fashions by Oshkosh B'gosh, Cheryl just smiles and eats her macaroni salad. Cheryl listens politely as her married friends giggle with faux embarrassment at their husbands' attitudes regarding foreplay.

"For Bob," Tiff says proudly, "foreplay is taking two steps through the front door. He's such a stud!"

Cheryl laughs but on this score has nothing to share. Cheryl lives in a different world, a world apart from Saturday soccer games and little drink boxes. While the wedlocked women speak of buying groceries in bulk, Cheryl says little. What she wants to talk about is her dream of hiking the old Hippie Trail.

"The Hippie Trail," Tiff says later, shaking her head. "Cheryl must be very unhappy."

The women agree that Cheryl should join them for a weekend at the lakehouse. The husbands and kids will be there too. They'll spend afternoons on the 60-foot sailboat, "The Tax Break." They'll spend nights drinking punch and playing Pictionary on the screened-in porch.

This, the women agree, will convince Cheryl that happiness lies in domestic tranquility—with a husband and family. All they need to complete the scene is a good single man to invite out for the weekend.

"Tiff, I have an idea," says Karen. "What about that nice young man Kevin who plays first base on your husband's softball team?"

Thus begins Corporate Headhunter's quest. She's looking for a few good men or one great one. It's like there's a job opening—Chief Operating Nice Young Man of the Cheryl Corporation—and the vacancy needs to be filled by the best available man. The sooner the better. The Corporate Headhunter will go to extremes to get him. She'll tell the truth about Cheryl or lie about her, depending on the guy's attitudes about the Hippie Trail and whatnot.

So here we are, the Kevins of the world, the unsuspecting dolts. We have successfully passed the initial Nice Young Man Test without even trying. We wear a nice shirt to work and our grammar is all right, so that pretty much aces it right there.

As the headhunting pursuit thickens, we Kevins emerge as merely a walking, talking checklist of requirements. College degree? Check. Religious affiliation? Check. Nice paycheck? Check. Volunteer work? Check. Knights of Pythias? Check. No criminal record? Check. Nice hair?

Check. Good skin? Check. Health and dental benefits? Check. A 401K? Check. No serious mental health problems? Right-o.

We are the perfect match for Cheryl. If not perfect, then a reasonable facsimile.

Left unexplored were things such as mutual attraction.

The Big-Game Hunter

The Big-Game Hunter will not rest until she has removed the single man from his natural habitat. She wants his head on a wall. She lives for the day when she sees the heretofore single man stuffed uncomfortably in a tux, waiting for his bride to wedding-march herself right down that aisle.

The Big-Game Hunter diverges sharply from the Corporate Headhunter in male-procurement philosophy. Though misguided, the Corporate Headhunter is philanthropic at heart. She wants only to initiate her friend into the happy sorority of Stepford Wives.

The Big-Game Hunter, on the other hand, has her crosshairs on the single man. She's going to poach that sumbitch.

The Big-Game Hunter despises the single man. He is a threat to her happiness. He gives her husband ideas. She believes that by age 25 a guy should settle down and get boring. He should tuck in his shirt and work around the house on Sundays, before dinner. He should be in bed by 10—with his wife, who is probably asleep.

But the single guy threatens her little Shangri-la. Occasionally he stops by to join her husband for a fine ale on the front porch. She hears them talking and laughing because her ear is against the wall. She believes these porch pow-wows lead to other dangerous activities, such as ballgames and fishing trips. She'll have none of this.

In a veiled attempt to separate this scalawag from her husband, she tries to fix him up with one of her coworkers, Sheila. Sheila can best be described as a secretary with hair.

When that relationship fails, she tries again and again to find a mate for the man she calls Lucifer. There's Kelly. Terri. Maggie. They can best be described as Kelly, Terri, Maggie.

The single guy wonders why the Big-Game Hunter never extends an invitation to double-date. She never invites her newly paired couple for a night of cheese dip and charades. She sets the trap, but wants nothing to do with the captured prey.

He asks his friend about this glaring oddity but the friend says he never noticed, blunted as he is by years of marriage to this woman.

The Garage Phenomenon

It's a day that comes in every married man's life. It's inevitable, like love handles and the Business Section.

The Garage Phenomenon.

The Garage Phenomenon usually occurs on a crisp, clear Saturday morning. Birds are singing. Children are playing. You—the single guy—stroll happily to your married friend's house to see if he wants to play basketball. He's a good friend, plus he's the only one on the block with a hoop.

You dribble your old rubber Spalding onto the driveway. You notice your married pal in the garage with a handful of cardboard boxes. His face is white. His eyes are glazed. The life is gone from his step.

"Want to shoot some hoop?" you ask, thinking he might want an escape from domestic drudgery.

"Can't today," he drones, without even looking at you. "I have to move my baseball card collection to the garage. My wife say there's no room for it in the house."

You notice that she's already cleared off a shelf beneath the Weatherbeater Paint. You observe the water marks left over from last year's spring rains.

"Can't you put those on a higher shelf?"

"No," he replies wearily. "It's already filled with my record albums."

You look up to see The Beatles' "White Album," only now it's the Beatles' "Off-White and Dusty Album." It's so warped, it's more suited to serve chips and dip than to place on a turntable.

As he wedges the boxes onto the shelf, a 1974 Hank Aaron autographed card falls to the floor. You pick it up and remember fondly the day 20 years ago when he brought it back from the All-Star Game. He told all the guys how Hammerin' Hank signed it during batting practice. Hank even gave him a pat on the head.

The card became the most coveted in the neighborhood. Kids came from other neighborhoods just to see it, kind of like the Christ child. You offered half your baseball card collection for that one card. He wouldn't part with it. Never.

"You dropped this," you say, handing it back to your buddy.

"Oh. My Hank Aaron card," he says, nodding at the sight. "You can have it if you want."

"No," you reply, far too merciful to accept it. "You'd better keep it."

He puts the last of his cards on the shelf. He stands and wipes the sweat from his brow. He appears finished.

You ask again if he'd like to shoot hoop.

"Can't," he says. "I have to move my caps to the storage shed."

Getting Dressed Up

Single men dread getting dressed up for one reason: We have to get dressed up for it.

Our fashion phobia usually originates in a particularly sour sartorial night in early adulthood. It happened when we went out in a $500 Armani suit and $8 earth shoes. We had on one blue sock and one black sock because we put them on in the car. Lucky for us we never took off our blazer. Our date might have noticed we had to hold up our pants with an olive green web belt with the Boy Scout emblem on the brass buckle.

No matter how hard we men try, we fail. We live in perpetual fear of fashion faux pas so heinous, people will hand us their loose change. We have these waking nightmares that one night our date will answer the door and then promptly slam it in our face. From inside she will shout, "You're not wearing that, are you?"

From outside we reply, "Actually, I had planned on it."

Most single men don't get fashion, except that the tag goes in back and the fly goes in front. The only guys who get it are the guys with high cheekbones who model for J. Crew. They look great and they're wearing free clothes. We wonder why they're always pouting.

The rest of us remain clueless as to haute couture. Just when we're getting used to one fashion, a new one comes along. What gives?

"I know earth shoes used to be in style," we tell our friends. "Shouldn't I have received a memo from the Dexter Shoe Company telling me not to wear them anymore?"

Equally confusing are women's fashion magazines—Vogue, Bazaar, Mademoiselle. Men don't understand how a woman can wear a dress she saw in a magazine, then be upset when another woman at the party is wearing a dress just like it.

Men have the opposite reaction. If two guys are at a party, and they're wearing identical shirts, they are immediately drawn to each other—in a manly way. They smile, cross the room and slap each other on the back. One guy looks back at his girlfriend with an expression that says, "See, I told you it was okay to wear this shirt."

That's one reason men enjoy sports—30 teammates all wearing the same thing. They don't have to think about what they wear. And never they have to feel goofy about it.

The big difference in how men and women look at clothes is that women look at clothes. Men don't. To men, clothes are little more than a tool, something to protect us from the elements and keep us from getting arrested for public nudity. That "No Shirt, No Shoes, No Service" mandate also plays heavily in our decision to dress ourselves.

When it comes to clothes, men and women have different ideas. For example, women have boxes of stuff they call their "winter clothes." To a man, "winter clothes" are summer clothes with a jacket.

When women say "I don't have anything to wear," what they mean is, they don't have anything they want to wear. They look into a closet full of garments and find nothing that appeals to their particular mood.

When we hear this phrase, we conjure up images of naked Tahitian women sitting with their equally naked villagers. "The National Geographic photographer is coming today," they say, "and I have nothing to wear!"

When we men say we have nothing to wear, it means one thing: Our laundry basket is full.

A married man has a distinct fashion advantage over the single man—a woman who watches for possible fashion pitfalls. His wife is a sentry on the fashion watchtower, checking for plaids with stripes and ties with stains.

It's a privilege of marriage that begins on his wedding day. He is dressed better than he ever has been. This signals a change in his fashion perspective.

But for the single man, getting dressed up is like Pee-Wee's Big Adventure. Each time we go out the door, we risk a big fat "OOPS!" Too often, our favorite fashion combo has become stupid-looking since the last time we wore it.

Only upon our own funeral can we guarantee we'll be dressed for the occasion.

Women Who Try to Change Men

We know a guy named Bill. Bill started dating a girl. We can't remember her name. This should tell you something. It is foreshadowing.

About two weeks after he started dating her, we saw Bill at lunch. We were eating the customary cheeseburger. Bill was not. Bill was eating a bowl of diet broth.

We said, "Bill, what's up with the diet broth?"

Bill said, "Aw, what's-her-name's got me on this new diet. She wants me to lose weight."

A month later we saw Bill at lunch. He was eating the customary cheeseburger. We said, "Bill, what's up with the customary cheeseburger?"

He just smiled and kept chewing. We knew she was gone.

THE MAKING OF THE SINGLE MAN: THE LITTLE KID IN TV LAND

We're men. Barring unforeseen surgery, we'll be men till the day we die.

Before we were men, we were boys. It was a compulsory phase, like driver's ed. Boyhood was a sort of apprenticeship for manhood, a training ground for manhood's frequent ups and downs as directly pertaining to sex.

Sex has always been a big deal to humankind. We just didn't know it at the time. Our parents had sex and we showed up some time later. Yet for several years we remained blissfully unaware of it all. Boyhood marked the one time in our lives when celibacy was fine with us.

But something was going on out there. People were doing things we weren't doing. We saw commercials on TV where men seemed interested in women for reasons other than a game of freeze-tag. We saw ads in magazines where men and women rode together on tandem bikes. They seemed to be enjoying it. Why?

In stores we saw little ceramic statues of two naked people embracing. We wondered why two naked people would hug. Maybe they were comforting each other after their clothes got stolen.

As we got older, we started to catch on. Men and women liked each other. They kissed, touched and then disappeared. It was called sex.

But on the topic of sex, nobody was talking. Not our moms and dads, anyway. We had to learn about sex from alternate sources, the tutelage of the streets.

There was always one kid—usually his name was Howard—who knew a lot about sex. From Howard we learned that when men and women sleep together, the man sleeps on top. Howard couldn't give a reason for this, but he knew it to be true.

For kids growing up in the electronic age, there was one other source of education—TV.

From TV we began to learn about love, sex and women, and how they relate to one another.

TV or Not TV? That is the Education

The Walk Of Shame marked our first bout with the boot, our first taste of the ouster. It was TV, however, that introduced us to unrequited love. TV taught us that sometimes, love is a one-way street.

Call it the Petrie Principle—Petrie as in Laura, not Rob.

We learned early—on afternoon TV reruns—that a woman coveted is seldom a woman obtained. By the time we tuned in, Laura had already married Rob. Jeannie already had a master. And Ginger ignored our amour by turning her attention to Gilligan's sidesplitting antics. She never even knew we existed. None of them did.

It is safe to say that no kid ever consummated his crush on Ginger Grant, or did the Frug with Marsha Brady. No kid ever slept in the same room with Laura Petrie, even in separate beds. Instead, we boys found satisfaction in watching them through a window called TV, a sort of sanctioned voyeurism. We learned to look but not touch. We were Peeping Tommies.

TV helped cut the emotional umbilical cord between us and our moms. Sitcoms placed other women in prominent roles in our lives for reasons not remotely maternal. Our moms gave us Twinkies and soft hugs; Jeannie and Ginger gave us something else entirely: an indefinable longing. We wanted to see them each day for reasons that were new to us. We loved how Laura cried, "Oh, Ro-o-o-o-b!" when she was upset. We loved the way Jeannie stayed perky in so many ways.

We loved them…but they did not love us. Each day they left after half an hour. That quick desertion marked our first experience with a common male malady: admiring a woman from afar. It is the pain of passion unreturned, a pain we'd experience periodically into our adult years.

But it also taught us that just as one woman left, another arrived. That was a pretty good lesson too.

TV Signals: Sex Ed and the Little Kid

Today's single men grew up on TV. We were the first generation to feed on a steady cultural diet of tube. We learned lessons from those shows. We learned from Father Knows Best that father knows best. And we learned from The Dick Van Dyke Show that Laura looked great in Capri slacks.

Indeed, our amatory awakening occurred right there in front of the boob tube, watching Laura or Ginger or Jeannie do her thing. As we got older, that indefinable feeling in our heart began to relocate to a place decidedly south.

It was like, "Hello, hormones!" One day you come home from school a regular kid and by nightfall you're a post-adolescent with a penchant for spending too much time in the bathroom. You're watching Gilligan get the seven stranded castaways in another fine mess when suddenly you take notice of Ginger Grant singing "poo-poo-pee-doo" in that tight sequined dress. Suddenly you're feeling special stirrings you've never felt before.

The moment Gilligan's Island becomes Ginger's Mainland is the moment a boy becomes a man. At least he begins to become a man.

Our early tube years had been spent watching age-appropriate shows like Romper Room and The New Zoo Revue. Suitably, these shows were heavy on rudimentary education and light on things like cleavage. If the guest star of Sesame Street (Rita Moreno) had good legs, we didn't notice. We were busy following the bouncing ball, or laughing at Bert and Ernie.

The shows did not appeal to our prurient interests because we didn't have any prurient interests.

By the time we graduated to Leave It To Beaver, we began to appreciate the feminine image. When a woman was pretty, we knew it. Beaver Cleaver's teacher, Miss Landers? Pretty. Laura Petrie's neighbor Millie? Not pretty. Ethel Mertz? Fat.

Yet we lusted for no woman. If a woman was pretty, we just thought she looked nice—nice as in not mean. We had no intention of taking Mrs.Cleaver to Miller's Pond to unhook her bra.

Then there was Ginger.

It all changed with Ginger.

The Ginger Years

The makers of Gilligan's Island did a good thing when they created Ginger Grant, the sexy Hollywood starlet marooned with six others on a desert isle that had no phones, no lights, no motorcars.

A curvy redhead of cartoonish perfection, Ginger Grant symbolized sex before we boys really knew what sex was. We knew something significant lay beneath that sequined dress. We just didn't know what purpose it served, other than holding up the dress.

As years went by, we were increasingly committed to finding out.

A lot of guys liked Mary Ann, the cute Kansas farm girl with the forever smile. But Mary Ann was just Ginger with training wheels. She was a Ginger Starter Kit.

Ginger had the kind of body that little kids in the '70s noticed. She had curves and breasts. To boys back then—in the pre-aerobics era, when skinny chicks were just skinny chicks—the classic hourglass figure represented womanhood. Had we training in such matters, Ginger would have been a fertility symbol.

Mary Ann? She looked like a little girl, and we had plenty of those around.

To a boy in the throes of fledgling sexuality, Ginger was the object of our vague, pointless longings. We wanted her. We just wouldn't know what to do with her.

Say this for Ginger. She got the ball rolling.

Boob Tube: No Sex Allowed

TV censorship didn't much help a boy in his pursuit of sex education. If we were growing up with TV today, we'd be fathers by age nine, so befitting its name has the boob tube become. But back then, nobody on TV was having sex.

TV was like a documentary on plant life. Take Gilligan's Island. With the exception of Mr. and Mrs. Howell, all the castaways were single and apparently heterosexual. Yet the Skipper cast nary a glance at Ginger. The Professor never performed any "science experiments" on Mary Ann. Mary Ann never seduced Gilligan on "the other side of the island." And not once did Gilligan jump Ginger's bones when she made him move furniture by blowing in his ear. The eternal milquetoast, Gilligan crumbled against Ginger's overt sexuality.

That oft-repeated scene gave male viewers cause to inflate their own sexual identity. They thought, "If Ginger batted her lashes and blew in my ear, I'd take her straight back to the hammock."

Every red-blooded guy in America watched Gilligan's Island and thought, "Whoa! Five single people on a desert isle and they're not doing it? What about moonlit nights and tropical breezes? Did the Pope fly to the island with Wrongway Feldman? What do five of seven castaways do for relief? Are they just shy? Do Gilligan and the Skipper sit around listening to Mr. Howell's bawdy tales of sex with Lovey? And if masturbation became an Olympic sport, would the Island Nation of Gilligan win the gold?"

All legitimate queries. But as kids, we thought nothing of it. There wasn't any sex on our island either.

Then there was Bewitched. It featured ad copywriter Darren Stevens and his wife Samantha, a bona fide nose-wiggling witch. Samantha could crank out whatever sorcery she might need merely by wiggling her cute little proboscis.

Turn Mrs. Kravitz into a fox terrier? Done. Help Darren with the Johnson account? Done. Turn water into wine? One chardonnay coming up.

But Darren, a mere mortal, forbade Samantha from using witchcraft for any reason whatsoever. Including sex.

Stupid, stupid mortal.

In issuing this edict, Darren proved that he wore the pants in the family. Unfortunately for Darren, it appeared he never took them off.

Meanwhile, post-pubescent guys everywhere were thinking, "Uh, Darren? Let's get creative here, Darren! Ever heard the phrase '…like a horse'? How about Samantha in triplicate? How about sex on the moon? Sex all week? Sex all month? Daaaarrrren!! Use it or lose it, man!"

Darren demonstrated his mortality by assuming the role of rank idiot. Like other TV men, he apparently was also a eunuch. The only thing Samantha ever wiggled was her nose. The most fun Darren ever had was getting the Johnson account.

It didn't matter who played Darren—Dick Sargent or Dick York. To us, they were just two useless Dicks.

For us kids, it confirmed what we already knew. There was no sex in marriage. We certainly saw no evidence of it.

Equally frustrating was I Dream of Jeannie, starring the aptly surnamed superbabe Barbara Eden in the title role of Jeannie. If we were Adam, and Eve had looked like Barbara Eden, we'd have baked her an apple pie and made two tubs of cider.

On the show, Jeannie lived in a bottle at the Cocoa Beach home of Major Tony Nelson. Major Nelson got his magical roomie by picking up some flotsam on a beach and rubbing it three times. Out popped a Jeannie. It wasn't a big blue Sinbad-lookin' Jeannie. It was the best-looking Jeannie on the East Coast.

So what did Major Nelson do? Nothing.

And that was the problem. Here he had a blonde genie who called him "Master," wore a frilly JogBra and granted his every wish, and he acted like he was at vacation bible school. All he could do was hang out with his pal Roger and plan a few space missions.

Lonely men in Montana get mail-order Phillipino brides with fewer credentials for domestic servility. But Major Nelson? He never even asked Jeannie to rub lotion on his back. Jeannie was frisky, too. She'd been cooped up in that bottle for like 6,000 years, certainly enough time to make autoeroticism a blasé pastime. What's more, thanks to a rigorous program of lying around on throw pillows, she hadn't lost her stunning figure. To top it off, the inside of her bottle looked like a bordello.

By the time Jeannie popped from the bottle, she was hot to trot. Even Gilligan would have looked good to her. Instead she got a choir boy. Major Nelson never did a thing with Jeannie. Any other guy would have been up to his armpits in throw pillows and cocoa butter.

Poor Jeannie. She probably plopped down on her pillows each night and sighed, "Is it me?" Meanwhile, every guy in America looked at Major Nelson and asked, "Why isn't it me?"

We dreamed of Jeannie.

Perhaps the worst offender was The Andy Griffith Show. It featured an asexual sheriff, Andy Taylor, with a young son, Opie, but no evidence whatsoever of the woman who gave birth to the boy. They lived in the Mayberry, N.C., the town without sex.

Each citizen of Mayberry had his or her reasons for remaining celibate:

Aunt Bee—too old, too lonely and too busy baking pies

Opie—too young, too innocent and too busy learning lessons of morality

Barney—too afraid, too fragile and too busy locking himself in the cell

Howard Sprague—lived with his mom

Floyd the barber—forgot what sex was

Gomer—never knew what sex was

Goober—his name was "Goober"

Finally there was Otis, the town drunk. Otis was perhaps the only man in history who got tanked but kept his sex in check by locking himself into the courthouse jail cell.

From Mayberry, N.C., we learned that decent people don't have sex.

The television of our youth was rife with asexual relations. Mike and Carol Brady had six kids but no sex. June and Ward merely kissed each other goodbye. Rob and Laura slept in separate beds. We'll never know just how Richie Petrie entered this world. By stork? And what about little Ricky? Where'd he come from? Was he a stocking stuffer? The most sexual thing Lucy and Ricky ever did was sing "Babaloo" together.

We watched these shows, little knowing the effect they had on us. Perhaps subliminally they suggested that sex lay ever below the surface, seemingly within reach but never quite within our grasp. That was a pretty good lesson too.

The Charlie's Angels Years…and Beyond

We wanted our own TV about the time we realized our small penis might have a bigger purpose.

If we had our own 12-inch, we wouldn't have sit under a blanket in front of the family console to watch Charlie's Angels. Terry-cloth shorts were vivid indicators of boyish interest in Jill Munroe. A boy in the midst of pubescent awakening didn't want Mom to see his growing excitement.

With his own TV a boy could enjoy another fine episode of Charlie's Angels in the privacy of his own room. Under those astronaut blankets he could get a pretty good feel for how he felt about women.

The trifold object of his interest? The Angels three: Jill Munroe, Kelly Garrett and Sabrina Duncan. (Sabrina, as you'll recall, was the smart one.) The Angels were everything we boys wanted in a woman. They were beautiful and they seemed really nice, except if somebody broke the law.

As boys, we were big into "nice."

Nice as the Angels were, they quickly became the new target of our junior libido. Nothing was sexier than Jill Munroe dashing from her Ford Cobra II to apprehend an industrial saboteur. Sabrina, the smart one, could read the guy his Miranda Rights, but Jill looked great in tight blue slacks and bright pink lip gloss.

Later, little Jimmy Dugan's older brother told us that people on soap operas had sex. Right there on TV. The next week our school saw a significant drop in attendance among male students. Several sixth-grade boys suffered soap-operaitis.

Feigning illness by placing the thermometer under hot water, we got the day off. A little man's sabbatical. The day, we believed, would be much more educational than another day of long division and stories of Johnny Tremain. We checked the local listings for the soaps that sounded sexiest. To us, the young and restless, the clear winner was The Young and the Restless.

We grabbed a handful of Oreo cookies and took our customary spot on the den carpet. We watched the show. All the people seemed so serious. They were a lot more serious than Gilligan. There weren't very many sidesplitting antics.

But we weren't in it for sidesplitting antics. We wanted to see sex.

It must've happened during a commercial break. When the show returned after the All-Temperature Cheer commercial, Lance and Tina were lying in bed beneath satin sheets, but they were just talking.

But we did notice that Lance and Tina's shoulders were bare. That was a start.

COMING OF AGE: AN INTRODUCTION TO LOVE AND SEX

The Early Years:
Feeling Our Way Through Puberty

We learned a lot in school. We learned that Dover is the capital of Delaware. We learned that math is for people who like math. And we learned that our nation's founders were white men who did no wrong.

What we didn't learn about was sex. Sex was something you didn't do in school. Presumably you'd need a hall pass or a permission slip from your parents.

No, sex was something you did outside of school. Like all good things, it was extracurricular.

Attraction to the opposite sex occurred at different times for different kids. Some kids were lovers right out of the gate. Some boys were junior-level Don Juans by kindergarten. For show-and-tell, Kenny Kitchens showed the class how to French kiss. Ms. Carmichael put a stop to it by taking Kenny's tongue off the phonics chart and placing it back in his head.

Other boys were still engrossed in Marvel comics in 8th grade when suddenly they got thumped by a big old hormone. Their voice dropped three octaves and they sprouted a bumper crop of peach fuzz. They also began to take notice of little Jenny Davis for reasons other than her uncanny abilities at kickball.

Meanwhile, information spread from kid to kid—birds-and-bees by word-of-mouth. In junior high we learned once and for all that a man and woman "do it." It seemed gross at the time, especially when we realized our parents might somehow be involved. We also learned that Darla Jones had started her period. According to sources, this meant she was doing it.

By 8th grade, informal sex-ed classes were being held in dark hallway closets during chaperoned parties, two students to a class. Boy and girl would disappear from the cookie table and return eight minutes later, having enjoyed an inaugural session of "Seven Minutes in Heaven." This comprised two seconds of opening and closing a closet door and 6 minutes 58 seconds of harmless kissing beneath a woolen coat.

Spin-the-bottle served as an effective group tutorial on smooching, not to mention an unbilled primer on the spread of infectious disease. A bout with the common cold was fair tradeoff for the chance to liplock with Joy Jeffers, the prettiest girl in school.

To kiss Joy Jeffers in a game of spin-the-bottle, you had to pay the piper. You had to kiss the ugliest, gawkiest, ungainliest girl in school, who, according to tradition, would grow up to be a supermodel. Spin-the-bottle not only was a study in random physics but a lesson in democracy. Spin-the-bottle was the most democratic game on earth. Everyone had a chance to kiss everyone.

Whenever we kissed Joy Jeffers, we wanted it to last forever or until curfew. It felt so good it was like Christmas morning. It gave us a weird burning sensation in our chest. Later we had the same feeling when we just thought of Joy Jeffers. We had the feeling a lot.

We wanted answers for these feelings. Sex was distinct from these feelings. We wanted to be with Joy Jeffers, walk with her, hold her hand. We were sure that sex was something else entirely.

Sex was for naked people.

We wanted to learn about sex, yes, but not as it applied to Joy Jeffers. Joy Jeffers was too good to be associated with something like sex.

Sex Education: A Home-Study Curriculum

At home we explored sex on our own, usually on Saturdays when Mom was at choir practice. We looked up words in the dictionary. Mainly these were words we'd heard from Howard, the kid who knew everything. We looked up "penis:"the male organ of sexual intercourse.

The definition of vagina was more confusing: the canal between the vulva and the uterus. It sounded like a waterway between the Tigris and the Euphrates.

Other words weren't in there. For example, there should have been a word between "fuchsin" and "fucoid." Maybe our dictionary was old, as the word was probably new.

We looked up sex in the Encyclopedia Britannica. If the encyclopedia could supply our report on Eli Whitney's cotton gin, surely it could do a fair job with sex, which was no less important to the population of the South than the cotton gin. But the encyclopedia made sex sound like biology. There was a male. A female. An egg. Sperm. Fertilization. Mitosis. Gamete. Chromosomes. Fetus. Placenta.

There wasn't anything about boobs.

One place to find boobs was National Geographic. It was exempt from the definition of pornography because the breasts were foreign and frequently in the company of spears. Another good place to go for breasts was public television. Public television was an ideal cover for our educational pursuits. We'd tune to I, Claudius or Masterpiece Theatre and pretend not to notice when Monty Python's Flying Circus or The Benny Hill Show came on with occasional depictions of topless English lasses. For a long time it seemed like all topless women were African, South American or English.

Messages came from many sources: TV, books, magazines, movies, radio. We began to understand double entendres and sexual references in songs, such as Led Zeppelin's "Lemon Song," which, according to the lyrics, had a young man fall right out of bed when a young woman squeezed his lemon.

As for books, it required several more years to understand not only why Dick chased Jane but also how Puff fit in the picture. There was a lot of symbolism going on. Other books made more sense. On Wednesdays after school we'd raid Mom's bookshelf for Sidney Sheldon novels. We got pretty skilled at skimming over superfluous plot-oriented text to get to the sex parts. Words like "quivering lips" and "throbbing member" caught our eye. If we were ever to get involved with a beautiful counterespionage agent in Paris or Milan, we'd know what to do: Invite her up for a drink and unbutton her gauzy blouse, which would highlight her firm, upswept breasts.

Movies were a good source of education—if a kid could manage to sneak into an R-rated film. Sometimes a man and woman on-screen would get dramatically undressed to a Burt Bacharach song. This was fun to see, but sex ed took place less on the screen than in the seats. Typically the back row of the theater was filled with young couples in love. They had been to see the movie eight times but hadn't seen it once.

Movies, like closets, were a good place to get close to a girl. A guy could even cop a feel. A boy never actually watched a movie unless he was with other boys. With a girl, he was always plotting, worrying and wondering what to do with his arm and hand. Placement locations included his lap; his Cola; her thigh; her hand; interlocking arms; and the favorite, draped over her shoulder. A boy with long arms and long fingers had a decided advantage here. Stubby guys with stubby fingers could only hope to feel her clavicle. But tall guys could drop the smooth move all the way down to the top of the girl's breast and maybe beyond, way down to the promised land—the brassiere.

Playboy Magazine: A Boy's Life

So exotic was the image of a naked woman, we spent much of our free time considering it. We had glimpsed images of partially clad women—mostly on boxes of Mom's feminine hygiene products. That gave us an idea of what nudity looked like. But we needed to know for sure if nudity was as naked as everybody said it was.

It was, in retrospect, the anatomic equivalent of mankind's early fascination with the moon. He knew it was out there. He'd seen it from a distance. It tantalized him on many nights. But he'd never been there, never touched it, never explored its mysterious peaks and valleys.

The Dark Ages lifted the day our friend Bobby discovered his dad's Playboy stash out in the storage shed. Bobby quickly became a valued friend.

Indeed, in every group of friends, there was one kid whose dad hadn't thrown away a Playboy since 1952. In our case it was Bobby's dad. Bobby's dad was our favorite dad. We called him "sir" quite a bit.

Bobby's dad had stacks of Playboys stashed in a dark corner of the storage shed behind the metal file cabinet, next to the tool box. The storage shed soon became a favored hangout. We'd sit there under a dim light bulb that hung bare from a naked wire, enjoying the age of enlightenment. Grown men may read Playboy for the preseason football polls, but boys look at it for the pictures. It is the best education a boy can sneak. Our health books in school had color illustrations of the urethra. Playboy had photos of what mattered—the skin of a woman.

It was weird. Finally we had seen pictures of naked women, and they were women, man! They were nearly as old as our moms! They looked like secretaries. Naked secretaries. Huddled in the storage shed, we mulled the reasons that so many secretaries would pose naked for a magazine. It didn't seem very lady-like.

"They probably need the money," Bobby finally surmised. "They can make a hundred dollars."

We nodded and turned our attention back to the magazine, unfurling the Playmate of the Month centerfold like some great scroll. We read to each other the vital information regarding Miss July. Her name was Toni. We giggled at Toni's turn-ons: "I like skinny-dipping under a full moon," Toni confided.

To which one of us would reply, "Hey, Toni, you can skinny-dip under my full moon anytime."

We talked a big game, though not one among us had been beyond second base on the famed four-base chart of sexual conquest. We were but 12 years old and still fascinated by our frequent spontaneous erections, which too often occurred in the middle of math class.

"Jimmy," Miss Peterson would say, "come to the board and solve for w."

Never mind that we couldn't solve for w even if we had been paying attention. There was a more pressing concern—and it was pressing on our zipper. As every boy well knew, there was but one way to handle the unwanted woody: Think about football.

Traditionally, thinking about football is the fastest way for a male to lower the mainsail. (What males did before the advent of football, we don't know. Perhaps they thought of the Peloponesian War.) But here's how a boy would do it: He'd envision muddy linemen fighting it out in the trenches, a running back soaring over the top, and by the time the running back landed in the end zone, the unfortunate erection had been replaced by a more suitably flaccid member.

We are convinced that one reason football remains such a popular spectator sport is because, as boys, we spent so much time visualizing it.

We looked forward to many things: the big game on Friday night; summer vacation; birthdays. But mostly we looked forward to our first Naked Girl Sighting—an actual naked girl. A kid can see only so many Playmates on four-poster beds before it starts looking like the same picture, over and over, from five different angles.

By now, we knew that boys who still rode a bike with a banana seat rarely if ever saw naked women. That privilege was reserved for worldly men who drove cars with bucket seats. How then, we asked ourselves, could we ever hope to become that worldly?

Knowledge was the key. We had to attain knowledge.

One day we jumped the backyard fence and cut across the alley to the one true source of knowledge—Bobby's house. Bobby had this older brother, Ben. Ben had this treehouse. The treehouse had cheap pile carpet that covered an old wood floor. Under the carpet was something Ben had found while rummaging through the neighborhood dumpster.

A magazine called Penthouse.

We quickly discovered that Penthouse had a specific target audience: grown men. It gave us a head-start on becoming grown men ourselves. Letters from readers provided detailed descriptions of sexual escapades in elevators, dressing rooms and cruise ships—with co-eds, co-eds and co-eds. It was the sex gospel according to Steve B., Rick G. and Mr. Name And Address Withheld By Request.

With the Penthouse letters, we'd struck the motherlode of sex-ed.

What better way to learn about sex than from some Fuller Brush Man who felt compelled to record his adventures in a small Midwestern college town?

It was in Penthouse that we learned the following things about women:

1. All women want sex even more than men do.
2. All women are capable of having 10 to 12 screaming orgasms in succession.

We planned to carry this scientific data into adulthood, until such time that we could confirm it for ourselves.

Moving Violations: Hands-On Experience

At 16 we got a license to drive. The driving test included parallel parking but not parking. We found this interesting because parking—in the sense of "parking"—might also involve a parallel maneuver that could result in a serious accident. A guy had to know when to put on the brakes.

A lot of us guys didn't have to put on the brakes. We weren't going anywhere—at least not there. We moved from movies to moving vehicles not for more leg room but because we were expected to. The change of venue was a male tradition. At 16 a guy goes mobile. He goes from theater seat to back seat. He goes bumper to bump 'er.

It is an American rite of passage. We had seen Richie and Lori Beth go to Inspiration Point on Happy Days. We had seen teen movies in which boy and girl park at Makeout Holler or Hickey Hill in order to discover more about each other. Now it was our turn.

The first thing to do was get a car. The next thing to do was get a girl.

We realized early that high school girls were auto aficionados. Maybe they didn't read Car & Driver, but they knew cars—and drivers. They knew that boys who drove green Gremlins were no match for boys who drove black Trans-Ams. They wanted to be seen in a cool fast car, not some guy's mom's '76 Buick Le Sabre with lipstick-blot tissues in the front seat and a coat hanger jammed into the broken antenna.

It seemed unfair at the time—and still does—that good-looking girls went to guys with good-looking cars. A kid could be a straight-A student on his way to Yale, but if he drove a hand-me-down Buick Skylark, he still ran a distant second to the kid who got a D in wood shop but whose dad owned a Pontiac dealership. That kid drove a sleek Trans-Am with a Pioneer speakers in back and a foxy girl in front. The straight-A kid drove a Skylark that still smelled like his grandmother.

One way to combat the bad-car syndrome was to double up with a friend who drove a better car. Guys with better cars had instant friends. It's the same thing as adults who have pools and boats.

A parking double-date could be awkward. You sat in the back seat with your girl. Your friend sat in front with his girl. Three weeks before, you had made out with his girl and he had made out with your girl. This was before your girl was your girl and his girl was his. You both knew this. It didn't matter.

What was awkward was the proximity. Something so private—making out—was performed so publicly. It was like bathing in the Ganges. Other people saw you. You made out in the back seat while they made out in the front, 18 inches away. It wasn't exactly Romeo and Juliet.

If you got slightly off-kilter you could blow in the wrong girl's ear. You could kiss her fingers before realizing her fingers were his fingers. The hair on his knuckles would give it away.

On rare occasions a kid could borrow a car. Maybe it was his brother's car. Maybe his brother even knew about it.

Whenever a kid got a good car, he had to get a girl to go inside it. A good car couldn't go to waste. That'd be like if your parents left town but you didn't throw a party that eventually got 12 kids grounded. It would be a waste of a house.

Likewise, when you got a good car, you had to operate in accordance with the unwritten rule of teenage irresponsibility. You couldn't drive the car to a Young Life meeting. You had to park it somewhere, then make out. It was imperative.

With a bad car you headed straight for Makeout Holler. With a good car you took her to a movie first. It made it seem like a date. A date was like a deposit on parking. It made her feel special. It gave her the impression that you'd spend your allowance on her. It made her feel like a lady when you didn't make her pay for gas.

After the movie you'd ask, "What do you want to do?" It was rhetorical. You both knew what you wanted to do. But asking legitimized it. It made her think you weren't "out for one thing"—not directly anyway. It showed you were willing to do two or three things before you did that one thing.

You drove to Makeout Holler. You pulled slowly onto the gravel parking area. Pebbles crunched beneath the tires. Dust danced in the white glow of the headlights. You turned off the engine. You left the radio on. It played softly. For once it played softly.

The car smelled of sweet perfume.

You turned to her and said the only sensitive thing you could think of: "It's a beautiful night out."

She looked through the windshield, into total darkness, and said, "It probably is. If it weren't so dark out, it would be easier to tell."

You had a decision to make—the kind of decision that would follow you well into adulthood. "How," you asked yourself, "do I bridge the gap between her and me? How do I get from here to there without it seeming like from here to eternity?"

Kissing wasn't a problem—if you were already kissing. Making out was a snap once you were making out. The challenge was getting started—getting from here to there with some semblance of suave.

It wasn't just the cup-holder that sat in the way. Or the retractable armrest. Or the lap belt. It was presentation. It was the packaging of intent.

Your intention was, of course, to kiss her like nobody's business. You both knew it. Kissing is a mutual thing. It takes two to tango, and she wanted to tango as badly as you.

But for propriety's sake—to play to the illusion of respectability—you had to think of a subtle way to start it. A kind word, perhaps. A gentle gesture. To dive straight across the front seat into her lap would paint you as the Neanderthal you probably were. And, the implication that she would even accept such an overt overture would sully her substantial virtue. You had to think of something better than that.

It was a game—a weird battle of the sexes—that we'd continue to play into adulthood. We play it even now: Lust packaged in a pretty bow of propriety; animal need disguised in the odd veneer of human masquerade.

It is a two-person performance: We're both frisky, but if we pretend we're not frisky, then it's OK if we are. We can slobber all over each other.

"You look tense," you said finally, looking across the dark car at the pretty girl. "Would you like me to massage your shoulders?"

Love and Sex: A Comedy of Errors

In high school we fell in love constantly, as if love were part of the curriculum. Sometimes the girl knew we loved her. Other times we never bothered to mention it. We were happy to hide in our locker and watch her walk to math.

Our capacity for love was elastic. The frequency with which we fell head-over-heels was gymnastic. We could bounce from a doomed romance to a torrid affair in the course of a school day. Between homeroom in the morning and band that afternoon, anything could happen in the heart. It was a free-for-all.

The first day of each semester was like Christmas. We couldn't wait to see which girls were in our class. Maybe this would be the year we'd get a class with Joy Jeffers. Maybe there'd be a foxy transfer from Jefferson High, or a foreign exchange student from California. We were ready to fall in love at the ring of the bell.

We got our class schedule and held it in our gaze, as if almighty love lay cryptically in its letters and numbers—4th Period. Algebra. Rm. 242.

"She could be in there," we thought in the happy clouds of a daydream. "She could be in that class!"

It felt so good to have a crush ever-ready, love in the holster like Quick-Draw McGraw. We could whip out a crush in no time flat. We wanted to feel it. We looked ahead, always ahead. Our hearts held life's big elixir, hope. There was always hope.

We hoped to find a girl at any turn. A trip to the fountain could become a date to the dance. We crossed our fingers when Ms. Tolliver assigned study partners—"Please please please put me with Sarah Sawyer." It didn't matter that the assigned topic was the wreck of the Edmund Fitzgerald. Love was in the air.

Alas, we got stuck with Ralph Putrigaard. But getting stuck with Ralph didn't dull our optimism. Each morning was a new day. A new day, not another day. We sat behind Sarah and smelled her hair. It smelled like spring sunrise. While Ms. Tolliver discussed the Smoot-Hawley Tariff, we daydreamed of strolling in the sun with Sarah, hand-in-loving-hand. Imagination made it a long walk. A good walk.

We were never afraid, never reluctant to dive in love for fear of getting hurt. We were not yet jaded, not yet clobbered by the cruel broken heart. That would come later.

Youth, we know now, was optimism embodied.

Saturday Night Fever: Adolescents on Patrol

On Saturday nights we cruised The Strip. We combed our hair and cruised for chicks. It was a tacit dismissal of those feelings we all had. We all wanted to fall in love. But on Saturday nights at The Strip, we just wanted to meet chicks—chicks from other schools.

Shiny cars gleamed in streetlights' glow, yellow and blue and gold. Horns honked and stereos blared, screaming snippets of songs as they passed. They passed like a concert train blaring a little ditty 'bout Jack and Diane.

We drove with windows down. Warm night air tossed our hair. So we combed it. We talked and laughed but mostly looked. Looked for chicks from other schools. A kid got extra respect for getting a chick from another school. The whole point was to kiss and tell. If you kissed and didn't tell, it was like you didn't kiss. The kiss wasn't the thing so much as the tale end of it. Key words were "…and then?"

Another way to quantify conquest was to collect phone numbers. In most cases a phone number wasn't a phone number at all. You had no intention of calling Mindy-I-Can't-Read-Her-Last-Name from Sacred Heart High School. A phone number was a merely a mark, a trophy, an elk head on the wall of post-pubescent triumph. At night's end the winner had a pocketful of paper. A special King Daddy Award went to any guy who got a number that included area code.

With chicks from other schools, time in dark cars on dark streets produced unscheduled visits to uncharted territory. Most of us had been to the movies. We had touched a bra, sort of. We had touched the top of it from the outside. It counted. We got lace.

But most of us had yet to visit what can only be described as breasts. We had brushed against them, rubbed elbows with them. Certainly we had stared at them. With friends we had pretended to touch them on the produce aisle at the supermarket, taking special pains to loiter near the ripe melons. We all laughed at this. But we had never touched actual breasts, as they were attached to actual girls.

Howard had. Howard had started touching breasts years before and had, on many occasions, told us so. He had described it in great detail, almost like theater-in-the-round. At night in bed, based on Howard's eyewitness accounts, we envisioned the breast so fully that we could almost feel it. Pillows came in handy.

Now, in the back seat with Susie Somebody from Hayseed High, we were suddenly getting up-close and personal with a key constituent of the female anatomy. Susie's tongue was halfway down our throat when suddenly she took our hand and placed it directly upon her bosom. We figured it must be a mistake. Maybe she wanted us to roll down the window. These things happen. We removed our hand and returned it to our lap, which of course was experiencing its own rumble in the Bronx. Susie retrieved our wayward palm and returned it to her breast. And there it lay, directionless, a ship lost at sea.

We had heard about this sort of thing—mainly from Howard—and now it was happening to us. It was unbelievable. It was our maiden voyage to the Port Of Cleavage. Finally it was happening! To us. To us! Our eyes were open wide, bigger than Penn 6 tennis balls. Our heart was booming. Booming! We were kissing her but realized we hadn't moved our lips in a while, so deep in confusion were we, so paralyzed by the unknown.

But the unknown felt good—like we'd imagined it but softer. Years of vague expectation had culminated finally in one moment of tactile clarity. It was so real that fuzzy fantasy had no place, no call in predicting it. It was better than a dream.

Fear gave way to courage. What the hell. Susie had done this before. That much we could tell. We weren't taking her to prom. We didn't plan to marry her. It wouldn't be like, "Mom, I'd like you to meet the girl whose breasts I felt."

We pressed onward. We moved our hand slowly, awkwardly. We squeezed and rubbed, pushed and pulled. "You're not milking a cow, lover," said Susie Somebody from Hayseed High.

Yeah, but we were feeling a breast. And it felt good. The achievement felt better than the breast.

To Do It, or Claim You Did It?

Canada was put on this planet for two reasons:
1) to give hundreds of hockey fans a place to live;
2) to give American boys a place to lose their virginity.

More accurately, Canada gave American boys a place to claim they lost their virginity.

Canada has become a geographic metaphor for anyplace that ain't here. And Canadian girls represent girls who aren't here to dispute claims of male conquest. They are the nameless, faceless phantasms who quell the shame of teenage male virginity, girls ever beyond the scope of confirmation.

After a summer vacation to the hinterlands, American boys could return home in mock triumph. They could describe to their friends their first coital encounter—without mentioning that it never happened.

"You don't know her," they'd say at tale's end. "She's from Canada."

You couldn't blame them for trying. You couldn't blame them for lying. The pressure was on. While parents rooted for abstinence by pretending their teenagers were still 12, teen peer-pressure tightened the screws on any kid still in possession of his virginity.

An erroneous claim of Canadian coitus was far preferable to the barbs suffered as a byproduct of virginity. For girls it was OK to remain chaste. For boys it was a sin unpardonable. If girls were supposed to remain virgins and boys were not, who exactly were we to do it with?

There was but one answer. Canadians.

We just wanted to lose our damn virginity and get on with our lives. We'd heard of French boys whose dad got them a coming-of-age concubine. That would be fine—anything to get it over with. It wasn't so much that we wanted to have sex but to have had it already. We wanted it behind us, not vague before us.

We wanted to follow our heart, but our loins kept getting involved. Rather, it was the expectation that our loins should get involved. We got a feeling when we sat behind Sarah Sawyer, and it had nothing to do with "doing it." She was beautiful, yes, but the attraction went beyond the physical to something deeper. We felt silly, but somehow a big hug sounded better than sex.

We withstood the taunts of Howard. Howard was usually off in his Camaro anyway, experiencing some chick from the alternative high school. As far as we could tell, none of the cool girls at our school ever really liked Howard. Howard never went to homecoming. Not once.

We figured our day would come—next week, next year. Someday, at long last, we'd have sex under our belt. Someday and forever, we wouldn't be virgins anymore. That's what mattered.

Meantime we followed the heart's little compass, pointing us ever in the direction of another crush.

Love 101: From Crayons to Perfume

Some kids had perfect school attendance. They were dorks. They made A's.

The rest of us attended school pretty regularly. It was the best option available. There wasn't much reason to stay home. Cable TV hadn't been invented and there weren't any naked people on soap operas. We checked.

Mainly, guys went to school because that's where the girls were. Whoever invented school had a good idea: Put boys and girls in class together and they might show up. They wouldn't necessarily pay attention, but they'd be there. We can only surmise that boys in all-boys schools had a thorough understanding of the Smoot-Hawley Tariff.

Even so, we didn't know how good we had it. We spent seven hours a day, five days a week with the best-looking age-group girls in our parents' tax-appraisal district. The girls were well-groomed and well-read. They had a comb in their pocket. They had books in their hand.

It was the deal of the century. There were tons of girls. Crushes galore. Sometimes a guy would have a crush on a girl and he'd take it a step farther: He'd admit it. Sometimes he'd discover that she, in turn, had a crush on him. What's more, she'd had the crush forever—two weeks.

Born of the mutual crush was true romance. Teen romance. Puppy love.

Sure, we had "gone with" girls before. We'd gone steady for brief periods, much like we'd visited our grandparents for the weekend. For example: One afternoon in junior high, Judi Johnson's friends stopped at our locker to tell us that Judi liked us. They said it in a way that only pubescent girls can: "Judi likes you."

In that instant, between homeroom and American history, we felt eight feet tall. Somebody liked us. It didn't matter that we didn't much like Judi. Judi was the girl with the square head. She smacked green gum. But it felt good that somebody cared.

Judi's friends then asked, "You want to go with her?"

Caught between swales of uncertainty and esteem, we replied directly: "Uhhhh…OK."

Each afternoon for a week, we walked Judi to Bus No. 2. We stared at the flat grass and asked her how math was going. She stepped onto the bus, and we waved goodbye. We phoned her every night to ask one question 12 times: "So…what are you doing?"

The passion ended when Judi broke up with us before 2nd-period science so she could go with Randy Wallace, the kid with the round head.

We felt something entirely different the day Lori Lewis sat next to us in the lunchroom—and it wasn't the Salisbury steak. It was a first-time feeling, like the first charley horse: "What the heck is this?"

We had had crushes before, of course. But always it was a one-way crush. This time, for the first time, the feeling was mutual. Lori sipped chocolate milk and looked at us with big brown eyes. We went straight to melt-down. Our insides felt like Dante's Inferno. Lori listened to things we said. She laughed at jokes we made. She agreed that Mr. Fuller, the health teacher, should be reminded that it is not pronounced the "Hypocritic Oath." She also agreed that Mr. Fuller should not shave in class.

And there we were, halfway through our mashed potatoes, fully engaged in puppy love. It was like some great god of love had given us a permanent grin. We couldn't stop smiling. When she touched us on the arm, we felt special and alive like we'd never felt before.

We finished our Little Debbie Star Crunch, and the bell rang too soon. We walked her to social studies and told her we'd call her. We meant it. It wouldn't be to ask her, "So…what are you doing?" It would be to ask her a million trillion questions, the answer to each we wanted to hear. She smiled as we said goodbye, right there at the door of Room 118. There was a long, long pause as, for the first and last time, we resisted the urge to kiss each other.

The feeling was so new, so different, so good. It felt like a warm, constant hug, like she was with us even when she wasn't. In bed at night, we didn't think about football. We thought about her. It made us look forward to tomorrow like we never had. We couldn't wait till the next day.

When we awoke each morning, she was on our mind. How did that work? Did she occupy our thoughts through the night, coursing lovely through dreams we did not remember? We lay on our pillow and smiled. The feeling followed us through the day. It never went away. It was warm and weird.

With her we did the things we always dreamed of doing but never did, both for lack of a partner and fear of reprimand from our friends. Now, for the first time, we walked hand-in-hand at the park. We giggled at that, because it seemed like a sappy afternoon movie on the fourth TV channel, the non-network channel. We wrote notes to each other, notes with little red hearts on them, signing off with "I LOVE YOU!" We didn't care if it was dorky.

Each night on the phone, we talked and talked. We couldn't hang up. Couldn't say goodbye. We fell asleep with the phone against our ear.

Alone at last, we kissed for hours. It marked the last time in our lives when kissing would be enough. It was enough to feel her lips on ours, soft and warm. We loved her lips because they were hers.

Finally the time arrived to express our feelings in ways more physical. Ways that were new to us. It wasn't a decision but a need, a progression. Kissing led to other feelings, greater desires. It was strange that emotion would manifest physically in groping hands and grinding hips. It felt natural.

It felt different, too. Before when we'd made out with a girl—when we put a hand on her thigh or chest—it was a quest, an attempted affirmation of our burgeoning manhood. It was a chance to see how far we could get, mainly because our friends were getting there too.

Now we were in love. Our friends had nothing to do with it.

Loving the First Girlfriend

Our first girlfriend had as much sexual experience as we had, which is to say, not a lot. We'd both been to the movies. We both knew the general location of coveted appendages, but after that, it was anybody's guess what to do once we got there.

What we lacked in experience, we made up for in enthusiasm. We were gung-ho. It was like we had made the varsity.

Sometimes we were too enthusiastic. Sometimes we investigated the opposite body at inappropriate times—such as before her parents had fallen asleep. Indeed, a lot of hands-on training occurred on the other team's sofa as The Tonight Show flickered the image of some unseen guest such as Gavin McLeod. We whispered sweet nothings in her ear. With the other ear she listened for footsteps.

It was novice lovemaking on the sly, tenderfoot romance wedged clandestinely between couch pillows.

On the nights we visited, her father was always hungry and thirsty. He'd come downstairs 12 times for a glass of milk and a sandwich. Whenever we heard Pop's footsteps, we'd sit up straight and comment loudly on how much weight Gavin McLeod had lost.

"Honey," her dad would call out as he ascended the stairs for the last time, "you need to batten down the hatches by midnight." It was already 11:40, and he knew it. His edict was a gentle exercise in paternal diplomacy, a euphemistic way for Pop to say, "The guy had better be gone in 20 minutes, or you're grounded for the next three years."

In retrospect, we realize he knew exactly what he was doing. He was looking out for his daughter—and probably for us too. He'd been 16 once. He'd played covert kissy-face in the parlor, disguising his sexual incursions with a game of parchesi. His final advisory was his way of issuing limited freedoms, like a warden granting furlough. He was giving us 20 minutes to French kiss but not much else.

Today, we'd like to publicly thank the little general, the stern but fair father who allowed his daughter and his daughter's boyfriend a small sliver in time to discover each other.

We took advantage. We discovered each other with the wide-eyed wonder of early explorers who bumped into islands they didn't know where there. With fresh hands we explored. We imagined what it must feel like, that body under those clothes. But for the time being, feeling soft fabric against her warm body was good enough—great enough.

We were fully clothed, but it still felt like sex—so much so that one night we finished prematurely something we weren't aware we'd started. This preceded the first time we ever washed a load of underwear ourselves.

Kissing could last eternal but for the fact we had to be home by midnight. At other times we'd steal away—perhaps after school or on a Saturday—to have more time alone. As we kissed and groped, our lips and hands told us there had to be more. Our heart told us that, too. We loved this girl, and we realized that touching her body was the perfect way to touch her soul. It was like God had invented an outside to give humans a flawless way to love the inside. It was cool.

Still, we were increasingly interested in the outside. Loving her soul made us love her body even more. In her company we developed a natural lean. We were drawn to her as if by great magnetic force. When we looked into her eyes, her lips were the next logical step. We were pulled to them.

One night we lay on her couch. The lights were off but for the bluish flicker of the TV. We kissed each other deep to the sound of Johnny Carson's monologue. Her dad wasn't feeling well and had gone to bed early. The time came to make our standard move.

We had attempted many times to slip a hand under her shirt and maneuver it toward her breasts. Always our thrust was met with her parry. We were turned back each time by armed guards just above the belly button. Her hand was an immovable object. Moving past it was like breaking into Fort Knox.

This time, as usual, we placed a hand on her warm belly and began moving it upward. We made it just north of the belly button and, by force of habit, stopped. Soon we realized we'd stopped on our own. She had offered no opposition. Rather than draw attention to this fact by mentioning it, we resumed the journey.

We had touched breasts before, of course, but not the breasts of someone we loved. Susie Somebody hadn't even qualified as someone we liked. Now we were close to touching the breasts of the girl we adored. Our insides churned like boiling water. Our heart beat like Tito Puente.

We moved ever upward. We made it to mid-rib and still got no opposition. We made to the bottom of the breast and got no defense. We felt the soft, smooth silk of her bra and the treasure it concealed. No protest.

We let our hand linger, there on the edge of paradise, afraid the dream would end for one bad move. Her body wiggled beneath us in ancient primal rhythms of need and big desire. She breathed fast and heavy, breath so hot like she'd been running and running. Hot slick sweat formed fast on our faces and bodies. She kissed us hard and wet, putting her arms tight around our neck and pulling us even deeper to her, as if she wanted us to crawl inside. We wanted to crawl inside.

It was time. Like a sprinter from the blocks, we burst toward the finish line, putting our hand squarely upon her breasts. We didn't think, just acted, basic desire having stripped us bare of reason and relegating us to actors on instinct. In minutes our clothes were gone, strewn on the floor in clumped heaps like innocence tossed aside. We lay naked and panting, not knowing what to do but wanting to do whatever it was. It was all confusion and happiness, and it felt too good to be true.

We lay caressing each other's bodies, inside and out, for the first time. The room smelled like sweat and love.

There was only one thing left to do. It.

Planning for the Big Event: Buying the First Condom

We didn't leave our first encounter entirely to chance. Or destiny. We took the Boy Scout approach: Be prepared. We bought prophylactics. Condoms. Rubbers. Raincoats.

We had seen condoms—or condom machines—ever since we were little kids, long before we knew their purpose.

We first noticed them on road trips with our parents. We were 9. We stopped at a truck stop on the interstate just this side of Podunk. We went to the restroom. On the wall was a metal box, upon it a photo of a woman.

She lay on her back on a bed. Her long blonde hair was all spread out on the pillow behind her. She seemed in considerable pain. It looked to be a chest wound. She was holding her breasts and appeared to be screaming. Maybe she had been ironing a shirt and missed. Maybe she had shut her breasts in a dresser drawer. It's all we could come up with.

Years later we caught on. After we discovered that people do it, we discovered that sometimes they do it with condoms. Evidently, a lot of the people who did it with condoms were truck drivers. We figured truck drivers did it more than anybody. We figured maybe we should be truck drivers.

Finally on one road trip, we made sure we had some quarters. When Dad stopped for gas at Billy Roy's Gas 'N More just this side of Hickville, we high-tailed it to the restroom. We put two bits in the slot and turned the knob. Out came a small package. We unwrapped the clear plastic and undid the little box.

It was an illustration of an ugly skinny man holding his thin erect penis. At the bottom was a joke we didn't get. We put 50 cents in the next machine. Out came a package. We opened it. It was a rubber. Our first rubber. It looked like a weird lemon slice in lemon juice. We put it in our pocket.

When we got to Grandma's house we panicked. We flushed it down the toilet. We didn't want Mom to find it and start asking questions. They would be questions we couldn't answer even if we wanted to.

By high school we'd opted to forego the solo purchase for buying in bulk. A bulk buy was proof that a guy had balls. First, it offered vague testament that he might be doing it—doing it a lot. Second, it took courage—a.k.a. balls—to stroll into a supermarket and buy a box of Trojans. The box was unmistakable. It showed a guy and girl on the beach, silhouetted against an orange sunset, locked in love's deepest kiss. It sure wasn't a box of raisins.

One thing we feared was the price-check. We'd approach the checkout lane with our box of Trojans as well as two diversionary purchases—an Ace Unbreakable Comb and a box of Q-Tips. These were inexpensive but important pieces of merchandise designed to draw attention away from the condoms and thus ease our embarrassment. We didn't know why we should be embarrassed. If a fellow teenager witnessed our transaction, it would make him think we were doing it. That would be good. If an adult saw it, it would define us as responsible young men taking measures to prevent bad things. That would be good too.

Still we were embarrassed, a shame only magnified by the gripping terror of the price-check. The price-check could expose us publicly as libertines, like a Biblical stoning of an exposed prostitute. We lived in fear of the nightmarish scenario: A guy in a red vest would look at the box and, finding no price tag, turn to the microphone. In a strong voice belying his timid appearance, he'd say: "We need a price-check on Trojan Deluxe condoms with the reservoir end plus—and I quote—'raised ribs for her maximum pleasure.' That's a price-check on Lane 4 for Trojan condoms for the young man in blue jeans and white Izod shirt, who stands in judgment before God. Thank you."

The other big fear was that we'd see one of our mother's bridge partners.

Still, for whatever reason, we bought the family pack of Trojans, as if we had sex each day before and after school. In truth, we could've taken the rubbers to school and sold them on the interscholastic black market to other kids who wouldn't use them. We could've blown them up to use as decorative balloons at the Friday pep rally. We didn't need them. But we kept them. Kept them all. Just in case.

We hid all but one rubber in the bottom dresser drawer, under the clock-radio warranty. We carried the other rubber in our wallet like people carry a roadside flare in their car, seldom if ever to use it. It just stayed there, like a library card.

We toted that rubber so long it left a ring on our wallet, a sort of bas-relief symbolic of our chastity. It stayed there forever. It was like we were doing a science experiment to determine the half-life of latex. That condom was Jurassic. A condom ring was solid evidence that a guy was still on the inactive list, a latter-day hieroglyph that said unequivocally, "Ha-ha! This guy's a virgin!"

Logic eased anxiety. We knew a journey of a thousand miles requires shoes. That initial condom purchase was a rite of passage in itself, a big step toward the promised land. The New World.

We endured great hardship and shame in preparation of our deflowering. We paid our dues and waited patiently for induction to the rank of Romeo, like a minor-league pitcher awaiting his call-up to The Show.

Alone in our room at night, we'd pull out our rubber and stare at it.

"Man," we'd think. "I'm this close!"

Lost Not Found: Virginity

As expected, the call was not expected. Nor was it welcome.

It was the phone call. We knew it would happen someday. We just hoped we'd be the guy making it.

What's true now was true then: A guy wants to see his friends do well but not better than he. He wishes well for his pals but not that well. Honest congratulations are typically bestowed by one on a higher or equal rung of achievement. From the bottom looking up, it's all envy.

And so it was with us. It was one thing for Howard to do chicks in his Camaro. We'd give him that. But frankly, a guy didn't want his best friends to score if he himself was getting shut out. We were waging an earnest if unspectacular battle to see who'd lose his virginity first. It was a cold war.

No one was sufficiently desperate, brave, knowledgeable or rich to hire a hooker. No one had the kind of naughty neighbor we'd read about in Penthouse, the lonely housewife who vacuumed naked and swilled Jim Beam all day. And we were still so mystified by the whole process as to pursue it with great trepidation. No one was diving headfirst into sex.

We thought about it, of course. As a group we discussed it. We had conversations as to what it might feel like, with opinions ranging from a Slip 'N Slide to creamy peanut butter. But no one was betting on it happening to him that week. No one was trying to out-Howard Howard.

In fact the phrase "happening to him" befit our mind set. We figured sex would just sort of happen to us someday. We wouldn't "do it" so much as have it done to us. To "do it" would imply that we were adequately seductive to cause it, as if we could look at a girl and her pants would fall off...that we'd chill a bottle of Dom, stand silhouetted in the smoky doorway and proceed to lie with her, taking her to climactic heights she'd not imagined.

No, rather, we knew our debut doink would be the product of serendipity, a sort of lucky-charm intersection of dual destinies, a his-and-hers tryst preordained by Eros or Aphrodite or Bob Guccione or some great omnipotent force connected to sex. Either that or we'd get lucky. This was the one time in our lives when lucky meant lucky.

To predict it would require clairvoyance beyond our grasp. We'd have to cross that bridge when we got to it. For some it was a bridge too far, for others a bridge over troubled waters. It was a bridge that we were both afraid and anxious to cross—a bridge from the Old World to the New World.

Then it happened. It was a Saturday morning like any other. We were eating Frosted Flakes and ignoring our mother. The phone rang.

Mom answered. She paused, then said to the caller, "My word, David. You sure sound like the cat who swallowed the canary!"

We looked up from our flakes.

"Phone's for you," Mom said.

We took the receiver with great reluctance. We gave her a look that said, "Mom, please go away."

"It's just David," she said, wondering why she should leave for a phone call from our best friend.

"I know," we replied. "But it's private."

Mom went outside to look at plants.

We put the phone to our ear. David shouted so loud we had to jerk the phone away. "Duuuuuuude!!!" he screamed joyously, victoriously. "Duuuuuuuuuude!!! Duuuuuuuuuude!!!"

We knew what "Duuuuuuuude!!!" meant, but we played dumb.

"Yeah?" we asked. "What is it?" Of course we knew what it was.

"Duuuuuuuude!!!" he shouted, even louder this time. "Duuuuuuuuuude!!!"

"What?"

"I did it!!!" he screamed. "I did it!!! I did it!!! Last night!!! I did it!!!"

We swallowed hard. We knew. We knew he did it. He finally did it.

"Did what?" we asked, feigning ignorance.

"It!!! It!!! I did it!!! Last night!!! I did it!!! I got laaaaaaaaaiiiiiid!!!"

The Brady Bunch dealt with basic sibling rivalry, but it never dealt with the issue of a guy faking happiness for a friend who got laid first. Dobie Gillis never had to hear Maynard Krebs shout, "Duuuuuuude!!!"

We'd been educated by TV, but we were left in the dark on this one. We had no idea how to handle it. All we knew was this: We should have felt good for David, but we felt bad for ourselves. His triumph spelled our defeat. His achievement emphasized our futility. Our buddy had gotten a promotion, and we were still sweeping floors.

We were speechless. We tried to think of something to say besides "screw you," because David would have replied, "Ha-ha! She already did! Hoo-hoo!!"

So we gave him a tepid, "Hey, that's great."

He didn't hear us. He wasn't listening. He listened only to the resounding echoes of his own conquest, the booming concussions of his Big Bang reverberating through the cosmos of his own life. You couldn't blame him, but you could hate him.

"Man, I can't believe it," he said. It was weird, but we could actually hear his smile. "I finally did it! It was grrreeeeat!"

Our cereal was getting soggy.

Then, in tempered curiosity, David asked, "Have you ever done it?"

He was pretty sure we hadn't. He knew we would have told him. Still, he wanted to double-check, to confirm that he was the first to plant the flag.

To mask our chastity, we lied.

"Yeah, well, sort of…I mean, yeah…you know…I had it in once…I had it in for like three seconds, you know, but her mom walked in…you know, but yeah…I mean, I pretty much did it…it was in there…I mean, I know what it feels like…."

David really knew what it felt like. We needed to know. We had to know. David's phone call was an exclamation of his new manhood, a victory lap. Now the race was over. David basked in the thrill of victory. We wallowed in the agony of defeat. What made us feel worse was that we felt this way at all. Did it really matter that much? Evidently it did.

Later we mulled the implications of David's conquest. Strangely, it made us feel as different as he felt—different in a different way.

We were strangely sad. Our world of baseball cards and innocent crushes was gone forever. David had changed everything for us in one night. We looked back at the childhood we were reluctantly leaving behind, unable to return to the boy who once ruled the world from the sandlot. Our friend had leapt the threshold into manhood and, with him, had pulled us to the brink.

A Great Loss: When Virginity Goes Bye-Bye

For every man it is different. His deflowering may come at the hands and hips of a friend, a lover, a stranger. He may lose his virginity to a virgin, a veteran, a paid professional. He may be in high school, in college, in love, in lust. He may wait for marriage. He may wait for 8th grade. He may wait forever. He may become a monk.

For every fellow there are different moral, ethical, religious, social and personal implications. For every man the burden is unique. Some must answer to their God, others to themselves, others only to their friends. Others must answer to a magistrate on charges of solicitation.

The questions "Should I do it?" and "Should I have done it?" are phonetically similar but thematically divergent. One is about expectation, the other about gladness or regret. Each fellow has his own set of cause-and-effect concerns relative to his introductory experience. The first time is the first time forever. It is a permanent memory, good or bad. Good or bad, it can keep a guy up at night.

The act itself assumes greater consequence than a mere merger of two people. Feelings beyond orgasmic are intractably connected to it, feelings that occur before and, in particular, after the act. It is a uniquely human characteristic to attach such significance to nature's primal function.

For humankind, the bearer of reason, sex goes way beyond the physical. And that's why the first time is such a big deal. It begins and begets a lifetime of the most enjoyable, confusing, miserable, wonderful, terrible, emotional, primitive, blissful and necessary activity on earth. It.

LOVE, SEX AND THE SINGLE MAN

Sex and the Single Man: A Brave New World

Age brings change to the single man, and not just in the form of love handles. College, career and money have upended the high school status quo. The high-school babe-magnet with the Firebird now has a big gut and a bigger alimony payment. He's bald, ugly and drinking his way through rehab.

The dork who drove his mom's Le Sabre discovered synthetic aluminum. Now he lives on a private island with three naked women. A fourth is on the way. It took him years to realize those Penthouse letters were embellished or fabricated altogether; but since he moved to the private island, he's realized that not everybody concocts those wild tales of carnal adventure. He has written eight letters himself—all of them true. A ninth is on the way.

The fact is, it's not high school anymore. This is grown-up sex with grown-up consequences. It is removed from the age of discovery into the age of cause-and-effect. Sex is no longer a rite of passage. The scope has broadened to include all manner of considerations. Sex is tempered by the possibility of consequences that, in the happy darkness of virginity, we had never imagined.

Some say sex is the reason single men stay single. Others say it's why single men get married. Obviously it depends on how much sex a guy is getting, and from whom.

Some believe that a single guy avoids wedlock for one reason: It would interfere with his goal to amass as many sex partners as possible, as if it's an Olympic sport.

For some single men, this may be true. Yet too often the single man's sex life is mistaken for an exaggerated stereotype used for a cheap laugh on a Thursday-night sitcom. Not all men refer to their genitalia in the third-person, as if it has a life of it's own.

Isn't that right, Goliath?

PART I

Sex in Relationships

First Date Sex: Women are Right About R-E-S-P-E-C-T

The woman is right. We won't respect her in the morning. We won't heep honor upon 'er if we're on 'er on our inaugural date.

Here's a simple rule: A girl should not have sex with us the same night she tells us her middle name or hometown. We can't exactly put her on a pedestal if she's lying next to us two hours after she told us she's from Omaha. This is first-date information. Such information dispensation should remain separate from sex for a grace period of at least 48 hours.

We won't think she's Jezebel, but neither will we nominate her for Cedar Park First Methodist Church's Annual Woman of the Year Award. We'll still think she's bright, attractive, charming, if in fact we thought that before. We'd still like to spend a week with her in Cozumel, or even a weekend in Nuevo Laredo. We'll still like the way she laughs and the way she somehow locates our groin even when she's asleep. We'll still like the jigsaw fit of our sunrise spoon.

But as we lie there, staring at the morning ceiling, one thought remains: How many other guys has she similarly engaged on the first date? The question isn't fair, but who said men were fair?

Frankly, we were a little surprised when she whipped that condom out of her purse with the nonchalance of someone taking a Dole Fruit'N Juice Bar out of the freezer. We had been politely perusing her CD collection when, suddenly, we turned to see her extracting that invitational Trojan. We figured she wanted to do one of two things: make water balloons or have sex. The fact that she proceeded to unbutton our trousers with her teeth convinced us it wasn't water balloons she wanted.

Still it bothered us. Was this a regular part of her first-date regimen, like ordering dressing on the side? Or was this a rare event bestowed on a fortunate man? Were we a special guy whose sex appeal toppled the walls of her resolve? Or were we just a stand-in, a stunt man available to perform necessary physical feats? Did all her first dates get lucky?

Even when a guy gets lucky, he wants to feel special—somewhat special, anyway, as if she didn't pull his name out of a hat. Or get him free with three proofs of purchase of Rice Krispies Cereal.

He wants to feel like she picked him for him, that she likes him. Girls do not have the market cornered on feeling used. We men don't like feeling used unless she uses us really, really well.

That said, we confess that men do apply double standards to first-date sex:

Double Standard No. 1. We won't respect a woman in the morning—BUT we see nothing wrong with our behavior. We won't respect her but we'll respect the ourselves even more. She gets demerits, we get bonus points. She gets a bad reputation, we get a good one.

Double Standard No. 2. We won't respect her in the morning—BUT we'll gladly let her sleep with us if she wants to. We don't want her to let a little thing like our respect stop her from making us happy. It's her life. We're just part of it—for now.

Double Standard No. 3. We won't respect her in the morning—BUT if she's cool, we'll gladly see her again and again. We'll still like her, but we'll never introduce her to our mom.

Double Standard No. 4. We want her to spend the night—BUT we don't want her to spend the morning. We want her to leave before daybreak. For a guy, the worst thing is to wake up to a girl who wants to spend the day at the zoo.

Generally, a man takes a woman on a first date because he likes her, not because he's for a Mattress Dance. He wants to have a good time, but not that kind of good time. Not necessarily.

He wants to know a good woman better, maybe start a relationship. He won't subvert the possibility of romance by rubbing her thigh under the dinner table. A guy pulls that move, he might as well get a take-home box because that affair is over.

Granted, many women mask their sex-overdrive in the candied cloak of a respectable first date. These women have numerous first dates but few second dates. They camouflage their whopping libido in a public display of decorum—dinner and a movie. A nice date is proof, they believe, of their moral decency. Yet a more accurate description of the date is dinner and a movie and a lay.

They have just enough self-respect to render the inevitable romp a man's reward for buying them some large buttered popcorn. It amounts to an unindictable escort service, payment rendered not in cash but foods and services.

We know women like that. We've taken them out. Once.

Here's the deal: If a girl beds us on the first date, we got lucky and she got lucky but she's out of luck. We won't be calling her again unless it's 2:16 a.m. and we're soused. If she was interested in us romantically, she literally blew it. She sabotaged potential for the immediacy of a thrill. Not that we turned it down.

Frankly, nothing so disappoints a guy as first-date sex with a woman he truly liked. Her character is not what he'd hoped. Once the offer of sex is made, he doesn't run the other way. He just wishes the offer had never come.

Sex, Love and Choices: The Life of a Boyfriend and Girlfriend

On a perfect planet, a love affair would proceed on a predetermined course toward sex itself, much like a game piece on a Monopoly board. It would move according to plan toward the appointed round—a sort of A then B then C, thereby subtracting the ceaseless uncertainty regarding the appropriate time to tango.

Metaphorically, at least, we'd know that each spring we'd swim upstream, make a loud clacking noise and then wait as our mate came willing and able. Sex would occur in a kind of mate-by-numbers format, according to a preordained sequence of mating-ritual events: dinner, movie, first kiss, first fight, first make-up, first time to share an ice cream cone, etc., until the designated time of our pioneer union. It would be easy as pie.

Like reading the Time Life book on do-it-yourself plumbing, we'd just follow instructions:

Man: "Honey, according to the manual, we'll make love for the first time a week from Thursday!"

Woman: "I can't hear you, sweetie! I'm down here fixing the U-joint!"

Notwithstanding the Brave New World implications of master control, such a system would make life a hell of a lot easier. Often it's better to be told what to do than to figure it out for yourself. As for sex, it's dicey enough when it's happening regularly, let alone when it hasn't happened yet. For a young couple in love, a launch date is hard to determine. When is it time for the First Time? You can't exactly stick her back in the oven if she isn't ready.

Alas, there is no schedule, no docket for a young couple's maiden voyage on the Deflower. The couple is left to go it alone.

Sex in the Relationship: Inevitable, But When?

A human relationship is not subject to a governing body that dictates its progress. There is no higher authority that declares when a couple of people become "a couple," unless the girl is pregnant and the higher authority is holding a shotgun. Or unless she insists on a joint checking account. But we're jumping ahead of ourselves.

Some say a couple should approach the First Time in thick mystery. It is that uncertainty that makes for good foreplay. What fun would it be, they ask, to have the First Time scheduled like a dental appointment? Mystery is good. It keeps the fires burning.

If there were a predetermined number of dates before sex occurred, men might ask the girl to validate a card after each date to make sure they got credit toward their prize. This would be as romantic as getting a free Soap 'N Rinse after 10 fill-ups.

As it is, the First Time is TBA—To Be Announced. In any fledgling affair, countdown to liftoff finds an assortment of starts and paces. In a question of sooner or later, one partner may choose the former, the other the latter. Timing is of the essence.

Yet even to the most sex-perplexed couples, "it" eventually becomes a matter of "when," not "if." (For younger less experienced participants, other matters include "where" and "how.")

Men are generally acknowledged to operate on a different schedule regarding commencement. For a great many men, there is one ideal time to begin having sex—AS SOON AS POSSIBLE.

Right freakin' now!

Even though we know sex too soon can ruin a relationship, we're often willing to take that chance. This is a character flaw unique to men. We know this and we accept this.

We learn soon enough, however, that women operate on a wholly different timetable. They have the patience of Job's wife. They could sit through a literary reading at Whispering Oaks Retirement Center—

"James Michener: A Complete Retrospective"—before they'd even consider granting visitation to their privates. In fact, many women determine the depth of our love by the length of our wait. The longer we wait in the lobby, the more we want them. That's the theory.

Thus it's two people on two timetables moving at two speeds toward one destiny—It. Given the absence of instruction, the procedure can be painfully awkward. It might require several attempts to finally and successfully remove the underwire bra:

Woman: "No no, sweetie. It unhooks in front—in front!"

Man: "I think I just sprained my wrist!"

It might require several months of earnest begging before a greater gift is bestowed. And then, after all the genuflecting, the guy's not sure what to do with it. It's like the instructions are in Japanese.

Man: "Does this feel good?"

Woman: "It would feel better if you clipped your nails."

The uncertainty is contagious. Both partners feel it. The more nervous one partner gets, the more the other partner wants to run and hide.

Woman: "Are you sure you're ready?"

Man: "I think I'm going to puke."

But at long last it happens. Clumsiness is cured by a shared gung-ho attitude. Opening-night jitters give way to the old college try. Errors are, in the lexicon of sports, "aggressive errors" and "rookie mistakes." Bruises heal. Happiness lasts. And from here it gets easier and better.

We learn that the wait justifies the reward, regardless its duration.

Sex and the Girlfriend: Learning to Please

Some men never discover the information on the pages of Cosmopolitan, and and that's too bad. Despite a girlfriend's discreet attempts at sex education—like placing on his pillow the article "Multiple Orgasm: 101 Ways He Can Make 'Em Happen!"—some men still prefer the wham-bam-thank-you-ma'am method of lovemaking, as originally demonstrated in caveman times. Perhaps "lovemaking" is the wrong word.

Conversely, we men of enlightenment take a continuing-education approach to sex. We figure the worse we are, the less we'll get, so sex is something we should get good at. Sex is something two people can do together, much like tennis. It can be a lifetime sport, much like golf.

Thus we learn to please our partner. At least we attempt to learn. We read how-to tips in men's magazines featuring photos of guys we wish we looked like. We see Chiseled Man in the accompanying photo and think, "If this guy needs help with sex, I'm doomed!" But we are heartened in the assumption that ugly people have sex too, because there are a lot of ugly people, and somebody has to be procreating them.

The most common sex tip concerns paying attention to her needs. Some men figure all she needs is this! This right here! Hoooo-weeeee!

We discover she needs more, much more. Tenderness, soft words, soft touch, plus the handy instructional booklet featured on page 223. The magazine claims the booklet will help our sex life. It will show us that women also enjoy sex, as it involves them jointly. The booklet costs $9.95, plus shipping and handling, and we think the word "handling" in this case is funny.

The booklet is self-defeating. She might not wait four to six weeks for delivery.

Also, we wonder how exactly we're supposed to read the thing in the dark, when we need it most:

"Honey, I'd know exactly what to do here if I could actually see Diagram 2-B."

We read more and more articles, each promising new insight. Most articles offer the same tips as the previous article, but in a slightly different order. Most are titled "What She Really Wants in Bed!"

The articles could also be titled "How We Can Really Get You to Buy This Magazine!"

We read more, learn more. We learn more about nouns that, in 9th grade, we looked up in Webster's New World Dictionary. Nouns such as "labia majora," which sounds like a Mozart concerto but isn't.

More importantly, we learn which verbs should be applied to those nouns—verbs such as "rub," "stroke" and "avoid."

We want to be a student of sex, valedictorian of whoopee. We want to be good in bed, but not so good that she thinks we've been practicing with someone else. We want to be good in bed with her. We want her to brag to her friends. We want them to tell two friends, and so on and so on.

As we get older, we learn to rely less on supermarket checkout-lane fodder and more on word of mouth—specifically, word from our girlfriend's mouth. The best person to teach us about our girlfriend, we figure, is our girlfriend. She can tell us more about her needs than some pointy-headed SoHo writer earning $5 per word to rewrite advice from last month's issue of Mademoiselle.

Honest communication provides better sex-ed than the article in the June issue: "12 Hot Ways To Make Your Ssssummer Ssssex Sssssizzle!" We already know what makes her sizzle. She told us, and then she showed us.

The education continues. We experiment. We gather empirical data. Subtle clues—like "Owwww! Not there!"—indicate we're not performing like a champ. Conversely, a shout of "Oh God!" is either an unqualified endorsement of our sexual prowess or spontaneous recitation of her favorite George Burns movie.

Sex is a dual tutorial. Each partner learns from the best teacher in the room—the other partner. It's the best way to determine if that high-pitched yelp is a response to orgasmic bliss or to a crushed solar plexus. Trial and error can be effective training. What popped the corn of a former lover might not butter the bread of the current girlfriend. It might give her a leg cramp.

We try different positions. Some are reminiscent of Amish couples while others are more gymnastic than the entire Belorussian Olympic Team.

One night in particular, we're twisted like a Rold Gold pretzel. It's like we're playing Twister in the buff. We look down at her and suddenly we get the impression we've seen this position before—from a different angle. Then we recall where we saw it; at a friend's lakehouse last summer during an impromptu screening of Naughty Nurses II: ICU Nude.

We start giggling in mid-thrust. We feel we're copying Lance Stagg, Porn Star. We feel ridiculous. But the position feels good.

We try other things, other methods, creams and oils, lights on/lights off, all to develop the perfect sex life with the girl we love. We win some and lose some. One night, after an especially energetic session, she informs us that she does not like rug burns or the taste of latex. "It tastes rubbery," she says. Nor does she believe the term "headboard" should be taken literally.

The discovery phase is mutual. We tell her, "Hey, that thing's not a toy! It might be fun to play with, but cool it with the kung-fu grip. There are nerve endings in there! It hurts when you bend it at a 93-degree angle. And if you need something to bite, try Wrigley's Spearmint." And then we have more sex.

Each partner jots the information in a mental notebook for future reference. We make more love, make more mistakes. One night, while applying the condom as directed, we accidentally shoot the little Trojan across the room. Pa-ting! It slaps against the wall and falls to the floor. We both laugh.

One night as we go to kiss her passionately, we stop just short of her lips to spit out a hair. It is a short hair, and we can't seem to get it off our tongue. We feel it, but we can't find it. Finally we find it but we can't spit it out. It's like somebody Super-Glued it on there. It feels like a permanent part of our anatomy, like ears. We both laugh.

And every time we laugh in bed, we love each other more. Laughter is such a turn-on.

The voyage continues. We are on the Ni§a and Pinta of sexual discover. Some things float her boat but don't float ours. Her Ni§a rides waves of pleasure while our Pinta is back at port.

One night we're doing that thing we do. It's the thing she absolutely loves, but to us it's like washing dishes. It's just a chore. But it feels so good to her, she's practically singing the soprano solo from "Madame Butterfly." She's absolutely wailing, shakin' like a leaf on a fuzzy tree—and there we are, thinking about making a sandwich. Ham and cheese on rye. At this point, we're just a sex toy—just pull the string and watch us go. But that's OK. We love her. And she loves this. If she feels good, we feel good.

Unlike the voyage of Columbus, our exploration moves toward no specific destination. We don't dance triumphantly after she reaches orgasm then call it a day. Instead we continue to learn and explore. We seek a lifetime of discovery.

We find that learning to please is pleasing. Mutual pleasure has nothing to do with simultaneous orgasm. Not necessarily.

A Male Secret: What We Think About During Sex

A man hopes his lover is not performing—in the thespian sense. A woman hopes her lover is—in the physical sense.

A man hopes his lover is not pulling a Katherine Hepburn, delivering an Oscar-caliber performance in the sack with dialogue such as, "You're the best." A woman hopes her lover is not pulling a Fast Eddie Felson, with dialogue such as, "Well, I'm finished. You?"

In a perfect world, women would never feign the joy of sex. Men would never rush their own. Women would never fake the Big O. Men would make sure they didn't have to.

We said in a perfect world.

In sex as in golf and tennis, timing is everything. The problem is, sometimes sexual mechanisms need to be recalibrated. Respective male and female sexual clocks often run at different speeds. Too often, a man's clock is a stopwatch, a woman's a sundial. And in a battle of stopwatch and sundial, the stopwatch wins. The stopwatch gets there first.

A man can finish what he started in a matter of seconds. Originally, this quick-finish ability allowed the man—as hunter and protector—to plant to his Paleolithic seed and quickly resume his duties of killing mastodons and fending off warring tribes from raiding the tribe's clothesline.

Times have changed. Humankind has evolved. A man's quick-finish ability now allows him plenty of time to see the second-half kickoff or finish painting the garage. It is less an ability than a disability, at least for his partner.

These days, a thoughtful man must take deliberate measures to ensure his performance is an extended one. It should not be a cameo. A girl could get George C. Scott for that.

Women, of course, rarely finish too soon. If they do, they don't fold up the tent and call it a night. Some proceed to string together several more Big O's, much like a scoreboard on a Nolan Ryan pitching performance— O-O-O-O-O-O-O-O-O. Women are impressive this way—the way they can string together so many consecutive "oh's."

Often for a man, it is a battle of the bulge to deny himself immediate pleasure of the flesh. He must wage war against finishing too soon—hold his finger against the breaking dam—lest he face subtle ridicule from the girl's friends the rest of his life. In doing so, he must tread a fine line between too much pleasure and not enough. He must fight against a sequence of too much flow and, subsequently, too much ebb. He doesn't want to finish too soon, but he doesn't want to render himself incapable of finishing at all.

It can be a very delicate process. A man feels that tingle coming on within the first 38 seconds, he has to find a way to send it back to the bullpen—but not permanently. Thus he must wage psychological warfare with himself to prevent a premature launch of the Space Shuttle Steve. In the throes of ecstasy, he must take the most unnatural of measures: contain himself. He must constantly change his focus to alternately numb and reignite his senses, shifting frequently into Economy Mode to forestall the approaching climax.

If a woman could read his mind during sex, she might be shocked to discover a virtual one-man roundtable:

Oh, god, this is great! ...this is sooooo great!! ...In fact, it's a little too great...whoa, big fella...hold your horses, stud boy! ...emergency brake! ...

Economy Mode: Pace yourself...put it in cruise control...think of something else... That's it! Baseball! Yes, the Yankees look to field a quality team this year, with depth in the bullpen and a fine starting rotation, plus speed in the outfield and a couple of big bats....

Hey, hey! ...back in control...back on top of my game...I'm the man! ...feelin' good now, feelin' reeeeeaaaaal good, maybe too good...hey now, hoss!...whoa now, Trigger! ...fire in the hole! ...

Economy Mode: I've certainly noticed a move toward the long-shafted putters and a continued trend toward the jumbo drivers on the PGA Tour. Obviously, even among professionals, there is a tendency to drive for show and putt for dough...doughhhh...doooouuuughhhhhhhh!...

Hey, now! Is eeeeev'rybody happy!??? ...I am the MAAAAN! ...Somebody put me in a movie!!!! ...Hooooeeeeee! ...look at me go...Stud-O-Rama!!! ...whoooaaa, whoa there, stud...pass the potatoes! ...

Economy Mode: Slow it down now...go into the four-corner offense...that's it, pass the ball around, work for the open shot...be smart...don't rush it...wait for the open man. ...oh, no...oh no...somebody stole my ball!!! I can't get my ball back!!!

Got it! ...stole it back, ba-beeeee! ...Drivin' full-court now! ...coast-to-coast! ...drivin' the lane! ...goin' in for the jam! ...thank you, ma'am! ...gonna rattle the rim! ...gonna break the board! ...don't even THINK about blocking my shot! ...aaaand BOOM! ...He shoots, he scores!!!

A man's brain is a sexual thermostat, constantly checking itself against overheating. When too many impulses threaten to override the system, the brain releases a supply of asexual thoughts, allowing the man's nervous system to send a cooling-off signal to the nether regions. Once order has been restored, the brain reverts to the matters at hand. The process repeats itself until the man finally allows his orgasm to bypass the system.

The process is not a genetically inherited trait but rather a developed skill. It requires much practice to achieve the delicate balance. Many men never bother to master the craft. Those men usually get to see the second-half kickoff.

Those who do master the craft don't watch the kickoff. They have their own ballgame.

Great Sex, Bad Relationships

A CAUTION sign for couples who get too good at sex: Bedroom aptitude sometimes takes precedence in a relationship. The sex is everything Helen Gurley Brown said it could be, and more. It's so good, you spend a majority of your time getting dressed and undressed. Your conversations take place in the missionary position. You are so good in bed together, you could probably do a series of instructional videos.

There is just one problem. At some point, you have to get out of bed.

This is where the relationship falls apart. Off-mattress, the romance fizzles like a flat Coke in afternoon sun. Anywhere outside the bedroom, the relationship just plain sucks.

Each day begets an argument anew. If there isn't an argument by the time World News Tonight begins, you start one out of habit. You argue so much that friends no longer watch bad talk shows featuring fat women fighting over tattooed men—they just watch the two of you.

The upside of the stormy affair is the nightly session of wall-shaking, ground-quaking, bed-breaking, neighbor-waking make-up sex.

You: "I'm sorry."

Her: "I'm sorry too. Now take me, Mandingo!"

Sex becomes a drug to fix the infirmity of your relationship. You know the relationship is wrecking your life, but you can't wait for that next fix. That next fix will make it all better.

You know you can't stay with this person. You have to break away—go cold turkey. But the thought of leaving her leaves you clammy. Visions of sex withdrawal leave you scared. Each night you sleep with her in your arms, fearing the argument that daylight brings. Each battle eventually leads you back to bed in a cyclical path to another score. You wonder if a heroin addict feels any differently.

Great Relationship, Bad Sex

She is the first woman who ever shared your passion for old train stations and black-and white-movies. She doesn't think it's weird that you still subscribe to Highlights magazine and continue to laugh at the exploits of Goofus and Gallant. You love it that she has her own bat roost and plays first-chair viola in the local philharmonic. You're beginning to think you've discovered the perfect girl.

Then you go and spoil it all by jumping into bed.

Suddenly things don't seem so great anymore. She laughs at your smiley-face boxers and, worse, what's underneath. Despite your obvious displeasure, her bedtime attire is an old yellow T-shirt featuring a faded Jimmie Walker shouting, "DY-NO-MITE!" She also eats crackers in bed.

Worse, you've tried enough positions to become an honorary member of the Kama Sutra club, but nothing seems to pop the cork. Her yin zigs while your yang sags. The only thing she does well in the bedroom is put on a fitted sheet.

To her, sex is like C-Span—she can take it or leave it. She thinks oral sex means you talk about it—and she doesn't even like to do that. Worse, she takes the term "lay" literally, remaining stiff and motionless like a hoe—a garden hoe.

Sex with her is a chore, something you feel you must do in order to avoid becoming your parents—your sexless, Winnebago-driving parents, whose only goal is to collect another state-shaped sticker.

You ask yourself if you are making too much of this, if sex is really that important. After all, monks go without it, as do plants. But you realize sex is that important. It's very important. You are not a plant, though a lifetime with the sexless wonder might just turn you into the botanic garden.

A lifetime of bad sex is not the future you'd envisioned. You'd envisioned four decades of great sex complete with whipped cream and all sorts of squeals. You didn't envision life with June Cleaver.

Each morning, when you wake with her in your arms, you fear the sunset. The setting sun augurs another dark night of cold sex. No sex. You fear your sex life, or lack thereof, will become a life sentence with no chance of parole. You envision 40 more years of watching The Tonight Show out of the corner of your eye.

Sex, Love and Commitment: The Reluctant Man

As kids, we always got cool gifts from Gramps. While Aunt Velda gave us tulip seeds, Gramps came up with the goods. His gifts were simple and effective, like Gramps himself. We'd get a baseball. A model airplane. A silver dollar. We told him thanks and we meant it. We hugged his neck and smelled the Old Spice.

His greatest gift did not come in a box or bow. It did not come on our birthday or at Christmas. It came unexpectedly, when for the first time, Gramps regarded us not just as a grandson but as a man.

Late one afternoon, in the fall of our twenty-first year, Gramps took us to the city park. He wanted to have a good old-fashioned sit-down. A man-to-man, he called it. Gramps began telling us things he'd never told us before. Gramps started talking about sex.

"Eeewww!" we said. "You had sex?"

He cackled and sipped his Schlitz.

"Well, hell yes, boy," he said, wiping his lips with thick fingers. "How do you think your dad got here?"

We never imagined that Gramps had sex. Sex was for young people, beautiful people. Not for old people.

But according to Gramps, he did have sex. He said Grandma could back him up on this one.

We sat on an old log under a mulberry tree and talked. Gramps said he wanted to describe the sexual climate of his time, and so he did. The way he told it, the climate was pretty cold. He wanted to tell us how much easier we have it. We wanted to tell him it isn't so easy.

He knew that. His story served more as a primer and a lesson. It showed us that each generation has its unique circumstances regarding sex and relationships. We have ours. Gramps had his.

For Gramps, getting lucky didn't mean getting laid; it meant escaping the scrutiny of his sweetheart's parents.

Back then, single women didn't have their own apartments. They didn't have Girls Night Out. They didn't go to Cancun in squealing groups of five. Most of all, women didn't go around "spreadin' their legs at the drop of a hat."

At least that's the way Gramps tells it.

For Gramps, the first date consisted of an afternoon of light conversation in the family parlor—if, of course, the girl's father approved. Even if her pop permitted the afternoon rendezvous, he made sure to remain within earshot.

Saturday-night dates were just that—Saturday night only. A young couple had little chance of a waking together on Sunday morning. Sunday was reserved for Father Donavan's fire-and-brimstone condemnation of all things fun, not to mention the sideways glances of the entire congregation of Our Lady of Perpetual Censure.

At least that's the way Gramps tells it.

Scrutiny. The entire community was one collective watchdog. Social Mores had to be upheld, or else the entire town could be sullied. All the townsfolk, minus a few longshoreman, were in agreement: Sex must be reserved for marriage and marriage only. The Rotary Club even put a sign on the city limits: "Only Good Girls Live In This Town!"

At least that's the way Gramps tells it.

One way a young man could escape watchful eyes was to don the khaki for Uncle Sam. That way he could take shore-leave in Guam and pay a visit to Rosie's Good-Time Bar & G.I. Love Shack. Otherwise, he might be out of luck in getting lucky.

If a guy stayed home to mind the store, chances were he'd still be a virgin on his wedding night. This alone was probably reason to accelerate the courting ritual. Society's collective denunciation of premarital sex was enough to make any 16-year-old couple dive for the altar. Matrimony was the only sanctioned way a young couple could have sex without rotting in hell.

It was boy meets girl, boy marries girl, boy has sex with girl, boy gets to know girl, boy grows old with girl.

At least that's the way Gramps tells it.

Gramps could scarcely imagine courting in today's world—although he might like to try it.

It is a world of I.U.D.'s, edible condoms, cohabitation, girl-on-top. Unlike the men of yesteryear, few of today's men enter the honeymoon suite with virginity intact. Nowadays, the anticipation of unleashing a cooped-up libido is of little consideration in choosing a wife.

Gramps was right: We don't need to dash out and buy the cow when the milk is free.

Thus our march to the altar is not nearly so urgent as Gramps'. More liberal attitudes—and more liberal girlfriends—have taken the urge out of urgent. Today we can seek marriage without regard to sexual motives. We don't have to jump the broom to finally jump in bed. We can base a marriage on a healthy relationship rather than a starved libido. We can delay marriage until we know the match is perfect.

And delay we do.

We are often involved in a lasting relationship—one that lasts and lasts and lasts but, much to our girlfriend's dismay, never progresses to the altar.

Weeks dissolve into months, months into years. Like good champagne, the question remains unpopped. The diamond remains unpurchased.

Even this month's Cosmo can't seem to answer what is wrong. Why don't we commit? Could it be that sexual freedom has turned the delay into a virtual postponement?

True, sexual freedom does give us a reason not to rush matrimony. But the reasons to delay it are more complex:

A. The relationship really isn't perfect:

The relationship looks good from the outside. Friends think you're the happy couple. But from the inside, where it counts, something is missing. In the halls of your heart, an emotional Hoover Upright is sucking up passion like a lint ball. You have feelings for her, yes, but those feelings are feeling less like instinct and more like habit. The relationship is just another pack of Marlboro 100s.

You feel what passes for passion, but you figured on having more passion than this. Now it's just muscle memory. When the relationship started, it was a five-alarm affair. You had sex all the time. It was like Mrs. O'Leary's cow had kicked over the lamp on your loins. You had sex for breakfast, lunch and dinner. You had a lot of between-meal snacks. She was getting bow-legged and you were developing back trouble.

Now the most important tool in your sex life is Tylenol; her headaches are becoming more frequent. As for you, it's a lot of London Bridge Is Falling Down. You have trouble rising to the rare occasion. Sex is less of a want-to than an ought-to. It is less like hunger and more like taking out the trash. You're afraid that soon, sex will become a monthly entry in your day-planner, like a haircut.

"Honey, according to the schedule, we'll be having sex on Tuesday the 14th, from 6 to 6:20, right before the Yard Of The Month awards."

You ask yourself, Is this the way it's supposed to be? After a relationship moves into the extended phase, is passion phased out in a sort of forced retirement due to erotic downsizing?

You used to watch Hart To Hart on TV, and Jonathan and Jennifer were very cute and passionate, always sexy and well-groomed, even after Jonathan's requisite car chase and fistfight in a three-piece suit. If they could stay frisky, what with all that mayhem, why not you? They had been together for many years and still played footsies. Why can't you? Why can't you feel passion on a daily basis? You turn to ask her that question, but she's asleep.

The relationship is running on autopilot. The initial spark is a low blue flame bordering on ember then ash.

Sure the relationship is comfortable. It's like a big ol' beanbag chair. The two of you know each other's moves in parlor games such as Balderdash. On Saturday nights with friends, you frequently get the high score. At home you share a toothbrush. You drink milk from the same glass. Your hugs fit like two jigsaw pieces.

It is virtually effortless in its comfort—a movie-rental kind of relationship, where you snuggle on the couch and fall asleep before the movie's over. But it is not the perfect love you always wanted. It is a B-minus.

The minor flaws that at first you overlooked have, over time, become magnified. Her aversion to camping now seems prissy and extreme. Just once you'd like to camp with her instead of going with your old Scout buddies while she stays home to plant seasonals. Just once you'd like to wake her to watch the sunrise without hearing, "Oh, sweetie, you go. I want to sleep."

You just want to tell her, "I don't want to go! That's not the point! We need to go."

You hate to admit it to her. But you must admit it to yourself. You love her, but you are not in love with her. You are living on residual emotion. As for sex, it has its blinker on, and it's about exit the relationship entirely.

Silently stroking her hair in quiet concession to reality, you finally admit it: She is not the one. She is almost the one. But she is not the one.

To find happiness later, you must endure pain now. You have to end a good relationship to find a great one.

Like many men, you will put off marriage rather than give up what you have—freedom—for something you really don't want—imperfect marriage.

B. You have other worlds to conquer:

You'd love to sell your big-screen TV, move to the warehouse district, grow a goatee and paint for a year. You'd like to scale Mt. Everest because it's still there. You want to enter the Dakar Rally and place a respectable third. You want to write the Great American Novel or at least a pretty good one. The point is, you want to do something.

There is a world for you to conquer—a world right here on planet Earth.

Shackled to a desk in a corner office, you daydream of greatness. Your dreams are not the empty reveries of hollow men longing for a past that never happened or a future that has no chance. They are not the arenas of improbable hope. You already have the key to the executive washroom. So do other executives who wash their hands in an executive fashion. You want more. You still harbor Lewis-and-Clark dreams of doing something special. You hear the theme from Rocky.

You know that a future legacy is a work in progress. A legacy-in-the-making leaves room for improvement. Your legacy, you're sure, can be a legacy recalled and rejoiced, not filed away with the dusty obituaries of anonymous lives. You know too that if you do nothing, your legacy will be nothing—yet another eulogy to murdered aspirations and liquidated dreams.

What stands in your way is real life. It is the American male's standard grievance: "Well, if I didn't have to work, I'd fly a hot-air balloon around the world." A formidable obstacle to epic achievement is the 9 a.m. sales meeting.

Another hurdle to lasting greatness is the girlfriend—in particular the longtime girlfriend with crosshairs fixed on matrimony. A girlfriend has a special way of soaking up large chunks of free time. She is like a job that way. On a Saturday when you could be preparing your kayak for a solo trip across the Atlantic, you're holding hands at the zoo. You're sharing a blue sno-cone and watching the lemur do backflips.

You have to admit it's fun. You love it. And you love her. Love isn't the problem—or maybe it is.

You were a single guy when you met her. You were living large. But you fell for her on the spot. It was soap-opera fast and soap-opera deep.

"Not now!," you thought. "I'm single! Single!"

You tried in vain to deflect the frontal assault of emotion, clinging by a fiber of independence to your solo status. You wanted to stay single—as in single—a helluva lot longer before putting down stakes with Ms. Right. But you met her way ahead of schedule. And now you're stuck on her, stuck like green on grass.

But in the Male Ego mechanism of your mind, you're experiencing technical difficulties. Ever since you were a kid, you wanted to be an astronaut or a cowboy or a sea captain. Captain Nemo called. Those groovy vocations were specific dreams indeed, but also representations of some primal need for rare adventure. Unfettered by society's expectations, you just wanted to do something cool when you grew up. Now that you are grown up, you still do. You want to do something big.

But in order to chase the dream, you must run from responsibility. At least you think you do. And responsibility includes your girl. In chasing his dream, Don Quixote had Sancho Panza, but Sancho Panza wasn't a girl. Thus Don Quixote could chase the impossible dream without having to stop first at the outlet mall. More importantly, he could hold a steady course to a self-centered goal without distraction. He didn't have to waste time with tender moments.

The fact is, you met her too soon. It is a forever affair that began when it shouldn't have, a premature launch that now threatens its forever potential. Your epic-achievement years were spent winning stuffed animals at the county fair, and it bothers you. You never had the chance to kayak or balloon your way to greatness. You were too busy being in love.

To you, achievement is a hike across the Himalayas. To her it is the Wedding March. Ne'er the twain shall meet.

Your married pals play softball. Slow-pitch. They have pleasant grins and double chins and their lives are like a ground-rule double. They seem happy enough. But you sense a vacancy in their lives, one filled previously by aspirations beyond the Methodist League Summer Slo-Pitch Championship. You wonder: Did the promise of simple love and easy sex end their dreams of adventure? Did thrillseeking end when skirt-chasing ceased? Did marriage soothe the savage beast?

You must make a decision. You cannot hold the girl in abeyance. A girl-friend cannot go on a layaway plan like a new couch.

Do you trade warm fuzzies for hard achievement? Do you trade the spoon position for the hunched-over position as you barf bacteria in the wilds of Bora Bora? Do you trade happiness for your idea of greatness?

You don't want to wait till it's too late, grabbing life by the heels as it passes. You don't want to wait till you're 55 to cruise Route 66...or 70 to sail the Seven Seas. Dwindling opportunity often finds its final refuge in the desperate attempt. A heroic endeavor begotten by midlife crisis often leaves a man crumpled in a heap, dead of a heart attack. More often, a dream put on hold becomes a dream put to rest.

You cannot allow that to happen. You have to decide now. Is it the girl? Or is it The Grail?

You know one thing: It's not that getting married will stop a man from circumnavigating the globe. But it will let a little air out of his balloon.

C. You might want to sleep with other women:

You love your girlfriend. Your conversations are masterpieces, like Bach symphonies without all the violins. Your laughter is shared, like all else in the relationship. Your days are like walks through great museums, so much you discover together.

You love your girlfriend. Even the sex is great. Twice she has read the Kama Sutra. She practices what it preaches. She believes that to give pleasure is to receive it also. And she receives it quite a bit. You are happy to oblige. You love making love to the one you love.

There's just one small problem. You're a man.

As a man, you have a major flaw: Fantasy and reality are separate but not equal.

Your sex life is heavenly. But your fantasies are out of this world.

And so far your fantasies are just fantasies, reveries yet unrealized. You've never had sex with a tall blonde supermodel backstage during a Christian Dior runway show, though you have imagined it often. You've never made love to a Radio City Rockette on the pitcher's mound at Yankee Stadium. You've never starred in a Triple-X movie under the alias "Randy Stallion." And you've never done it in an elevator.

You haven't done any of these things. And if you marry the woman you love, you never will—except for maybe the elevator. You'd have to push the right buttons.

For a woman, fantasy often involves candlelight dinner and tender sex with the man she loves. For a man, that is a very enjoyable evening—but it sure isn't fantasy. Fantasy is candlelight dinner and sex with the Laker Girls.

And for you, fantasy is no different. You're a man, and you have manly fantasies. You sure don't fantasize about gentle lovemaking on a heart-shaped bed with the woman you adore. That would be a cool thing to do, but it rates a 10 on the Fantasy Yawn-O-Meter. Nor have you envisioned a warm bath, soft music, ambient lighting, tender sex and yourself dropping to a knee to pop the question. If anyone's dropping to a knee in your fantasy, it ain't gonna be to pop the question.

Instead you've imagined sex with dazzling women in dazzling locations. Sometimes the women take turns; sometimes they perform as a group. Your fantasies are pretty flexible that way.

You've imagined sex in the surf at Big Sur; she calls you "Big Sir." You've imagined yourself a Miss Universe Pageant judge, promising your vote to Miss Costa Rica in exchange for an early peak at her talent. She blows horn. You've even had the prison-guard-in-the-female-prison fantasy. In your version, the prisoners take you hostage to protest the fact that their prison-issue bras are way too small. You perform with amazing stamina for a man your size. You are a naughty little hostage.

Your fantasies are not merely imagined trysts with imagined women, however. Your fantasy life also provides a framework that anything is possible. It leaves the door open for the Laker Girls—which is unlikely—but also for the girl next door, which is very likely, as if you haven't noticed her dancing nude in front of the window lately.

Your fantasy life provides more than recreation on lonely nights. It is a harbor for probable and improbable fantasies alike. It gives you a reason to stare at the Victoria's Secret catalog and think, "I'll never make it with the blonde chick in the seamless contour bra, but what if…?" It also gives you a reason to ogle the aerobics instructor at the gym and think, "Hey, it could happen. It really could." So what if it never does. It's the thought that counts.

Indeed, your fantasies feed the engines of optimism. They let you to think that maybe this, at long last, is your day to meet the saleswoman in the strangely deserted men's clothing store. And like Steve B. from Akron, it is finally your turn to write a letter to Penthouse that begins:

I never thought it would happen to me. But there I was, trying on some red Jockey briefs in the dressing room, when suddenly there was a gentle knock on the door. I opened it to see the beautiful saleswoman, her full lips trembling.

"I just wanted to see," she said huskily, "if those briefs fit properly."

Within two seconds, they did not fit properly. They were way too tight in the crotch. So I took them off and said, 'Perhaps you'd like to place these on the bargain rack…."

You know it doesn't hurt to dream. In fact, it feels pretty good.

Your optimism is continually fired by bikini-waxed images from the mass media. You're bombarded by Baywatch, the Swimsuit Issue and NC-17 movies with bad dialogue but good bodies. Riddled by these slick skin-toned images, you have been systematically seduced by the possibility of seduction. Sex is the carrot at the end of the stick, and Hollywood is holding the stick. Hollywood supplies the notion—misguided but fun—that what happens to James Bond could happen to you. You have seen Agent 007 and his lengthy his roster of conquests, and you know you can do just as well just as often.

"I'm sorry, Miss Galore. I didn't catch your first name. But I see by your nudity that it really doesn't matter."

Likewise, in real life, you imagine your own brand of Bondian conquest. Ever since puberty you've imagined a glorious sex life—glorious but not unreasonable. You've imagined the French girl in a French bikini who drops her top and asks you to apply some Bain Del Soleil to her St. Tropez tan. You've imagined the buxom divorcÇe who asks you to carry her groceries, then suggests you follow her home for your tip. You've imagined the girl who comes to your house in nothing but a trench coat without you asking, "Why don't you come to my house in nothing but a trench coat?"

Fantasies are fanciful relative to their absurdity. You know you won't spend an afternoon at the Playboy Mansion pool playing Marco Polo with Miss April. But you might meet that French girl. You realize that a retouched Miss September will never waltz down Main Street U.S.A. to pop into your hardware store looking for a good nail. But you might have a chance at Missy from the mail room.

Either way, it doesn't hurt to dream.

Still, some men allow images of airbrushed centerfolds to determine their destiny. They will throw away a happy future for a slim-to-none chance at that free-thinking saleswoman. The possibility is enough to make them discard a life of definite love and trust for a life of indefinite sin and lust.

You ask yourself, "What about me? Will I trade love for lust?" You wonder what exactly is the ultimate fantasy—a woman to have and hold? Or four women to have and hold? A woman to love? Or a woman to do in a dressing room?

You know one thing: The moment you marry, those fantasies are forever fantasies and no longer minute possibilities. Marriage places fantasy squarely in fantasyland, a place where possibility is forever laid to rest.

You know, too, that if you don't marry her, and you start chasing wild island fantasies, you just might change your tune. You might fantasize about gentle lovemaking on a heart-shaped bed after all. You might fantasize about conversations that are masterpieces.

PART II

Sex Outside the Relationship

The One Night Stand: Every Man's Right—and Sometimes His Wrong

The one-night stand is something of a misnomer, partly because nobody ever stands until it's over, and then rather quickly.

In fact, a more appropriate tag might be the "one-night lay." It's not like "The National Anthem" is played each time just before sex begins. There's no 7th-inning stretch. Nobody shouts, "Down in front!" There really isn't much standing at all.

Apart from its bad name, the one-night stand has gotten a pretty bad name. It is oft interpreted as vile and reprehensible. And again, it is generally the female participant who bears condemnation while the male reaps praise for his warrior-like conquest. In society's post-sex valuation, the man generally gets better marks. The woman goes straight to hell.

People often interpret the one-night stand as a slap to decency, morality, Jerry Falwell, the Christian Coalition, Ward Cleaver and the institution of marriage itself. They argue it's not what God had in mind when he created man, woman and night. They argue that sex without marriage is wrong, and that sex without knowing the partner is stupid.

But let it be said that the argument will continue till doomsday, for there will always be plenty of people to argue it. If not, it won't be for lack of trying. People will have sex with people till people cease to exist. If there's one marketing slogan that applies to life itself, it is this: Just Do It.

Humans will do just that, even if they have to take a cab in the morning.

Cause and Effect: The Ups and Downs of a One Nighter

Stripped to its basics, the one-night stand is a consensual union between two people who, for the minimum requirement of one night, actually like each other—enough to strip to their basics.

Come morning they might hardly know each other. An introduction might be in order. But that night—hooo-weee!—that night they have a thing going, baby! They are Cleopatra and Marc Anthony, lovers in the heat of the night—lovers still discovering new things about each other, such as first name and last name.

Popular perception of the one-night stand is that of a quick, selfish, sweaty affair in an alien bed, destitute of affection and based solely attaining the Big O. Sometimes this is the case. Sometimes it is not.

Sometimes a guy and girl converse more deeply than in terms such as "oooh." Sometimes they talk about books and movies, then they get it on.

Wit and intelligence are especially attractive when accompanied by a nice butt.

The one-nighter is widely condemned, especially by married people who don't get to do it anymore. But in defense of the one-nighter, let us say this: It can create wonderful memories, if in fact the participants can remember those memories.

The one-nighter can also fill gaps of great loneliness and need. Need in this case refers to a frequently expressed need among adult males: "I really need to get laid."

For males, a dry spell of any substantial duration is cause for alarm if not panic. Men begin to question their manhood if they haven't actually used their manhood in quite some time. A one-night stand can reaffirm their strong male identity and carry them through the next dry spell. Many men tie self-esteem directly to sex; there is little of one when there is little of the other. For them, a rollicking one-nighter can fix all that. They can hold their head high.

Admittedly, the one-nighter can also create uncomfortable situations—for both male and female. As men, we are sympathetic to a woman's post-one-nighter stress disorder. It takes the form of an old joke:

Q: What's the first thing a sorority girl does in the morning?

A: Walks home.

Make no mistake, a guy is grateful when the girl is gone in the morning. He wants to do what he always does in the morning: sit on the toilet and read the sports page. He hates to wake to some semi-alien female chirping, "Let's go have breakfast!" These are words from morning hell. A guy hears that and 30 minutes later he's eating $8 eggs with a girl who's wearing one of his best T-shirts. Worse, he knows he'll never get the shirt back.

But—a guy doesn't want the girl to walk home. Her daybreak escape from the one-nighter shouldn't turn into a March of Dimes deal, where she's trekking across urban landscape like she's earning a dime per mile. Most guys can muster the decency to give the girl a ride home. Even when the whole world smells like snuffed cigarettes and his head is beating like a bongo drum, a guy can scrounge up some politeness—plus a big pack of lies about how busy he'll be for the next few weeks.

Duality of the Double Standard: Her Pain, His Gain

Given society's standard double standard, guys don't suffer the same shame as girls. A girl walks home wearing the clothes she wore the night before, she's branded a harlot on the spot. People honk, bad men whoop. It's sad. Suddenly she's Hester Prynne. Her ashtray sweater is her scarlet letter.

A guy, on the other hand, fairly struts home the morning after. The girl offers him a ride and he says, "No! No! I'll walk! I'll walk!"

It is a victory march, a celebration of fornication, public proof that he can swing with the best of 'em. People honk, glad men whoop. They respond for entirely different reasons. The sounds are not censure but a salute to the good fellow's conquest.

"Hooray for you, man! Shame on her!"

The morning sidewalk is clear metaphor for the double standard. For a guy it is Macy's Day Parade, all pomp and glowing praise. For a girl, it is a march toward the Gates of Hell. Suffice to say that on the morning after, a girl walks much faster than a guy—record time vs. own sweet time.

But—those congratulatory whoops and honks awarded the male are based on the idea that his night's work was good work, that he is strolling home from Victoria's secret love palace. This is not always the case. Nor is it often the case. Actually it's never the case. If it were, he'd still be there, sipping a Bloody Mary on the sunny deck with a lingerie model on his lap. She'd be wearing a fine jacquard robe in a rich satin weave.

No, an honest morning appraisal of the previous night's activities is seldom a thing of beauty. Retrospective critique often reveals the awful truth: She was nothing worth honking over. On the other hand, she didn't exactly sleep with Fabio, and she knows it.

The Morning After: What Have We Done?

We must first acknowledge that one-nighters are often inspired by too much Jim Beam. Barstool judgment of beauty is 80-proof. Beer goggles turn Jane Hathaways into Jayne Mansfields, Mel Cooleys into Mel Gibsons. Few people look more beautiful than a woman at 2 a.m., unless it's a woman at 2:02.

Closing time brings out the best in a woman. It highlights her better features, such as the fact that she is there. Indeed, it might be interesting if beauty pageants were held at closing time: "You're all winners!"

A guy who brings a girl home for the pageant's talent portion risks a rude awakening indeed. Often he wakes, rubs his eyes and tries to focus on the nude outlander at his side. "Who the hell is that?" he asks himself. "Where the hell did she come from?"

Suddenly, last night's everybody's-beautiful buzz has given way to greater visual acuity. Eyesight has returned to normal. Last night's pageant winner is, in fact, Ms. Potato Head.

Strange how a beautiful woman can get so ugly overnight.

In such cases, most guys would rather flee their own home than roust the naked stranger. The typical escape is a note on his nightstand. The exit note is emblematic of the way guys in particular handle touchy situations: politely, but with one foot out the door. Men will avoid a face-to-face confrontation if a note will easily do. They'll risk his getting their TV stolen if it saves them the bother of explaining themselves.

On the left is what the typical note says. On the right is what it says between the lines:

Sorry I had to leave—I was hoping you had to leave.

I didn't want to wake you—because I didn't want to see you.

You looked so peaceful—as hibernating bears often do.

I had to run some errands—my main errand was to run away.

And I had some work to do—on my plummeting self-esteem.

Make yourself at home—for about three seconds.

Feel free to use the restroom—and wash the sheets.

Don't forget to lock the door—behind you.

Have a nice day—and a nice life.

We know how to write the note because we have read one just like it.

A worse fate awaits the man who beer-goggled his way into an alien bed. Come morning any number of things might happen, only one of them good: He finds his clothes, finds his keys and finds the door, careful not to upset the delicate construct of destiny by waking the girl before her appointed time.

Rather than wake her, he will gladly walk into broad daylight smelling like Discount Night at Miss Jessie's House O' Delight. He will gladly suffer the pious stares of nosy neighbors rather than the befuddled stares of the Unknown Lover as she emerges from her coma to find a complete stranger.

Indeed, a fate worse than bad breath awaits the man who selects his one-night consort at the tail end of Nickel Beer Night. He should have listened to his friend, who early in the evening had pointed at a woman across the room who looked like a sparring partner.

"She's about a 12-pack," he'd said.

And sure enough, five hours later, she was. Twelve beers turned her from sparring partner to pin-up girl in another classic case of beauty through chemistry.

The hard part comes at 7:17 a.m., when a dozen Bass Ales start knocking at the guy's bladder. He opens his red glassy eyes to see a wall he's never seen in a place he's never been. He shakes his aching head and tries to recall if maybe he fell asleep on a friend's couch. Nope, that framed "Footprints In Time" poem isn't anything a guy would have.

He tries to move but realizes he is stuck. He rolls over to see a hulking figure next to him. He wonders if he stumbled into bed with a Green Bay Packer. Wedged beneath this bigger figure is his right arm, caught like a twig under a collapsed bridge. This is what is officially known as a bad situation.

He cannot move his arm. He cannot escape. The only way out is to remove his arm forcefully, which might wake Sleeping Booty. He leans over to look at her face. He grimaces. Waking her would not be a good idea. She is two Rembrandts shy of a pretty picture. The guy tries one more time to extract his arm, hoping to flee the scene with some measure of dignity. He can't. He can't move without waking her.

This, in single man's parlance, is a Coyote Moment. A coyote, if stuck, will gnaw through its own limb to free itself. Likewise, a man held in limbo by a bimbo is said to face a similar situation: He'd chew his arm off rather than wake the slumbering beast. Better to lose a limb and save face. His self-esteem might remain intact, in fact, if he can avoid waking her and taking her to Waffle House for a pork chop.

Pinned under the wreckage, the guy mulls his options. He decides that for breakfast he will eat his right arm.

He decides, too, that if the girl starts looking for a one-armed man, he will chew off his left arm.

Singin' The Blues: The Soul of Remorse

Guys get morning-after blues too. Guy Blues aren't as blue as Girl Blues, but they're still blue. Guy Blues still qualify for the color wheel. They are a primary color.

Guys get the morning blues for the same reason girls get them—guilt. They get all B.B. Kinged because they feel bad about the night before. They don't always feel bad and blue. Sometimes they feel good!-like James Brown.

But at other times, for whatever reasons, they regret their actions. If they could change the course of human history, they would:

1) tell the Titanic to hang a right
2) tell Elvis to take up racquetball
3) alter the events that led to the previous night's coupling.

Regret is nothing new, of course. Nobody took out a recent patent on remorse. We imagine the caveman waking up in some strange cave and feeling a little glum about it. We imagine the Roman gladiator not so glad after all.

Sunrise has a way of shedding a whole new light on the previous night. The clarity of hindsight is hardly overrated. The cosmos reverberates still with uttered echoes of the male lament: "Oh man, I shouldn't have done that."

Contrary to popular belief, it's not all high-fives the next day.

For a guy, morning remorse generally occurs when he makes a simple realization: He likes the girl, not enough to start a relationship but too much to have done what he did. A guy feels OK about a one-nighter when, in retrospect, he can denounce the woman as a vile temptress and evil seducer of men.

But sometimes a guy feels like a bastardly, dastardly Don Juan—like he curled his handlebar mustache, slipped the girl a Mickey, laughed a wicked laugh and sweet-talked his way into her Posture-Pedic, only to crawl over the balcony at dawn leaving nothing but the scent of his Brut For Men. That's how a guy feels when—in the words of every country song ever written—he done somebody wrong.

A guy feels especially crappy when he sullies an especially sweet girl. Sometimes, on weird rare nights, a sweet girl falls head-over-heels for whatever charms the guy might possess. Even if he doesn't have any charms, she seems to find them. It's strange. On that one particular night—because of providential alignment of celestial bodies or because the guy is wearing Brut For Men—he can do no wrong. She adores him. She is stuck on him like Velcro. No matter what the guy does—trip over the pool table, spit dip in a cup—the girl thinks it's cute. And whatever he says, she considers it a philosophical jewel from the lips of the Occidental Gandhi.

He takes her home. They get naked. They sweat and moan in tandem. Deluded by images of slow-motion Hollywood sex, she thinks it's the beginning of a beautiful relationship. He thinks it's sex.

In the morning, as she nestles her head in the warm crook of his neck, she sighs a contented sigh. He thinks about what he needs to do that day. She says, "I hope it can be this way forever." Now he knows what he needs to do: Go directly to a confessional and seek absolution.

He feels like hell; she feels heavenly. He had sex; she made love. Their points of philosophical departure were vastly different, yet their physical destination was the precisely the same—the other person's groin. What to him was a fleeting pelvic moment was to her a physical expression of heart and soul. To her it was the first of many; to him, the first of one.

He is bluer than blue. He is Muddy Waters and John Lee Hooker and Blind Lemon and Howlin' Wolf, moaning out a sad chorus of sorrow in the Mississippi Delta of his soul. It was a night he'll always remember because it was a night she'll never forget. He can't escape one wrenching feeling: that he tainted this fine girl for the guy who someday will love her.

Someday, under questioning, she will lie to him or tell him the truth. It will be painful.

Nightclub Love: Fugitive Emotion

Sometimes the one-nighter is like a hot shower that gets very cold when the hot water runs out. What begins as steamy romance gets tepid overnight and frigid by daybreak. Love can end abruptly when a person has a chance to sleep on it.

Often it begins when the guy and girl make spiritual eye-contact across the bar. Intoxicated by booze and dual infatuation, they fall in love on the spot, like characters in a cable movie. By 11 p.m. they are holding hands; by 11:30 she has a leg draped over his lap; by midnight they are kissing in public; and by 1 a.m. they are ready to commit to each other for life, right after they order some cheese fries.

They are in looooove, baby. They can't believe their good fortune—that their soul mate should happen to be drinking in the same bar on the same night as they are. What are the odds? This is no ordinary fling. They like the same books and movies. It's love, bartender!

Were they not 1,300 miles from Vegas, they'd hop in the Chevy and go get hitched at Miss Tillie's House O' Nuptials.

Come morning, of course, they'd awake face-down in Room 212 of the Roll The Dice Motel to discover themselves officially registered as Mr. and Mrs. Dumbass. A good sign it wasn't true love would be the quick scan of the Las Vegas Yellow Pages for Miss Ellie's House O' Annulment.

It's a lesson many have learned: Not only does physical attraction ebb with the rising sun, so does love. Love isn't on the breakfast menu. It is a midnight snack.

Indeed, most people discover that nightclub love is a temporary membership to deep emotion, more feverish but shorter than the 24-hour flu. It isn't love but rather a good impostor, its disguise a cloak of fresh passion.

It feels like love. It has all the markings of love—desire, compatibility, and for now, fidelity. It feels great, which is its sinister nature. Abetted by heady fumes of momentary discoveries, nightclub love is a drug whose affects are temporary but intense, the heroin of the heart. It is a nocturne deep and lovely whose opiate ends at rooster's crow.

That 7 a.m. wake-up call is a real wake-up call. Boy and girl realize that, other than body fluids, all they share is a love for books and movies. They both like "The Sun Also Rises," but not when it rises on them. It reveals the ugly truth. They've lost that lovin' feeling. Nightclub love was a convenient cover for lust.

There's just one thing left to say: "It's the third house on the right."

To drop off a one-night girl in the morning is perhaps humankind's greatest breach of his informal contract with decency. It is a dual liar's society, a one-on-one symposium of great insincerity.

The passenger door swings open. The girl steps out. She looks back through the window.

"I'll call you," he says.

"You do that," she says.

The Upside of a One-Nighter: A Rare Beauty

Sometimes, upon morning inspection, a guy gets a sunrise surprise: The girl looks like Miss Venezuela. It's rare but it happens, even to guys who don't play for the Lakers. When it happens, a guy is tempted to take a Polaroid for proof.

Indeed, a veteran of the one-nighter operates under the blanket assumption that under the blanket will lie a whale of a girl. He's scared Greenpeace will show up to protest. To discover that she is a fair maiden is happiness visited.

A guy may ask why. Why, on occasion, does Joe Blow hook up with Aphrodite? There is an answer.

Women, like men, get an occasional snootful of the old firewater. Women, like men, sometimes ignore the Surgeon General's warning and booze it up like there's no tomorrow.

The cool thing for men is that women weigh less then men. Female tendency toward the bantamweight division is beneficial to the bigger, burlier gender. Given respective weight ratios and an equal amount of booze imbibed, men look better to women than women look to men. This is another way that nature balances basic inequities between the sexes, like how nature gives men testosterone but women the right of first refusal.

Thus on any given Saturday night, women are equally inclined to throw back a few. That's why rich ugly guys have beautiful girls. Rich ugly guys can buy beautiful girls a lot of booze. By night's end the rich ugly guy is not quite as rich, but he's not quite as ugly either.

As men, we can all benefit from the glassy-eyed stare. It makes us taller, darker, handsomer. Booze is like a gym that way. It turns us into a hunk.

So if it happens that a verifiable vixen goes home with a guy, he should handle it with standard protocol, which is to say, he shouldn't panic. First, it is important that he handle himself properly that night. He shouldn't put on Snoop Doggy Dogg as mood music. Nor should he tell her to stay on her side of the bed. He should say nice things about her beauty, because she's heard those things before and she's expecting to hear them again.

It is equally key that the guy handle himself correctly come daybreak, when he should do as the guy in the movies does. He should:

Wake up with the girl's head wedged lovingly in the crook of his neck; caress her amazingly well-groomed hair; kiss her gently on cheek; slide out from under her, careful not to wake her; put on handy pair of pants next to bed; zip them while revealing washboard stomach; make amaretto coffee while revealing rippling biceps; put on old flannel shirt, pet big happy dog; sip coffee on the patio; read Wall Street Journal as sun starts risin' above the horizon; notice that stocks are doing well; walk to back yard to make something out of wood; use circular saw to make a boat;

Fail to notice her when she emerges two hours later, sipping coffee and smiling at his masculinity; appear engrossed in boat project, careful to level the hull just so; look up finally to wipe manly sweat from manly brow; smile upon sight of her, for she is wearing his Van Heusen and nothing else; take her into his sweaty, muscular arms with a passion that would cause a TV movie to cut to commercial.

Proper morning behavior works like a coupon, redeemable for one additional night of passion. Morning decorum can take it from a one-nighter to a two-nighter at least. The guy might get a week out of it.

The One-Nighter: Lasting Benefits

For a guy, the one-nighter does offer benefits apart from sex itself. It doesn't offer a dental plan or a 401(k), but it does offer these perks:

1) It does not require alimony. When the guy leaves in the morning, she won't get half his stuff. He can keep all his old Doobie Brothers albums.

2) He does not have to meet her parents. Nor does he need approval from her grandmother, which is good, because he wouldn't get it.

3) If he spends the night at her house, he might get a cool T-shirt to wear home. It would be one more for the collection.

4) If she spends the night at his house, he might be more inclined to do laundry the next day—specifically, sheets and pillowcases.

5) If he spends the night at her house, he doesn't have to make the bed in the morning. This is nothing new, but at least he'll have a reason.

6) If she spends the night at his house, he'll finally have a chance to get rid of that crappy wine he got for Christmas: "Care for another glass of almond-roasted peppercorn cabernet?"

7) If he spends the night at her house, he can use one of her condoms, thus saving himself about $1.98.

8) If she spends the night at his house, and she is forgetful, he might have a new set of earrings to take to the pawn shop. Maybe he can get his guitar back.

9) If he is hoping someday to enter politics, he can get plenty of politician practice by categorically denying the affair ever took place.

10) He can justify not going to the gym that day by chalking up the encounter to a vigorous session of cross-training for total-body fitness.

These are small benefits, 10 tiny bricks in the unsteady edifice of compulsory justification. People use all manner of rationale to salve the post-sex conscience and plea bargain their way out of personal penitence.

Guys generally have more opportunities to do so. One-nighters are the male status quo. For a guy, it's easy to impress a girl for one night. He can use the same lines he used on the previous girl and they will sound just as sincere.

It is simple packaging and presentation, the idiom of an actor onstage. A guy has to make himself appealing, but only for a little while. It will take just a few minutes of his time.

By morning, of course, the act wears thin and wears off. Last night's good guy is replaced by today's actual guy. Morning is the backside of nocturnal compatibility. It is paradise lost.

Usually the one-nighter amounts to two people who, in the throes of chemical alteration, use a certain measure of compatibility to get—and justify—what they really want. Sex.

Usually it is sex minus emotional attachment. It feels good physically, but emotionally it is the Dead Sea. It leaves both partners wanting—wanting the warmth and comfort of a person who cares.

In making love, they fail to make love at all. They have sex.

The Price is Wrong: Paying a Toll for the Sex Drive

All too frequently, sex assumes executive veto power over the smart thing to do. When it might be right to call it a night, lust pulls rank on reason. It hits the override button on rational thought.

In the throes of a turn-on, a man's brain performs its most rudimentary functions. It does not do things like solve trinomial equations or operate a gas grill. It simply drives the man toward sex. It is the sex drive.

Under the veteran leadership of raging hormones, lust can cause a man to do very silly things. Often he will risk a month of consequences, or even a life of hell, for one trip to the tunnel of love. Whether physical or emotional, the toll doesn't always justify the trip.

But that seldom stops a man. Driven by lust, the guy travels on, ever in danger of another pile-up. This is a man's life.

The following are typical bad scenes—not bad sex scenes but bad post-sex scenes. Each is caused by man's inability to just say no, just say whoa or just say, "I gotta to go."

The Sting

You are in bed with a woman who is not your woman. She is a woman. That much you are sure of, for these things are hard to fake. It is exactly one minute 38 seconds after you completed the so-called sex act. The sex was great. The Russian judge would give it a 10.

You were spectacular. The French judge would give you a dix, but of course you already have one.

You don't know the woman well. In fact, you met her only three hours ago. You were at a bar called Lucky's when she sidled over and challenged you to game of shuffleboard.

"Loser buys," she said.

Sure enough, you bought. You bought a lot. You were a loser.

After the eighth straight trouncing at the hands of the illustrious foe, you realized you'd been had. You'd been sharked—sharked so bad that Roy Scheider should have been watching you through binoculars and shouting, "Get out of the game! Get out of the game!"

The woman, you later discovered, is the defending Tri-State Shuffleboard Champion. Her nickname is "Shuffles." She is the finest player you have ever seen. Twice she appeared on ESPN2 at 3:45 a.m. on a show called Sports You Never Ever Watch. The show was canceled because people never ever watched it.

Tonight, in a painful 52-minute butt-kicking, eight games of shuffleboard cost you $4 in quarters and $88 in drinks. After each victory Shuffles ordered a martini, sharked not stirred. Each martini cost you $7.95. You wished you'd heeded that NO WAGERING sign.

On the upside, you managed a pretty good buzz yourself. With each martini you got a beer, and by game six, Shuffles was looking better than good. You had to admit she wasn't exactly your type. She was a bit aggressive, one of those hear-me-roar women who appears on the cover of Cigar Aficionado with a phallic stogie clenched in her go-getter teeth, under the teaser:

BLOW ME!
Career Woman Tramples 387 Men On Her Way to the Top!

Still, despite her Katie Couric hairdo and Type A+ personality, she looked sexier and sexier as she racked up point after point. Rather than lose to her, you preferred to look at her. You were about to tell her you'd had enough shuffleboard when she grabbed you firmly by the right butt cheek. She leaned close and whispered hot in your ear.

"One more game," she purred. "Loser gets naked and winner gets nude."

"Here?" you asked. "On the shuffleboard? The sawdust would get in your..."

"No," she said, her breath still hot. "At my place. In my bed. Grrrrrrrrrr."

For the first time tonight, you would find redemption in defeat. You would snatch meaning from the jaws of a thrashing. You would come out a winner.

Now you are naked and she is nude. It is exactly one minute 39 seconds after you completed the so-called sex act. The bedroom air is redolent with residual whoopee. Silent, you lie proud, impressed with your performance. She, no doubt, is more impressed than you. At shuffleboard she is the master, but in bed you are The Man.

Your male ego—that delicate flower—had taken a pounding back at the bar. Shuffles had reduced you from macho to nacho; she had had you for lunch. Her dominance at shuffleboard, coupled with her impressive collection of martini trophies, had turned the tables on traditional gender roles. Her performance had rendered you subordinate in an otherwise masculine realm, and you did not take it like a man.

You were supposed to play the male lead, she the female lead. You figured to put your brawny hand on her fragile fingers, showing her exactly where to put the puck. "That's it," you'd say. "Nice 'n easy." Instead she wore the pants, then she gave you the what-for. "That's it," she said. "Dry, with an olive."

In assuming the lead role herself, she stole your manhood and administered a psychological castration. She turned you into a gelding.

Now you say nay. You are The Man once more. Basking in your own musk, reveling in your sexual prowess, you have reversed the emasculation. You are remasculated. You have been un-gelded in the most emphatic of ways. You gave her the Seattle Slew, which is exactly what she needed but what you needed more.

You are The Man because you made her feel like a woman. You did everything to please her, not yourself. You performed every trick you had ever read in Men's Health, every tip you had ever gleaned from Cosmo. You took your time. You lingered on good places.

Your centurion performance put the pigtails back on her. Made her feminine again. Now she would never threaten your manhood. From now on, you would be on top.

It is exactly 1 minute 48 seconds after you finished the so-called sex act. Her head is cradled gently in your arm and chest. Her face is warm and soft against the hard bulk of your biceps and pecs. For once she looks dainty, there in the safehouse of your hulking virility. You are Tarzan. She is Jane.

Suddenly you feel her move. She lifts your arm and sits upright. She runs a hand through her hair and pats you on the chest.

You reckon it's a love pat.

"All right, Tiger," she says, patting your rugged chest once more.

You smile in mock embarrassment, as if to say, "Shucks, 'tweren't nothin', ma'am. I's only doin' my job."

Your head is starting to swell.

"All right, Tiger," she says again.

"That's me," you say. "Grrrrrrrrrr."

You paw at her playfully. She doesn't smile at your cute little growl. Maybe she's just too tuckered, poor thing.

You reach to caress her face with the back of your hand, like you've seen in the movies. She blocks your hand and looks you straight in the eyes.

"When you're through doing Tony The Tiger routine," she says quite bluntly, "you need to get your tail out of here."

She is kidding, of course.

"'Scuse me?" you say, playfully pulling down the covers to reveal the rise of the Roman Empire. "The tiger can't leave until he gets some…you know."

You are so witty.

She doesn't laugh. "Grab your little clothes," she says, "and get you little ass out of my house."

"Do what?"

"Let me spell it out for you, fella. L-E-A-V-E. Go a-way. I'm through with you, little man. Done. I have no further use for you."

You stand silently, stunned by the reversal. Numb, unable to speak, you put on your jeans. You grab your underwear and, in a daze, put it in your back pocket. You leave the house in the dead of night, panties in a wad.

You don't feel much like a man anymore. Used and discarded, you feel like a tramp. You do recognize the irony: The woman took from you the two things that men often value most—money and penis. Coin and loin. She used them to her benefit, not yours. She played the game by different rules and won. She kicked your butt. You are a loser.

You wish you'd heeded that NO WAGERING sign. She is the finest player you have ever seen.

The Steam

You met her in a coffeehouse. It was poetry in emotion, the moments arranged like words in a sonnet, as if some cosmic bard had crafted the sequence of circumstance for every rhyme and reason to bring you two together. It was an epic. At least it seemed like an epic.

Through a veil of smoke and swirling steam, you saw her. She saw you. You locked eyes, and in that instant, it was like you locked lips, a quiet kiss that reached across the room. The coffee was roasting.

Drawn by a dual and inexplicable pull, you pushed past boys with goat-ees to meet at a table in the middle. You sat and stared at each other to a backbeat of bongos and Baudelaire. She was Keats and Yeats and Shelley, but not a thousand words could describe her. She was beyond verse. She was everything.

At some point—you don't know when—you began a conversation, a conversation without sound, for you heard nothing but a rhyming thump-thump in your chest. Her words were probably brilliant, probably poetry too, yet for you they merely formed a reason to watch her lips. The attraction was undeniable. It felt perfect.

She felt it too, as much as you. Leaning across the table, she took your hand in hers. You looked at her and she at you, connected by unspoken need.

"Let's go," she said, speaking finally.

"Let's go," you said, in perfect rhyme.

It is quiet now, soundless and still, the calm after the sex. The silence is a quiet chorus: The sex went beyond sex, to feelings that cannot rely on words for description, feelings that require sex to define them.

You are too weak to speak. The sweat on your body cools under the hum of the ceiling fan. The sheets are warm and soft, and so is she. You hug her gently. You kiss her softly on the cheek, wet and slightly salty. You love the way she smells, like April rain.

You smile. You have to be honest: This feeling is so strong, so intense, it almost feels like love.

Is that possible? Is the feeling really real? Or is it made of sexual leftovers, the enduring sensation, the waning flame? You aren't sure. You're a reasonable man. But you are sure of how you feel right now, whatever its definition or origin. You feel exalted, perfect, complete, shed of all worries and problems, above the world, stronger than wind, higher than air.

You are sure now. You know you haven't known her long, but you've known her long enough to know. A thousand words cannot describe her, but three words can describe your heart. You want to tell her: "I love you."

It is a feeling you've not experienced. Usually when the sex is over, euphoria fades fast to feelings unfed. Bliss dissolves to a drone. And you zip your pants and go, happy it happened but hardly fooled it will last.

Today is different. It did not end with climax but continues climbing still.

This is crazy. The emotion is too intense to deny. You know she feels it too. Like you, she is awed by it. Her silence is an ode to it.

It is time. You will take the lead. You will say what both of you feel. You will whisper that you love her.

You place your lips to her ear. You will whisper that you love her: "I…"

Suddenly she speaks, cutting you off at the pass. You don't mind. There is time ahead, years to come.

"That was great," she says, in a cute bit of understatement. "Really great."

"Yes," you say. "Great."

She lies silent, yet her feelings are profound in each breath she takes. She doesn't have to say it. You will speak for her. You will say it for two: "I lov…"

"Yep, you did me good," she says suddenly. She bites off the end of a fingernail and spits it to the floor. "You did me real good. You did me almost as good as this guy did me two days ago, right here in this bed. That dude nailed me hard."

"Huh?"

"Tino. I think his name was Tino. Whatever. Who cares? A name's a name. It's the ass what counts."

"Huh?"

"Big Italian guy. Gorgeous eyes, thick black hair, had an ass like an Olympic hurdler."

"Huh?"

She spits another nail on the floor. "We did it for hours. I mean hours. The freakin' walls were shaking like freakin' Jericho. The freakin' neighbors were freakin' screamin'. I had to throw a shoe at the freakin' wall."

"Huh?"

"But this guy, Tino, whatever. He was huge. He was a lot bigger than you, not to say that you're not big or anything, but this guy was huge. I mean freakin' huge. Normally I would've quit, you know, except that—god—I wanted it sooooo bad. You know what I mean?" You know what she means.

The Shock

You met her in your Wednesday-night photography class, "Seeing It In Black and White: The Aesthetics of Imagery vs. Actuality." You had a clear picture of her from the start.

She was cute, friendly, innocent, the kind of girl you see at a church picnic, then forget about. Her face was like a girlish image on a box of snack cakes: freckled, happy, big white smile. She kept her hair in a ponytail.

After forming your initial impression, you didn't pay much attention to her. You didn't pay much attention to anybody. You were there to learn f-stops.

One night after class, as you stuffed your Ansel Adams Day-Planner into your backpack, you overheard her talking to a classmate. She remarked that she could never schedule time in the school's darkroom. You casually mentioned that she could use the makeshift darkroom in your basement. She looked pleased and asked, "How about Friday night?"

A Friday night spent in a basement was not your idea of fun. "Sure," you said, lying, "Friday sounds great."

She arrived at 7:30. You told your friends you'd be finished by 9 and could meet them by 9:30. At 8:30, you went down to check on her progress. Her freshly developed photos were safely drying in a glow of red. She was admiring her work. You looked over her shoulder and admired it too.

You immediately noticed her well composed pictures. "Reminds me of the town square in Rancho de Taos," you said.

"It is," she replied, surprised. "I can't believe you've heard of that place."

The two of you shared stories about this forgotten New Mexico town. Your conversation drifted from the ancient church on the town square to early adobe construction methods. She told you about the year she spent in New Mexico teaching at an Indian reservation. You told her about the summers your family spent in the Sangre De Cristo Mountains. The conversation had twisted down many roads when you finally noticed the clock. Minutes had become hours. For the first time, you realized she wasn't wearing her pony tail.

You spent the next three hours together watching a meteor shower from the roof of your garage. Later, after the celestial fireworks show, you climbed off the roof. As you helped her off the ladder, you touched for the first time. Your unintentional embrace melted into a kiss. One kiss led to another, and another.

You moved inside to continue the shower of soft kisses. You both fell asleep on your couch. At 3 a.m. you awoke and suggested you move to the bedroom. You were thinking only of snuggling and sleep.

As you snuggled, her sweet smell kept you from falling asleep again. Slowly, the kissing resumed.

You awake at morning's light, both naked, in a natural, soft embrace. You kiss her on the cheek. She sighs.

You notice, however, it is not a satisfied morning-after-great-sex sigh; it is a worried well-here-goes-nothing sigh. You swallow hard. Your Male Warning Indicators have been activated.

"I have something to tell you," she says.

And it's like an anvil drops directly onto your gut. Your heart drops to your toenails. Your stomach ties itself in a square knot. You break out in an Arctic sweat.

This is not good.

On a man's list of SENTENCES I DO NOT WANT TO HEAR, the sentence "I have something to tell you" ranks just above a) "I'm going to kill you" and just below b) "You have a tiny penis."

The latter two sentences get right to the point: You have a teenie wee-nie and you are going to die. You can live with that.

But "I have something to tell you" is worse. It packs bad news but also dark foreboding, the forecast of doom. When a man hears it, he comes to several possible conclusions as to what the "something" might be. She might tell him:

1) "I'm trying to get pregnant."
2) "I tested positive."
3) "I'm married."
4) "I'm married to a Pittsburgh Steeler."
5) "I'm married to a Pittsburgh Steeler, and I think I hear him coming."
6) "I used to be a man."

You hope it's none of the above.

You hope it's not all of the above.

You know it's one of the above.

You know that in the next few seconds, your life will change—perhaps permanently. Depending on the news, you might soon be husband and father; you might soon be dead and buried.

You lie helpless, stripped of self-determinism, awaiting word of your future. You have relinquished control of your destiny, a puppet in your own show. Your fate is in the hands of someone you hardly know. Someone you wish you'd never met. You lie in bed, knowing not what lies ahead but wishing it would get here now.

You sigh. It is not a satisfied post-sex sigh. It is a worried well-here-it-comes sigh on the edge of the apocalypse.

You are briefly relieved by your own gallows humor. You think, "Will the defendant please rise?"

The End

You wake with a seismic headache. Your head registers 8.3 on the Richter Scale. The night left a bad taste in your mouth, like Lassie slept on your lips. You stink. You smell like last month's moonshine and last night's cigar. You are hot, very hot. You are coated in a thick syrup of molten morning sweat.

You look around the place, hoping for a clue. You don't know where you are. You'd like to find out. There's no map that says, "You Are Here." Where's Waldo indeed.

You are lying on a thin mattress on the bare floor of a bad mobile home. A single fan in an open window whirs, its rusted metal blades blowing wet woolen blankets of hot summer air into the dank. Brown stains and cat hairs cover the thin hard carpet. In the corner, an old cat sleeps on a pile of dirty clothes.

You feel sick. You look down. Beside you is a woman. You don't know this woman. From your angle she is average, like a naked woman in those still-life photography books that nobody buys because the models are friends of the photographer, not runway models with cocaine habits.

You wince. You wonder. Who is this person? And why am I with her?

It matters not. It's over. It happened. It's history. You just need to break from this personal Alcatraz and breathe clean free air. You will not do this again.

You stand and search for your clothes. If you can't find your underwear, fine. She can have it. Maybe she can clean with it. You just need to escape this sweat lodge before she wakes. Once you're outside the door, it will all be behind you. You will not do this again.

Zipping your Levis, you look to the floor. There between the Graceland ashtray and the empty box of wine lies a condom wrapper. You recognize it as your brand, and you breathe an easy sigh, relieved that even in stupor you managed good sense. You're safe. And you always will be safe, for you will not do this again.

As you bend to pick up your shoes, you examine the condom wrapper more closely. Suddenly you feel like someone just kicked you in the ribs. It is the sharp pain of abrupt shock, sudden terror.

The wrapper is unopened.

You feel sick. You are standing in the dirtiest, foulest place you have ever seen. You're sure the woman is no different. She is dirty and foul, and last night you put your formerly clean and virus-free penis inside her.

You feel sick. You have the virus. You are sure of it.

You have heard about this: When a person stares at death, his life flashes back. Now it is happening to you: Your life flashes fast before you—from Pony League to prom to last week's visit with Mom. It zips by like a bad short film. It is too quick, too dull, and you know you have more living to do. Life is what you do best. Perhaps your tombstone can reflect that.

You feel sick. You burst from the trailer door like a man paroled, stumbling down rusty steps into a yard overrun with high weeds. You breathe deep the heavy summer air like it's liberty itself. It is fuel to run on—to run from here to there. And there is free from here. Here is death.

You run and run, hoping to leave it all behind, hoping that sprinter's speed will place the experience squarely in the realm of a bad memory. Yet as fast as you run, you are gripped by truth, or what you fear is truth: Yours are futile steps on Death Row, the useless gait of a future corpse. For you know there is no escape. You're walking toward Old Sparky, shackles on. No matter how far or fast you run, the virus holds pace. It keeps up. It stays with you.

You've been handed a death sentence, you're sure of it. This is all you can think about, wrapped tight in paranoia. You have the virus. You, of all people. You! You're a dead man. You've known no fear like this fear.

You run on and on, away from the rusted AirStream, through thick weeds and black dirt, leaving behind the woman who destroyed you in the dark alley of your own stupidity. How could you have given your life to someone such as this? You don't even know her.

You want to cry, weep for a life that's here today, gone tomorrow. Stuff like this shouldn't happen to you—it happens to people it happens to, people in grainy obituary photos, people whose jig is up. Not you.

You want to apologize—apologize to a God you're starting to believe in big-time. He gave you a life and you sent it back like uncooked steak. Like you didn't even want it. Freaking ingrate. And you were one of the lucky ones. Other people get bad lives from the start. They are doomed from Day One. You had a life those people would love to live, and you trashed it. You blew it.

You stop running, out of breath but not permanently—not yet. You are draped in sweat and fear. You look to the sky, beyond high clouds, and ask The Man for help. It's been a long time. You haven't dialed his number in ages. You hope he's still listening. You consider blaming him, then you figure what's the use. You chuckle at the clichÇ, but not for long: You have only yourself to blame.

You breathe calming air, drawing hope where there is little. You think the best, only the best: Maybe you're OK. Maybe you're having a life lesson here. Maybe this is one of those "tests." God gives these tests a lot. Maybe you'll live through this thing, all the wiser.

Despite hope in quick flashes, you are worried still—so worried that later, you can't eat, can't sleep, can't think of anything but the life you may have trashed for a few moments you don't remember. You had always imagined death a noble passage from earth to the hereafter, a moment that represented your convictions, not your idiocy. You imagined it a moment of proud retrospect, not regret, a moment's reflection on what was, not what might have been. You imagined death the last chapter of a great book, your book, one in which you lived all your adventures, loved all your loves.

Now it's a short story, and the story is ending before it got good—before the one true love, before the weekend in Madrid, before the kids and grandkids. You think about all the cool stuff you'll miss, stuff you never considered before: naming the family dog; painting the picket fence with your boy; putting a Band-Aid on your daughter's first boo-boo. You think about hugging your wife and kids in a goofy family photo.

You miss it already.

OK, so what if you don't die? Death isn't all you fear. You might not get a death sentence but a life sentence: the other virus, the non-lethal one that can make life hell and sex burn. You imagine the despair of falling in love while carrying the poison that stays for life: Deep in love but hounded by the secret you hide, you wonder how to tell her—how to tell the one you love that something's not right.

Your imagine your relationship ever below the specter of a guillotine, the blade awaiting divulgence of your foul news. How could love be tempered so? How could a relationship survive that threat? How could love know full expression when trust is tethered to a lie?

You have never met the woman you'll marry, but she's out there, you know it. Rather you knew it. You have long imagined her face, a beautiful composite portrait of every feature you love: full lips, soft skin, lively eyes that are windows to the spark inside her. And now you imagine that face, its beauty wrecked at the moment she hears you say, "Honey, I have something to tell you."

How can you do this to her? You haven't even met her yet.

For days you hesitate to glance at your penis, afraid it might have a passenger it didn't have before. You stuck it where it didn't belong, and worse, you didn't dress it for the occasion. Now you fear every relevant virus known to man. You imagine them all grotesque and painful.

You know your stuff. You saw the "VD Film" in 9th-grade health class. You remember grainy images of afflicted GIs, young guys who let their loins do the walking in the brothels of Baden-Baden. You remember worse images: all that free-clinic footage they subsequently carried on their penis. It looked like cheese mold. You wouldn't want it.

One way or another, your life is over. If you don't die of the full-blown, you'll carry periodic reminders of your ill-chosen poke. Either way, your life won't be right. It will never be as complete as it should have been, your shot at the good life ruined by one reckless night, the future undone by an urge.

That's life. Life and death on Earth. Drunk on cheap and hormones, you allowed a nameless faceless woman to beat you, ruin you. Now she'll be with you always, till death do you part.

At the same time, you are calmed by the thought that, in all probability, you'll dead soon. This is your life, and you are entitled to your way of thinking. And your thinking is this: There's a certain serenity in knowing the outcome, a calm that comes in avoiding the storm of uncertainty. When you're dead, you won't have to worry about death anymore. There is a certain comfort in that. The bucket will be kicked. Then you can go about discovering what happens to a guy after he buys the farm. Heaven? Hell? Death has its pluses.

You have come to terms with your imminent demise. It's too late for you. You're dead. At least you'll be dead by Monday, Tuesday at the latest.

But hey—you can talk about this virus thing. Like everybody else who screws up his life, you can "educate the public." In helping some other hapless dude skip a premature appointment with death, you can find some meaning in the life you tossed.

You imagine yourself the New Martyr. Your slogan: "From Death, Life." You want to do the talk-show rounds and have teary-eyed women stand and clap for you, impressed by their own compassion. You want Montel and Geraldo and Sally Jesse to put an understanding arm around you, then at commercial sprint to the washroom.

You want to speak at high schools. You want 11th-graders to listen to you because they're missing algebra for this. You want to make them cry. You want to change their lives, at least until lunch.

You want to preach a message that sounds corny, but the message is true, you swear it: Sex is a passing thing. Love is permanent. Love never killed anybody, unless it was love gone bad. Sex can kill. You are living proof.

Your gloom has morphed into wisdom. You are the Confucius of the viral set. "From Death, Life." Your death shall have meaning after all. You want to shout it from the mountaintop:

Sex can wreck a life just as it can create one!

Pleasure isn't permanent, but consequences are!

Sex is a thing of the past as soon as it's over, but a future lasts until the day you die! And in a future there is hope—if your past hasn't screwed it up completely.

"From Death, Life." You feel so good about yourself, you could just die.

Later that day, as you walk to the U.S. Post Office to mail a certified letter to the producers of Geraldo, you run into the woman who murdered you. You turn your head quickly, shielding your face with the large manila envelope. But she has seen you already. She grabs you by the arm and turns you toward her. You can't look her in the face. To do so is to stare into the eyes of the executioner. You stare at the ground, which of course will be your home any day now.

"I sure had fun the other night," she says in a strangely chipper voice.

You say nothing.

"Cat got your tongue?" she asks.

"Cat hair."

She says nothing.

"I have to go," you say, turning to walk away.

"OK," she says. "But maybe you can over again some time."

You turn to face her, genuinely shocked. You want to tell her: You can't kill a man twice.

"Yeah," she says, "you really should come over and try it again."

"Try it again?"

"Yeah, try it again," she says, grinning. "I couldn't believe you passed out on me. I was looking forward to screwing your brains out."

You are strangely disappointed. You don't get to be a martyr anymore. On the plus side, you have your life back.

Later that evening you're at home. You have been granted a stay of execution. You're flipping through the TV channels.

The phone rings. It's your friend Bill. Bill asks if you want to go out tonight, meet some women. You say sure.

Life is what you do best. You're going to live it to the fullest, even if it kills you.

SINGLE MEN VS. MARRIAGE MINDED WOMEN

Times have changed. Growing up, we heard purple-haze tales of '60s carnal abandon and pelvic liberation. We watched the Woodstock documentary and saw imperfect strangers make love, not war, in the mud of Max Yasger's field. The message was clear:

If it feels good, do it.

Today's message is decidedly more muddled. While we're advised to wait longer for marriage, we're also warned that premarital sex might carry with it a viral death sentence. The message is clear:

If it feels good, it can kill you.

And so marriage does take on an elevated position relative to a date with the Grim Reaper.

This, at least, is medically sound. Ideally reserved for couples in love, marriage as safe haven from deadly disease is at least a healthy choice. We've seen it happen: men seeking refuge from AIDS by enrolling in forced monogamy.

Other men have similarly ulterior motives for marriage. Some choose a woman with big hands and a strong back to help in the farmhouse. Some choose a wife to bear a strapping young first-round NFL Draft choice.

Still others choose a trophy wife to look good at company functions. These fellows scramble to win the Good-Looking Girl Lottery. And this is where WonderBras, silicone and other cosmetic accouterments make their mark. They create good candidates.

Still it bothers some guys, this idea of marriage for reasons other than heart-pounding, palm-sweating, just-like-in-the-movies love. Many single men will relinquish independence only for the love of a good woman, not for safety and security or even nice breasts. They won't marry just because it seems like the smart thing to do.

Likewise, single men don't want to be snared into marriage by women who have ulterior motives of their own. We don't want to be lured, tricked, duped, forced, cajoled or otherwise persuaded into the permanence of wedlock by anyone or anything ingenuine. If marriage is a lifetime gig, a guy should get a little emotional about it.

But booby traps are everywhere. And single men fear them deeply.

Most of all, single men fear marriage-minded women who seek wedlock not for love's sake but for other, less than romantic motives. These women use many tactics and assume any of several identities:

1) The Self-Esteemer:

The Self-Esteemer has to marry because a) if she doesn't, people will think something's wrong with her and b) it will improve her status, especially if she "marries up."

We first met the Self-Esteemer in college, the girl from Yakima Town, N.H., who as a first-semester freshman had already embarked on a serious husband hunt. She pursued an M.R.S. degree with a minor in Social Climbing. She copied the class schedules of both the student body president and the starting quarterback; she followed the prez to poli-sci and the quarterback to lunch.

A lot of us campus proletarians didn't worry about M.R.S. undergrads. They didn't dig guys who worked nights at Big Bob's Burger Barn. The M.R.S. candidate spent her time near the Sigma Chi house seeking a Sigma Guy to cut her a piece of the Sigma Pie. Sigma Why? She preferred weekends sipping mint juleps at the boat club to Saturday afternoons quaffing Busch beer and tossing the Turbo Nerf. Most of all she enjoyed the campus whispers: "Have you heard? She's dating Biff Bannister, rush chairman."

Today the Self-Esteemer pursues any man who can supply her with immediate prestige. She's an attention absorber, a notoriety sponge. She wants to stride into The Riviera Room on the arm of Senator So-And-So and—she's always wanted to do this—"make every head turn." Power is her aphrodisiac, fame her turn-on. Her wet dream is to attend the Oscars with any leading man and stand there smiling as Entertainment Tonight's Mary Hart asks him where he bought his shirt.

Her own life has little consequence unless accorded by her beau. When she marries, she won't hyphenate. There won't be any of this "Ms. Jones-Clooney" business. She'll answer to Mrs. George Clooney or Mrs. Stephanopoulos or Mimi Kennedy. She fancies no greater honor than handing her newborn, Junior Van Damme, to the nanny as she welcomes the Better Homes and Gardens photographer to their seaside manse.

"Jean-Claude isn't here right now," she'd tell the photographer. "He's on location with Steve…Steve Spielberg."

Habitat: In quest of collateral notoriety, the Self-Esteemer hangs with fame. She attends mixers, socials, happy hours and wing dings at homes of the haut monde in a flagrant attempt to meet any man who can provide her with peripheral fanfare. It matters little how he treats her. So long as he escorts her to all the right places at all the right times, he can play golf all week and sleep with the babysitter

Modus Operandi: Maven of the celebrity cult, she bears no shame in her quest to bask in refracted beams of attention. She'll do anything to meet The Man—or at least a man who knows The Man. She'll actually say, "I'm your biggest fan."

Queen of the dilettantes, she boasts superficial knowledge of business and art. At parties she says impressive things like, "His dark abstractions are derivative of Dadaist nihilism," and "Money from an annuity contract owned by a person who dies goes directly to the named beneficiary without going through probate." She has no idea what it all means, but it sounds good and raises intended eyebrows.

If she fails to score a celebrity, she descends the scale of notoriety to high-profile attorneys, surgeons, CEOs and TV weathermen. She wants only to hear the whispers: "Have you heard? She's marrying Bret Brinkman, Channel 7 meteorologist."

Role Models: Carolyn Bessett Kennedy, Evita Peron, Larry Fortensky.

Not that we're famous. We'd have to somersault naked through the Oval Office during office hours to get famous. Or do like everybody else and get a talk show.

Guys daydream of fame. We picture ourselves calling Robert Redford "Bob" on the slopes at Park City; or cracking wise with Jay Leno as Isabella Rosselini giggles at our pithy observations.

But mostly we fancy fame for all the chicks we'd get. Not a man among us has watched some green-haired geek play phallic guitar to a bikini-wearin' MTV hardbody without thinking, "Jeez, alls I gotta do is get famous and I'd be kickin' em outta bed!"

It's true, too. We give you Kato Kaelin.

We hold out hope for our own Kato-morphosis. If Nipsy Russell can get famous, so can we. If Ric Ocasek can bag Paulina Porizkova, then we can land Winona Ryder or at least Wynnona Judd. All we need is to grab some airtime on E! or, failing that, claim we're the illegitimate son of Bob Redford.

Some guys actually put off marriage just in case they get famous. They don't want to marry their high-school sweetheart and then suddenly find themselves playing "Dirk" on The Bold and the Restless and becoming a national heartthrob. They don't want to be stuck with one girl when they can have the entire female viewing audience. Plus, alimony is huge when you leave your homespun wife for a Hollywood starlet. Ask Jim Carrey, who's about $8 million lighter.

Fame attracts women, but it also attracts problems:

First, what if by some quirk of kismet we do get famous? We'd have to eliminate Self-Esteemers who don't love us for ourselves, only for who we are and who they might in conjunction become. We'd have to hire someone to ask, "Where were you last year when he was nobody. Where were you when he spent Saturday nights alone, re-reading John Grisham novels to see if he missed the symbolism?" These troglodytes would probably fall in love with our stunt double.

Second, what if a Self-Esteemer dupes us into thinking she's a sincere person and we marry her? Let's say we're a local weatherman. What happens when a network guy—say, Al Roker—comes rolling in to the studio to do a promo? What then? Our loving wife glimpses that NBC lapel pin and boom!—she's all over Al Roker and his highfalutin "low-pressure trough." Fame is relative.

Mostly we fear the Self-Esteemer for this reason: If we get famous, we're absolutely sprinting to Winona Ryder's house. We'd hate to trample over an otherwise vertical Self-Esteemer. For us famous people, lawsuits suck.

2) The Gold-Digger:

She is determined to make money the old-fashioned way—by marrying it.

The Gold-Digger's mission is to get rich quick—in the time it takes to say "I do" to a good investment portfolio. Her objective is to awake each morning just as her husband is leaving to perform another lucrative round of liposuction. She will sip half-caf raspberry truffle from a Lenox china cup and watch Good Morning, America while doing breathing exercises on her on hand-woven Oriental rug.

She will bathe in a clawfoot tub of warm sudsy Calgon and proceed to the four-car garage, where she will choose between the sporty red Mercedes coupe and the four-wheel-drive Land Cruiser, which is very effective in handling speed bumps in school zones. Then it's off to buy an antique lamp at Past Perfect and join friends for overpriced salads at The Greenery.

That afternoon she will go to the club for a tennis lesson from Guissepe, the gifted young tennis pro. She will reapply her makeup and meet her husband at the Petroleum Club for the silent auction benefiting the Boys Club. She will act surprised to see the Society Page photographer there. She will kiss several people on the cheek and wonder if it's true what they're saying about Dr. and Mrs. Vandiver.

She will return to the English Tudor mansion she shares with her high-powered husband. She will take a red pill and a blue one and fret over her fleeting youth. She will slide into bed and kiss her husband on his Business Weekly.

Tomorrow she will purchase an end table.

Habitat: The Gold-Digger's territory ranges from the Galleria to classy watering holes where unmarried orthopedic surgeons go for post-op single-malt scotch and contraband Cuban cigars. Having purchased a junior social membership at Auburn Hills Country Club, she hangs around the 19th hole on Friday afternoons, frequently parading past the table of well-to-do scratch golfers.

On Saturdays she trolls Home Depot in the "nice" part of town, for she has no desire to marry a renter. She attends gala benefits in sparkling Victor Costa sequined gowns, careful to fortify her pageant smile with a few nips of the old brandy. On Sundays she attends Highland Park First Methodist and does her best to look sexy in a Christian-like fashion. At Uptown Market she buys lots of exotic foodstuffs such as arugula, careful to mention at checkout that "it's hard to cook for one."

Modus Operandi: In seeking a man of means, the Gold-Digger plumbs the provinces of rich men in the hopes of someday having a maid, a nanny, a Lipizzaner stallion and a secret lover of foreign extraction. She doesn't want a marriage so much as an extended shopping spree. She would settle for a husband from among the nouveau riche but would prefer old money, for it would do her well to have a surname of some civic clout. Someday she might have a hospital wing named for her.

She lives well beyond her means as a deposit on an interest-bearing marriage. She wears Bill Blass ensembles and drives a Lexus ES 300 as superficial enticements to marriageable moguls. She attends polo matches and symphony concerts to give testament to her breeding and good taste. There she gloms onto social spheres to which she is uninvited, laughing at jokes about insider trading and winking at men who wear Rolex. She shops the men's section at Neiman Marcus, loitering near the power ties and asking handsome executives, "Do you think this would look good on my nephew?"

Role Models: Leona Helmsley, Marla Maples, Klaus Von Bulow.

A girl would have to be a copper-digger or nickel-digger to target many of us poor single guys as her ticket to upward mobility. But we young bachelors do aspire to some degree of wealth. And if we do strike it rich, we hope to separate women with a heart of gold from those who merely dig for it.

We fear the female 49er who, if permitted, would exchange vows with an American Express Gold Card:

"To have and to hold, in sickness and in wealth, till death do us spend."

We prefer that a woman fall in love with us while we're poor. We can split a Chun King Egg Roll Dinner and talk about the future.

Then, if we get rich, we can hang out in a bigger house with better food while the love remains the same.

3)   The Desperada:

The Desperada will marry the first guy who shows interest, for she's afraid he'll be the last.

The Desperada is the human equivalent of an apartment vacancy, open to any number of applicants who fulfill basic requirements of steady employment and a good credit rating—but she'll take most any guy with a pulse. She hopes to marry a "good provider" who will "be there" for her—but she'll settle for anybody so long as the guy can chew his own food.

She believes a woman's place is in the home, preferably a nice home with walk-in closets—but she'll take a double-wide decked with velvet Elvis so long as it has his-and-hers hand towels. She'd prefer a handsome CEO—but she'll take any old Pete so long as old Pete comes home from the gypsum mine each day without ringworm, tetter or psoriasis.

The Desperada is the girl whose photo appears in the newspaper's Wedding Announcements page and you think, "Good grief, somebody married her?" Her head alone weighs 70 pounds, she has a helipad for a nose and she wears a wedding hat that doubles as a pizza tray. But yes indeed, some guy named Hank Terwilliger took her in thickness and in girth as his awfully wedded bride. His chicken-fried, double-wide bride. They will honeymoon at Arby's.

The Desperada isn't always a size 18. Sometimes she's a lovely but lovelorn lass whose beauty masks her desperate need for a big hug. She's the girl who answers the phone on the first ring, and when you say, "Sorry, were you on the other line?" she says no, and you're thinking, "Why am I calling you when nobody else will?"

You quickly discover why other guys don't call. After the first date she shows up at your door with 14 pounds of quality food she cooked from scratch, all in Tupperware color-coded by food group. She brings you a decanter of French Roast and a ceramic mug stuffed with Hershey Kisses. Suddenly you hear the weh!-weh! sounds from Psycho. Now you smell the coffee: This woman loves any man who so much as opens the door for her.

To the Desperada, a woman alone is but a woman alone, half a potential couple. When she meets a man, her heart gets too big too fast. A guy takes her out for ice cream and she asks which side of the closet is hers.

In bed at night, she reads Harlequin Romances and imagines herself in the arms of the forbidden Comanche "Redhawk." On Tuesday nights she watches made-for-TV movies with names like Lost Love, Found Love and Minor Obsessions, starring Donna Mills with William Devane as "Lance."

She would love to love a Lance, but all she wants is a guy.

Habitat: Anywhere and everywhere.

Modus Operandi: Anything and everything.

Role Models: Anyone who is married.

Single men have a fundamental fear of going stag a little too long. The older a bachelor gets, the more phobic he is about potentially permanent bachelorhood. He spends early adulthood playing the field effectively, dating a few vixens, resisting marriage, and suddenly he's 47 and still wearing tight jeans. He looks around and all the available women are either math majors at State U or bitter 39-year-old divorcÇes squabbling over visitation rights. He thinks, "I'm screwed! There's nobody left!"

He envisions himself a 92-year-old puny guy living alone in Pompano Beach with his pants pulled up to his armpits, eating cheese ravioli from a can and waiting for the kids from St. Pius School to make their monthly goodwill visit.

These, in order, are the most pathetic things on earth:

1) Aging rock stars
2) Aging athletes with no hope of employment as a sideline reporter
3) Long-haired hippie guys who don't play guitar
4) 47-year-old bachelors hanging out at singles bars and trying mightily to mine the hip-hop lexicon for something groovy to say to the 24-year-old blonde.

We fear the Desperada for one reason: At age 47, we might actually need her.

4) The Reunion Planner:

Her sole goal is to have a hunk husband to show off at her 10-year high school reunion. The Reunion Planner evaluates a man on the basis of obvious assets, most notably his muscle mass and—can we say this on TV?—his "package."

It matters not how he thinks or feels; it's what's outside that counts. He could deliver Meals On Wheels and read scripture to orphans and it wouldn't matter to her. He just has to look like Tom Selleck. As long as he exhibits no sign of male pattern baldness, he can kick dogs and push old women. The guy doesn't even have to talk. He just has to stand there and look good, like a mannequin or an actor on Baywatch.

Her life shall be rendered pointless if she attends the reunion with anything less than Chippendale. It is imperative that he resemble a well-oiled guy in a magazine ad for "male enhancement surgery." The value of her post-Jefferson High years is tied to one defining moment: going to the punch bowl on the chiseled arm of her buff boy-toy.

The Reunion Planner's life is governed by one principle: The measure of a woman is measured by the measurements of her man.

Habitat: The Reunion Planner patrols the domains of virile, athletic men who look like the guy in the Soloflex commercial. She works out at two fitness centers—one in the morning, one at night—to expedite exposure to muscular men with high levels of testosterone. On Saturday mornings she runs 5Ks just fast enough for beefcake men to run behind her and ogle her deliciously Spandexed butt. On Sundays she sits on the front row at the Levi Garrett Cowboy Church O' Christ, looking especially seductive when she kneels for communion.

Modus Operandi: She relies heavily on mutual attraction to a butt you can bounce a quarter on. She wears smudge-proof mascara to bed in case of fire and the subsequent visit of a brawny firefighter. At the gym she wears EstÇe Lauder Indelible Lipstick and that leotard thing up her butt, as if she's flossing. There she uses two standard introduction lines: On the bench press she asks, "You look very strong. Can you spot me?" and on the StairMaster, "How do you operate this silly thing?"

Role Models: Maria Shriver, Mrs. Howie Long, Lois Lane.

We appreciate a woman who thinks we're handsome, even if we've never appeared on the cover of Men's Health holding a 55-pound barbell in one hand and a bundle of carrots in the other.

But we object to the woman whose appraisal of us is based solely on our appearance. That would mean we're wasting time reading all these Stephen Hawking books when we could be doing calf raises.

We fear the Reunion Planner. Because no matter how handsome we are, no matter how studly we get, there's always a guy handsomer and studlier—a guy so virile, so masculine, he makes us look like Don Knotts.

5) The Wannabe Mom:

Obsessed with motherhood, The Wannabe Mom wants to match socks and coordinate carpools from here to eternity.

Her mission is to endure multiple childbirths and go to PTA meetings the rest of her life, so help her uterus. All she wants is to break water, give birth, pass placenta, nurse, feed, burp, rock, wipe, change, potty train and start all over again with the next little nursling. She wants to sit at tiny tables with other mothers and giggle at things their children do.

She has always been prone to motherhood. As a child she diapered her dog and cut the crust off her own sandwiches.

Now, at 22, she needs to put those maternal skills to use. She needs to start making babies now, while she can still lactate. She mustn't fritter her child-bearing years.

She's on a mission. She puts out an APB designed to locate not only a spouse but a sperm donor, for her biological clock is ticking. She needs a man who will begin breeding ASAP, for she is in rut.

To her, love is incidental. A man is but a plumber with tools.

Someday, her beleaguered husband shall fill a functionary role as thoroughbred sire: "Standing at stud, Mr. Bill Baker." He will plant the seed and watch it grow. He will be assaulted by monosyllabic dinner conversation and G-rated movies starring the Olsen twins. Occasionally she will ask him to hand her something.

For the Wannabe Mom, life without kids is life without reason. Her self-esteem is tied directly to her future progeny. Her quest is to bake cookies and drive safely to soccer games. She wants to send a clean change of underwear to her kids at Camp Winnemucka. She wants to tickle little people until they pee.

Once married, the Wannabe Mom cares nothing of sex appeal, only that her body perform functions necessary to motherhood, such as rocking.

In bed, if the moon is right, she will sometimes roll over for another round of procreational sex.

Habitat: To complete her ovarian destiny, the Wannabe Mom roams bookstores, continuing-education classes and lecture series to meet a mature man who can provide immediate fatherhood. Though raised Presbyterian, she attends St. Thomas Aquinas Catholic Church, for she delights in the Pope's strict prohibition of birth control. She brings lovely desserts to potluck suppers, convinced that the quickest way to a man's heart is through his taste buds.

Other hangouts: Knights of Columbus social mixers, Promise Keeper rallies and Utah.

Modus Operandi: Upon meeting a man, she makes quick inquiry into his potential as a stud. Her purpose is to ensure quality conjugation of DNA in order to form a more perfect union and ensure domestic tranquility. She examines his family tree to determine the pedigree of his lineage—and to see if the family is hiding any cretins in the attic. She has a checklist of congenital defects she wishes to avoid in hopes that her offspring get into Yale. She wishes not to offend but makes speedy inquest as to impotence—just answer yes or no. She requests an affidavit as to sperm count and suggests that he wear loose-fitting boxers instead of tightie-whities.

Role Models: Mrs. Walton and The Old Woman In The Shoe.

It's not that we mind frequent sex, just frequent sex accompanied by graphs, charts and "Barry White's Greatest Hits" to ensure fertility. We have needs, not just seeds. Will we have to do it in a Dixie cup?

We need a balanced life. We're not out to form our own baseball team here. Nor do we require 16 able-bodied sons for labor in the rice fields. Just the regular 2.5 kids is fine with us. Plus a dog.

What we really want is a wife, not a Young Life director. We believe the "to have and to hold" part applies to us in every phase of husbandhood not exclusive of the missionary position.

We fear any woman who suffers a pathological need for materfamilias. We want to be loved as husband and father, not just some doofus who can fertilize an egg and install a child-restraint seat.

6)   The Marriage-Minded Miss:

More than the rest, the Marriage-Mind Miss was "Born To Be Wed." She is a preordained spouse—not a Wannabe Wife but a Gonnabe Wife. Like a gymnast groomed for the Olympic Games, she was groomed for a groom.

Her parents, Dave and Sue, emphasized the hallowed institution of marriage by calling each other "hon" and frequently cooking dinner together. Later, Dave washed and Sue dried.

Home was a sort of prep school for wedlock. The walls of their pleasant house on Thistleberry Hill sported hand-stitched signs that read "Happiness Is…Being Married," plus several photos of Dave and Sue in love despite various bad hairdos.

To further prep their daughter for wedded bliss, Dave and Sue spent leisure time at home caressing each other's neck.

Every aspect of the little girl's life stressed the importance of matrimony. Her Barbie never lacked Ken. Her Weebles wobbled but they didn't divorce. In kindergarten, instead of making mud pies at recess, she was behind the gym marrying little Jimmy Dugan in mock ceremony. In grade school, she was the first girl to "go with" a guy. She made him dress better than usual.

In high school, she wore pantsuits and carried an umbrella. She went steady with the same guy for four years. Her boyfriend, Rick, was a business/finance double major at Evanston University. Throughout high school she wore a "promise ring." Nobody was sure what a promise ring was, but everybody figured Rick had something to do with it. The summer after graduation, she broke up with him when he accepted the Stanford Fellowship.

In college she performed various sorority functions like painting homes of poor people in broad daylight. This, according to plan, would look good on her bridal resumÇ. While denouncing college guys as "out for only one thing," she dated a litigation attorney. She had serious designs on marriage and a kidney-shaped pool. The lawyer, she later discovered, was preparing himself for marriage by already being married to somebody else.

Today the Marriage-Minded Miss regards both relationships as basic training, boot camp for marriage. Now she is ready for a lifelong commitment that includes a house, kids and full privileges at the country club.

"I want the fairy tale," she tells friends. "I want it all."

She wants the perfect marriage, the perfect husband, the perfect kids playing with the perfect dog in the perfect yard in front of the perfect house on the perfect street next to the perfect neighbors with perfect gardens and perfect golf swings. At the very least she wants it to look perfect. Her grandmother is watching.

She wants her life to resemble a Norman Rockwell painting in Anytown U.S.A., where every day is a block party with burgers on the grill and old Doc Johnson on the fiddle. She wants to pat her kids on the head and give them juice in little boxes.

She wants to take a cruise with her handsome husband and find a 14-karat diamond ring in her Dom Perignon, because "nothing says I love you like diamonds," especially when you're drunk on a boat with the man who pays the mortgage. Once a month, on Fridays at 4 p.m., she wants her husband to surprise her with flowers and sex.

All this she imagines in bed each night as she leafs through Bride and Groom, to which she has a lifetime subscription that hasn't done her any good. Every two months she makes out a list of bridesmaids. It's always the same list, though much to her increasing chagrin, only the surnames have been changed.

Habitat: The Tri-M is looking less for true love than perfect marriage—at least her concept of perfect marriage. Love would be a bonus, like finding that extra french fry at the bottom of the Burger King bag. Love is good, yes, but it's secondary to finding a man who meets the prerequisites of the perfect husband: stability, money, good looks and the ability to fix things. He doesn't have to make her laugh, but he does have to buy her a Volvo. She won't be marrying any brilliant young painter with a fondness for three-month sabbaticals. No sir. If she falls in love, it will be a carefully plotted love designed to produce a good marriage that includes Meatloaf Night.

Thus she plumbs the territories of stable, responsible men. Dave and Sue put her through med school—well, one year of med school—because med school is a great farm system for responsible men. They deliver babies but don't have time to chase skirts. Perfect.

Modus Operandi: To the Tri-M, a woman isn't happy unless happily married, like her mother, her mother's mother and her mother's mother's mother. Marriage runs in the family. All the women have done it.

To sanctify Granny's memory, the Tri-M must marry well and marry soon. Great-great-grandma's wedding dress waits in storage. It's a size 6, and she mustn't gain weight. She endures tremendous family pressure to marry while her flower is still in bloom. To hit 28 unmarried would mark her as the family's first spinster.

Thus the Tri-M doesn't go to singles bars except once yearly with friends to drink fruity drinks and pretend not to notice good-looking rogues wearing mock turtlenecks. She believes a man who spends his time drinking the devil's brew is not a man who could be trusted to fix Junior's trike.

Her method is simpler. She is Barbie, and she is looking for Ken. Come out, come out, wherever you are. It doesn't matter who you are, as long as you are Ken.

Role Models: Barbie (with Ken), June (with Ward), Harriet (with Ozzie), and her parents, Dave and Sue

We fear the Tri-M. We dread her. We cannot possibly live up to her idealized, June Cleaverized perception of marriage. Nobody can, except perhaps Ward Cleaver, and when you think about it, would anybody really want to marry Ward Cleaver? Daily preachments on doing one's best might grow stale. It's like, "Loosen up, dude. Lose the tie. Eat in front of the TV for once." Sometimes Mr. Right is all wrong.

Likewise, any marriage would suffer the burden of the Tri-M's emphasis on perfection. Norwegian cruise? "Can't go, honey, haven't finished the fence."

Walk on the beach? "Been so busy phoning from piano recitals, grew some serious love handles."

It scares us. Here we are trying to carve out a niche, find a unique identity, and the Tri-M doesn't care. She doesn't seek a man for his own identity. She has already established an identity for her man, and any candidate must first fit those requirements. Only then will she fall madly in love with him in the preordained fashion.

The single man hopes for love and maybe marriage. The Tri-M hopes for marriage and maybe love.

THE GENDER DIFFERENCE: ENGAGEMENTS AND WEDDINGS

A wedding marks the end of the single man.

It marks the end to disposable income spent on disposable activities—road trips, fishing trips, poker chips, skinny dips. An end to making Friday night plans on Friday night. An end to independence.

To a woman, a wedding symbolizes the beginning—the beginning of being a couple. To a man, it symbolizes the end—the end of being single.

A wedding does not spell the end of the man himself, of course. It merely spells the end of his carefree bachelor days. The man goes on, perhaps better and happier than ever. But the moment the church bells ring, his single life is forever put to rest. Ashes to ashes, dust to dust.

We, as single men, know all about it. We ask not for whom the bells toll; they toll for our friends. Indeed, as we men get older, we see more and more of our friends get married, for richer or for poorer.

We see it. It doesn't mean we have to like it. It doesn't mean we have to hate it, either.

The Announcement

In breaking the big news, men and women go distinctly different routes. From the moment the proposal is made, the bride-elect and bridegroom travel separate paths of disclosure and duplicity.

First, consider the way a woman announces her engagement:

It is noon Tuesday at Soups N' Salads 'R Us. Sunlight filters past green ferns and brass rails as Days Of Our Lives plays in fuzzy images on the big-screen TV. Ten women enter the restaurant for their weekly group lunch. They hug. They exchange hairdo compliments. They sit.

One of the younger women, Suzy, takes a seat at the end of the table. She sits but says nothing. Her friends notice that Suzy has a strangely joyous look on her face. That, they believe, could mean only one thing.

"This is it!" they think. "Suzy's going to order Roquefort!"

Alas, Suzy orders the standard eight strands of Boston Leaf Lettuce with lemon squeezin's. She eats with her right hand and places her left hand on her lap. On her ring finger is the bauble that symbolizes her approaching nuptials—a diamond ring so big, it looks like an interplanetary tracking device. Not by accident, Suzy has decided, will The Ring be seen. She will choreograph the unveiling so that everyone sees The Ring in one exalted moment.

Suzy waits for a moment of silence (this requires patience), then with her left hand picks up her napkin and dabs lemon squeezin's from her lip. No one notices the maneuver, so Suzy keeps dabbing and dabbing until finally sunlight strikes her ring and sends out a beam of light like an SOS from a passing ship.

Women stop in mid-sentence. A fork drops. The room goes silent. Sally Jesse haircuts swivel as every woman turns to see…The Ring.

The Ring!

THE RING!!!

Squeals spill from lipsticked lips. "Ohhhhhhhh!" The women rush to hug Suzy. They gasp, jump and hug. "Ohhhhhhhh!" They grab Suzy's hand and stare at The Ring as if it has a life of its own. "Ohhhhhhhh!" Complete strangers—women all—practically do flip-flops across the floor to offer congratulations. Philippe the gay waiter begins to cry. "Ohhhhhhhh!"

Scarfing the all-you-can eat garlic bread-n'-minestrone special, three men at corner table ask, "What's all the ruckus?"

Compare that ritual love-in to its masculine counterpart, when Joe announces—confesses might be a better word—that he is soon to jump the broom.

It happens like this:

Joe asks Suzy for her hand in marriage. Suzy says "Yes!" Ecstatic, she returns home to begin planning the rest of her wonderful life. Joe goes home to make a sandwich.

The next day Joe goes to work. After work he plays touch football. He says nothing to his friends about his impending wedding. Instead, he goes out for a pass.

For three weeks Joe says nothing to his friends. He doesn't want to ruin their day with news of the approaching apocalypse. Soon, however, rumor of his proposal begins to circulate.

"You won't believe this," Tom says to Bob, "but I heard from Phillipe the gay waiter that Joe's getting married."

Bob falls to his knees. "Noooooo!"

They call Joe for confirmation, but Joe doesn't answer. They leave messages on his answering machine:

"Say it ain't so, Joe!"

"Hari-kari, anyone?"

"Does this mean we're not going to the movies?"

On Saturday afternoon, Joe shows up for the touch football game. On a third-and-four at the 50, Joe catches a pass on a button-hook pattern. As he turns to run, several of his own teammates tackle him. They won't let him up until he answers the question. "Are you getting married?"

Finally, almost apologetically, Joe breaks the news: "Guys," he says softly, staring at the ground, "I'M GETTING MARRIED."

A timeout is called.

The wind blows cold across the barren field as 20 guys sit in stunned silence. Somewhere in the distance a lonely dog howls. Joe lies on his back, wide-eyed and worried, hoping he won't have to call a piling-on penalty.

After two minutes of funereal silence, Bob asks the obligatory but extremely crude question: "Did you knock her up?"

Joe says no.

Finally, Joe's married older brother offers congratulations, but only because it's the polite thing to do. He gives Joe one of those manly, good-to-see-you-again, one-armed bear hugs.

"Congratulations, Joe," he says for lack of something genuine.

The rest of Joe's friends give him a handshake, mumble something imperceptible, then walk around midfield in shock. Tom shuffles over to the field house, where he lowers the flag to half-mast. Bob staggers to his car and pulls out a black arm band.

Sadness reigns as the tribe of single men know that one of their kind is leaving the pack and will never walk with them again in the happy hunting grounds.

The Abandonment

For men—single men especially—a friend's revelation of approaching wedlock causes real feelings of abandonment. It is a desertion most disturbing. It recalls the time when we were 8 years old, and our best friend moved away. We didn't have anyone to play with.

It recalls the time when we were 12, and our best friend started hanging out with some other kid. We knew he had found a better pal. It was—and is—a terrible feeling, to be deemed second-rate.

Now, each time a friend matriculates to the fraternity of married men, we feel likewise betrayed. We feel neglected, abandoned. Our fun and games just aren't fun enough anymore. Our time together is no longer special. It's like the time you tickle your little nephew, and he doesn't laugh anymore. It's all over.

And so it is with our betrothed buddy. Even before his wedding, we begin to mourn his passing. His life flashes before our eyes. Our soon-to-be wedded chum becomes the object of retrospection, another settler in the clan of Remember When. We are left only with a mental album of memories and no hope for a future together. We talk about him in past tense.

We recall with fondness the times we shared, the road trips, the silly nights, the laughter. We recall the roadie to Florida, when we stopped at a Biloxi truck stop and peed on each other's feet under the stall. We recall the time we played golf and found 46 range balls—and needed every one of them to finish the round.

"Uhhhh…mulligan!"

We'll miss those times, miss them terribly. We wish we could call a mulligan right now. Soon, the only time we'll see him is when we're invited over for Ritz crackers and board games.

"Yahtzee!"

With every marriage, a single man is extinguished. He is put out for good. He can't be sort of single, somewhat single, single three nights a week. It's not that we want him to be single, or even to act single.

It's just that we want our old friend back. We want him to come out to play.

The Countdown

Now that the word is out, our pal slowly morphs from bachelor to bridegroom. He becomes a spouse-in-waiting, a husband with training wheels.

His friends see less and less of him. He no longer brings the beans to the all-guy Sunday night barbecue. Now, at the end of the night, there's extra beer. He no longer participates in that most bachelor of enterprises—lounging around. He never sits, never kicks his shoes off. He is on one endless errand, forever picking up something for his bride-to-be and always leaving to "drop something off."

For the first time, his life is sucked dry of free will. He's too busy being productive to be a bachelor. He's getting married.

He has a new peer group now: his future mother-in-law. He's always meeting her for lunch and a trip to Crate 'N Barrel. She invites him over for coffee, and he accepts. They sit and talk.

"So," she asks, "when can I expect my first grandchild?"

He takes long walks with his future father-in-law. They both stare at their feet as they shuffle through the woods. "Dad" does most of the talking. His words are mumbled but his point is made: He isn't gaining a son, he's losing a daughter.

"A man's duty is to his family," the father-in-law tells him. They walk silently back to the house.

While the bridegroom unwittingly separates from his friends, the bride-to-be has never needed her friends more. Her wedding is the day they've always dreamed of—they've been planning to plan it since Chi-O rush. There are bridesmaid dresses to hem, shoes to buy, hair to do and weight to lose.

The groom's buddies, on the other hand, are less than enthused about their part in the upcoming production. In general, men regard a friend's wedding with such indifference, they hardly prepare for it at all. Men prepare more for a short jog than they do a wedding.

For a wedding, they do as little as humanly possible. They don't lift a finger. They don't break a sweat. They don't buy a thing. Everything is rented, from head to toe. It's one of only three times in life when a guy rents shoes: prom, wedding, and bowling.

Despite the ease of men's wedding preparation, they still grumble about it. They have to spend one hour on a Saturday afternoon trying on a tux, a suit of such tailored precision that is has adjustable pants. Their only consolation is that they don't have to wash it. When they're done doing the Chicken Dance, they can give it back.

The Bachelor Party

Few women have ever witnessed an entire bachelor party. Those who do go by the name Porsha or Starfire. Men like it this way. We like to treat the bachelor party as if it's the former People's Republic of China, a closed society whose secrets are known only to those who dwell there.

As men, we want women to believe this one central fact: The legend of the bachelor party is true. All true. It is a men-only affair whose entrance requirements are heavy levels of testosterone and the unique ability to wear a necktie on your head. You should also be able to hold your liquor and at least consider having sex with a professional.

A woman, we like to think, just wouldn't get it.

The bachelor party is Men's Night Out, we tell them—The Final Night Out. "So go unwrap your satin teddies and your pink camisoles or whatever it is you do at your lame-ass bachelorette party. Go club-hopping in your condom-covered bridal veils. Go kiss the best-looking guy at the bar. Go stand on a table and sing 'I Am Woman.' Go do whatever your cute bachelorette friends tell you to do on your last night as a naughty single gal. Go share your dirty little secrets and talk about—tee-hee!—penises."

We're men! And by gum, we're going to act like it—at least for one more night. That frozen concoction will help us hang on.

The bachelor party, we tell them, is the most important night our lives. It is one final, glorious night where best friends leave in arm-in-arm, whistling as if we're off to build the bridge over the River Kwai. In our everlasting attempt to reaffirm our masculinity, we love to show 'em we're off to war to fight it out in the trenches of bachelorhood one more time. Brotherhood, we tell them, is the essence of the bachelor party.

It is the irony of life as a single man—the dichotomy of illusion vs. reality. Men are funny this way. For men, life is the existential equivalent of stuffing a sock in our jeans. We want to prove how manly we are, even if we have to fake it. The bachelor party is immensely helpful toward that end.

In the typical disguise of true intentions, we men give the impression that the bachelor party is an important rite of passage from the joys of single life to the rigors of married life. It is the final show of solidarity among bachelor pals, the culmination of the informal fraternity of single men, Game 7 of the stag lifestyle. We are comrades in arms, soldiers fighting the good fight, and we are not going gently into that good night.

We are single men, hanging out with our nearly married pal, smoking, drinking and whooping it up, but there in the midst of it all, amid all the twists and shouts, we secretly wonder if he is going to be happier than we are. But no, we won't let on. No sir, we won't let on.

"Beer bong!"

We won't let on to women, either. We won't let on that a bachelor would ever question the stag lifestyle, nor any of its fringe benefits. With the bachelor party, we emphasize to women two very important things: The single life is the good life, and thus we relinquish our pal only with great reluctance. He is passing from a great life to a dull one—from doing chicks to doing dishes—and we are marking the occasion with one serious party. He is going out with a bang.

"He's yours now," we tell the women with eyebrow arched. "But we give him up under formal protest. If it turns out that you don't want him, we have first dibs."

Thus the bachelor party has become a near-religious observation of that reluctance, a protracted display that we're hanging on to our pal by the fingernails. We don't want to let him go, but we will because, dammit, we love him. We love our friend. Hey, how 'bout those Bears!

For lack of a better way to show our loyalty, we take him out, get him drunk, buy him stogies, feed him beef, take him to a titty bar, buy him additional shots of liquor, buy him table dances, give him a woody and generally embarrass the hell out of him. This is a man's way of showing his affection, a true loving embrace disguised in sordid macho behavior:

"We love you, man! Now get yer ass up on stage and let Bambi give you a whuppin' you'll never forget! Hooo-weee!"

In our efforts at Clint Eastwood machismo, we forego any attempts at sweet reminiscence. Our final occasion together as friends—the Last Supper of the Disciples of Stag—should be spent remembering the good times: fun in the treehouse, the first double-date, the state football championship. Instead we spend the entire time staring at a half-naked 19-year-old who will pretend we are the most important men in her life so long as we feed her dollar bills.

Indeed, the titty-bar phase of the bachelor party is an attempt to show our betrothed buddy just what he'll be missing:

"Lookee there, my soon-to-be married friend! Put yer hands together for DesirÇe on center stage, dude, and kiss it goodbye!"

What he'll be really be missing is this: A pair of scientifically upgraded breasts that belong to a 19-year-old part-time college student working to make payments on her Toyota Camry.

The bachelor party is the last hurrah. It is a symbolic parting of the ways: a chance to show our unfortunate pal what he's giving up, and a chance to confirm what we as lucky single men get to hold onto: Good times. Freedom. Sex with lots of women.

Secretly, we want him to be so overwhelmed by our presentation that he summarily rejects his fiancÇe and rejoins us in the Clan of Single Men. We want him to renounce his engagement and declare his loyalty to us, his true friends, the most important people in his life.

We had hoped the bachelor party would do the trick: It would show our friend exactly what he was leaving behind. It did.

Now he is convinced. It's time to move on with his life.

Spinning miserably in bed that night, depressed and alone, just before the whiskey-induced fuzz fades to sleep, we wish we were him.

The Wedding

Once upon time, a man awoke on the morning of his wedding day. He decided to spend the day hiking with friends. They would scale a mountain and be back by oh, say, 5 or 6. He'd have plenty of time to get ready for his wedding. He already had his clothes laid out. His socks had been pre-matched. All he'd have to do was shower.

When he returned from the hike, he called his bride-to-be. He was scraping volcanic ash from between his toes when she answered. He asked what she'd been doing. She said she had spent the day getting her hair and makeup done.

"Wow," he said, examining a chunk of magnetite from under a toenail. "You're going all out for this!"

Men just don't get weddings.

It's just part of being a man. We don't get weddings, even though we constitute a good 50 percent of the marriage itself.

It doesn't matter if we're a groom, a groomsman or an innocent bystander. We're men, and we just don't get weddings.

It's really not our fault. We plead not guilty. In our formative years, our one impression of a wedding was of Dad complaining how the whole thing would make him miss the Alabama-Auburn game. We thought, "How bad could this be?" Then Mom shipped us off to the bathtub and sentenced us to five hours in our Sunday best.

As we got older, it got better. As teenagers we saw the wedding as a chance to sneak beer from "Chester" the bartender at the VFW hall. Chester would smuggle us a lukewarm Pabst in a red plastic cup. We'd stand in the corner and suck it back in two quick gulps. Then, for reasons that were exciting and new, we'd sprint to the dance floor to do the Hokey Pokey. That's what it was all about.

A year or two later, our older brother told us how easy it was to score at a wedding. We chugged leftover champagne and started hitting on cousins twice removed.

Today, for the single man, the wedding has evolved into a number of things: a reunion of old friends; a pageant of new girls; a waste of a perfectly good Saturday. The wedding can be work, play, or just plain Purgatory. But typically, the single man justifies his wedding attendance by shamelessly indulging in the traditional reception benefits of wine, women and song.

For the groom, however, those days are over. He doesn't get to pal around and drink beer anymore. He doesn't get to hit on girls. He is getting married.

Fortunately, some apostle had the foresight to make the family of the bride responsible for the wedding. If it were the groom's responsibility, the whole affair might be held in somebody's back yard around a barbecue grill.

"Guest book to the right! Pork 'n beans to the left!"

Later the best man would pass the veil for beer money.

Men tend to have trouble understanding the expense and effort that goes into a wedding. For instance, even the groom pays little attention to his attire. Here he is on the most important day of his life, and he rents—rents—a tux used the week before by a guy named "Booger" at the Cedar Valley High junior prom.

The woman, on the other hand, wears a priceless one-of-a-kind dress that has been worn just once—on her mother's wedding day. The wedding gown is a garment of such beauty and elegance that entire magazines are devoted it. It is enough to make grown women cry.

For a bride, a wedding is show business. It is her day, the one time in her life when all eyes are focused on her, when everyone turns to view the bride as she walks angelic into that good chapel.

The groom just stands there in his rented raiment and waits.

For the single man, an afternoon at a wedding is not exactly a 50-yard-line seat at the Rose Bowl. Our perspective of the wedding usually hinges on our relationship with bride or groom. For the young bachelor, there are various reasons to attend a wedding, and reactions and emotions associated with each—reactions and emotions exclusive to the single man, especially one who contemplates his own possible date at the altar:

1) You Are Dragged There By Your Girlfriend:

A girlfriend is nice to have and hold. She is good to have around. Like hackey-sack, she provides countless hours of good clean fun.

However, a girlfriend can also subject a boyfriend to sudden schedule changes and long weekends of overtime. A boyfriend often must go above and beyond the call of duty, even when he doesn't want to.

That is what's happening now. You do not want to attend an upcoming wedding, but orders have been issued from the top. It is the wedding of a woman who worked with your girlfriend five years ago. Five years ago. You ask your girl, "Isn't there a statute of limitations on this sort of thing? Don't women cross each other off the list if they haven't shared a slice of cheesecake in the last half decade?"

Well, mister, just for that little comment, you're going.

On Saturday, the Seventh of Octobour, she drags your insensitive male butt to the wedding. This is the punishment phase: You will watch a man you've never seen marry a woman you've never seen, and then you will eat cake.

You enter the Christ The King sanctuary and stand in the foyer, jingling your keys, shifting your weight, restless, like a kid held after school. An usher approaches, plastic smile plastered to his plastic face. "Friend of the bride or groom?"

"Neither," you reply.

Your girlfriend pinches your arm, which confirms you are not dreaming.

"Friend of the bride," she says to the usher, polite as ever.

The guy takes your girl by the arm and turns to walk her down the aisle, leaving you behind. You're thinking, "Wait a second, pal. She's mine.

Hands off!" You want to wipe that stupid grin off his face, but suddenly you think the better of it. You're in church, and there's probably a rule.

You sit in the middle of a long wooden pew. Organ music is playing already. This means only one thing: The church is under an Ave Maria Watch.

You sit there, hands in your lap, back erect. For some reason—you don't know why—you always sit erect at weddings. You do the same thing when you're pulled over by a cop. You wonder if there's a connection.

Throughout the church, women whisper. Men sit silent. There are no Coming Attractions to keep them occupied. Women look at other women, judging them from head to toe. Men look at their watch.

You notice your girlfriend nodding, smiling and waving at numerous women. She even waves at women she hates. This is what women do. You wave at nobody. This is what men do. Seeing a guy at a wedding is like seeing a guy at the Think Hard Impotence Clinic—attendance is a sign of weakness, and you do the other guy the favor of pretending he's not there. There is only one reason you would wave at another guy at a wedding: If he were walking the aisles selling peanuts and beer. "Yo! Right here! Large Bud and a bag of unsalted, and make it snappy!"

You look at your watch, thinking of the weather outside. The day is sunny and warm, with a nice breeze from the south, which means you could easily carry the sand trap on No. 5 at Shady Oaks.

You make a mental return from the course in time to see the best man fishing around in his tux, like he's looking for his money clip. He pulls out a ring, and maybe he's thinking it's more like a pair of handcuffs. He hands it over anyway.

The bridesmaids lean to see. The groomsmen stare at the floor. Your girlfriend reaches over and puts a hand on your knee, then slides it halfway up your thigh. Yowza!

"Do you take this woman," the pastor says, "to be your lawfully wedded wife?"

"I do."

Your girlfriend grabs your hand.

"Do you take this man," he says, "to be your lawfully wedded husband?"
"I do."
Your girlfriend holds it tight.
"I pronounce you man and wife. You may kiss the bride."
Your girlfriend squeezes your hand, now tighter than ever. You realize that she has a very firm grip on you.
You look at your watch. You wonder when your time will come.

2) Groom Is A Little Brother:

The strange thing about little brothers is that they grow up. They become adults with adult-like lives. You thought your little brother would remain a little person all his life, primarily for your benefit. This would give you several decades of brotherly pleasures such as fishing for crawdads. You could watch movies like The Apple Dumpling Gang without fear of embarrassment, for your brother would always be at your side, a little guy forever.

You discover, however, that little brothers are subject to the laws of nature too, like everyone else you've ever known. You find that Mother Nature doesn't bend the rules to accommodate big brothers who still want to play catch. Little brothers age in accordance with the chronological order of things. They grow like weeds.

One day you're helping him build a Lincoln Log fort and the next day he's marrying a former USC cheerleader with a degree in mechanical engineering. One day you are lord of his universe, large and strong, commanding his awe and whipping him at H-O-R-S-E, and the next day you are sitting in the first pew of First United Methodist, secretly lusting after his bride.

You can't believe the speed at which the little guy went from boy to man. He was a meteor.

You weren't finished playing army with him. You weren't finished playing ball. Here he is a man, and you want to give him another piggy-back ride. You want to have another pillow fight. You want all that and more, but cruel time kidnapped him and gave him a new identity.

Now you're looking for the rewind button, and all there is is fast-forward.

Reality hits hard: The days of crawdads and baseball are over, moved to memory's attic. He is your little brother, but the little guy is gone.

You wanted him to look up to you always, to regard you not as superior but older and wiser still. Now he is your equal. Like you, he is a man. You are older, merely older, and wondering if you should grow up.

3) Groom Is A Distant Cousin:

Distant cousins are peripheral people. Like satellites, they hang on the edge of your universe, occasionally sending back photos of the Grand Canyon.

"Saw Hoover Dam yesterday, Grand Canyon today...awesome! ...makes you feel so insignificant! ...wish you were here!"

Wish you were here? That's a curious sentiment. You see each other exactly once a year to exchange cheap Christmas gifts such as golf calendars. You fall into each other's "oops-better-send-one" category of birthday cards.

But for the sake of family relations, you continue your cousinly correspondence and promise to visit next year. Next year comes in handy because next year is always next year.

One day you trundle to the mailbox to check out the new pizza coupons. You leaf through equal-or-lesser-value-free offers—yada-yada-yada—until you come across a personal letter. You're excited. It's not often your name is written in cursive on a small mother-of-pearl envelope with a raised insignia of an American Beauty rose. This, you reckon, is no invitation to the Harley-Davidson Club's annual Panty Toss N' Brassierre Fling.

You open the envelope. You mutter, "Hmmmm." It is an honest expression of bewilderment. Someone you have never heard of is requesting the "honour of your presence."

"Who the hell are Mr. and Mrs. Jackson Clay Cadwallader?" you ask yourself. "And who the hell is their daughter Tiffany Ann Cadwallader? And why on earth do they request the honour of my presence at Davis Avenue Presbyterian Church at seven o'clock in the evening of the twenty-seventh day of the month of January in the Year Of Our Lord Nineteen Hundred And Ninety-Nine?"

Puzzled, you do that thing people do when confused by a letter—turn it over and look at the back of it, as if the back held some secret decoder to the letter's hidden meaning. But alas, the back bears no mystic secrets. You look at the card once more.

It is hard to read. The script is very fancy, as if a feather-quill pen had been dipped in India ink and guided in the noble strokes of English literati. You'd prefer that it were typed and double-spaced.

Finally you look toward the bottom of the invitation. There is another name, a name you don't recognize: "Weatherby Theodore Mayfield."

Weatherby Theodore Mayfield? You don't know any Weatherby Theodore Mayfield.

You do know a Teddy Mayfield. He's your cousin.

And then it hits you squarely. Of course! Your cousin! Your Hoover-Dam, golf-calendar cousin! Weatherby Theodore Mayfield—a.k.a. Cousin Teddy—is getting married. Son of a gun! And he wants you to come.

Well, why not? What's one day of your life to grease the gears of family relations? Cousin Teddy thought well enough to invite you, so why not bestow him the honour of your presence?

But who's kidding who. You know exactly why you're going to Cousin Teddy's wedding, and it has nothing to do with Cousin Teddy. It has to do with bridesmaids.

Emotional bridesmaids. Vulnerable bridesmaids.

You've been around the block. You're thinking, "Wedding schmedding." It's the reception you want. Free margaritas and boiled shrimp can make for a very good night, even if you do have to wear a name tag. But what really makes a reception cook is an impressive lineup of bridesmaids. In particular, unmarried bridesmaids.

In everyday life a bridesmaid is no different than any other woman. But once she dons that taffeta dress, she's ripe for picking. No greater combination of factors could benefit the single man: The bridesmaid is single; she is dressed to the hilt (or so she thinks); her hair is done by a pro; her makeup is perfect; she just witnessed one of her best friends get married and, to top it off, she's tanked on Carlo Rossi.

Thank you, oh Father, for these gifts we are about to receive.

You stand there, invitation in hand, grinning at the thought. You sign the reply card, slip it in the tiny envelope, slap a stamp on it and send it away. You'll be there. Bridesmaids beware.

Later you realize you didn't notice the location of Davis Avenue Presbyterian Church. You scan the card once more while smiling in silent reverie. "Cousin Teddy's getting married," you say to yourself, contended. "Son of a gun."

Cousin Teddy's getting married.

In Minnesota. In January.

Son of a bitch!

The Aftermath: The trip to Minnesota cost you $1,484, plus a persistent pain in the lumbar region. Aunt Petula suggested plenty of liquids.

From the cornish game hen you got food poisoning, and from Aunt Peg's plastic-covered sofa you got a rash. You also had to rescue Granny Peterson from an eight-foot snowbank after she mistook it for the ladies room. You lost a shoe.

As for the bridesmaids, all were married but one, and she spent the evening eating Cream Cheesies in the corner with her silent, suspicious boyfriend. There were whispers that she was having "some problems." Not with eating, though. Not with eating.

As for Cousin Teddy, he got hitched without a hitch. In the eight hours you spent at the wedding festivities, you were able to say exactly two words to him: "Congratulations, Teddy." Which came out to $742 per word.

Anyway, he'll like the Pebble Beach Golf Calendar. It is this year's model.

4) You Are A Secondary Friend:

After a guy graduates from college, he spends the next 10 years of his life on Postal Calligraphy Alert. Every few months he leafs through his mail and there, between the phone bill and the delinquent-payment notice, is an envelope that looks strikingly like the Magna Carta. It is yet another wedding invitation from a college chum.

This, you discover, is the post-graduate price for numerous college friendships. It is a high price indeed. In many cases, it is more expensive than college itself.

The irony is obvious. One reason a guy goes to college is so he can get out and make scads of money. Then, after graduation, he spends a great deal of that money going to the weddings of friends from college.

Thus for a decade, a college degree is just a break-even deal. You learn to earn—and you earn to fly Delta.

The problem, of course, is not the close friends who are getting married. You love those guys, and you'd attend their weddings regardless of location, cost or circumstance. No, the problem is the Secondary Friend who is getting married.

The Secondary Friend is the guy who, throughout college, dwelt perpetually on the second tier of friendship. You seldom hung out, just you and he. Always there were lots of people around, joking, talking, laughing; he was just one of them, always included, always welcome, but not always vital. You like the guy, but you wouldn't stop a bullet for him.

If the wedding of a Secondary Friend is nearby, no problem. You'll put on a tie and blow a Saturday. But if it's in Baltimore or Bug Tussle—

problem. You feel obligated to go. Other friends will be there, and you don't want to be labeled cheap, poor or just plain crappy.

Q: "Why isn't Bob here?"

A: "He's cheap, poor and just plain crappy."

The real reason, of course, is cash. Dinero. Wampum. You're not poor, but frequent wedding attendance is cutting into your enchilada money. The fact is, 2.8 was your GPA; it's not your annual millions. You do not have your own infomercial. You do not have a trust fund, other than Grandad's silver dollar. And unlike the classmate who never came to class, you were not taken No. 2 in the NFL Draft.

You do not have that kind of money. And the money you do have, well, you'd like to use it on your own wedding, not somebody else's. You'd like to take your future bride to Oahu, not Lake Ufalla. You want a real wedding and a real honeymoon, not cheap substitutes.

You do attend plenty of Secondary Friend Weddings, those that take place in the immediate vicinity—that is, within a 60-mile radius of your front porch. Usually you decide to go at the last minute, primarily out of guilt that you had already decided not to go. Inevitably, just as you're walking out the front door for a round of golf, you mutter the mantra of guilt-stricken man: "Awwww, crap, I'd better go to the damn wedding, dammit." It is not a poetic mantra.

Because of your last-second epiphany, you're always 3.7 minutes late getting to the church. After putting on your shoes in the car, you're another 2.2 minutes late getting into the church. After an additional 2.4 minutes spent perusing the names in the wedding register—"Cool, Dave's here"—you sneak in through the sanctuary door. But of course the door has a squeaky hinge—eeeeeeeeeeeeeep!

Worse than a standard eep, the church-door eep has an awful echo that sounds abundantly similar to a civil defense siren. Once the horrid sound has faded to its final reverb, you notice that everyone has turned to identify the perpetrator—everyone except Grandma Greisenschmidt, who didn't hear it.

You nod in slight embarrassment—"Yep, it's me. Hidy ho!"—then skulk quietly to a seat on the back row. You sit, then quickly stand to take a seat on the second-to-last row. You do this each time you go alone to a wedding, and you know why: You don't want to be mistaken as a church elder or choir director who just happened to wander in from next door. By sitting on the second-to-last row, you send a signal that you're at the right function, and you know it. You are here, in attendance, and you want credit for it. It's like a bartender taking notice of your tip. It counts.

Now, sitting alone on the second-to-last row, you are manifestly identifiable as the Single Guy: always late, always straightening the tie, always smoothing the hair, always checking the watch, always looking around, always oblivious to the ceremony itself. But at least it's for credit.

In an extended visual promenade, you look across the center aisle. On the other side, also seated on the second-to-last row, is another Single Guy. You know this because he is smoothing his hair, straightening his tie and glancing at his watch. He looks up and sees you. You nod at each other in a quick, manly, downward movement of the head. It is a tacit acknowledgment of shared status: "Greetings, my fellow Disciple of Stag. Live long and prosper."

Later, midst a wedding-induced daydream, you chortle at a sudden thought: When invited to a wedding, a single woman almost always brings a date. Not so a single man. To the single man, to be seen alone is not an aspersion upon his good character. It is not an offense punishable by pity. Going solo is merely going solo—it does not mean the man is pathetic or even herpetic.

Secondly, the single man does not need to subject someone else to excessive boredom just to ease his own. He can take it like a man.

Lastly, most importantly, and to his everlasting credit, the single man wants to attend the wedding in good standing, shake a few hands, meet a few aunts, eat a few sandwiches, then drink booze and seduce bridesmaids until he runs out of both. He can't very well do either if he's lugging a date around. The drunken pursuit of shapely bridesmaids is the single man's reward for enduring a solid hour of tedium—two hours if it's a Catholic wedding. A good-looking matron of honor—make that maid of honor—is a real feather in the single man's cap. Nothing says "Score!" like taffeta on the floor.

The ceremony nears its end. You watch your Secondary Friend exchange vows with his Primary Girl. You do so briefly before taking another look about the sanctuary. Scattered throughout are several college pals of the primary, secondary and even tertiary variety. You don't recognize some guys until they turn their head sideways.

"Jeez," you think, looking eight rows ahead, "that's Phil!"

The back of Phil's head is balder than it used to be. His legendary tan has faded to a banker's pallor. When he stands, you notice that his once Greek-godly physique has devolved into a sagging middle-aged vessel. Gravity is kicking his ass. His butt looks flat and weak, his shoulders narrow, his expression tired. Phil was a swimmer in college. Babe magnet. Then he got married. Now it looks like he's been doing the 6-Meter Couch Crawl for the past five years. You watch as Phil puts his right arm around his wife. You notice how old his hand looks.

It is striking confirmation that the years have passed.

They are salesmen now, Phil and the gang. Salesman and division managers and brokers and teachers. They have lives far different, far apart, from your own. They are married. They have mortgages. They look like their dad.

5) You Have A Job To Do:

Being a friend is like turning 18. You are officially registering for the draft. The wedding draft.

Friendship means possible, nay, imminent conscription into service. It will happen. Draft Day will come. Someday, as an enlisted man, you will serve in official capacity at a friend's wedding.

For duties performed you will be paid in patÇ and chicken strips.

Traditionally, a man's official role in the wedding is in direct proportion to his rating on the groom's Friend-0-Meter. A 6 rates you an usher; a 7-9 rates you a groomsman; and a 10 rates you the best man.

A score of 10 is rarely bestowed. Mostly you're a 6 through 9.

Usher:

An usher is the worst wedding-related job a guy can hold. It's like being the last guy in the Jackson 6 when they decide to make it the Jackson 5. You are left on the edge, an outcast, shamed for evermore, the shame inflamed by the fact that your name occasionally comes up in conversation: "Oh yeah. I remember that guy. He was an usher at your wedding, right?"

Most of all, usher means average. Ordinary. Mediocre. Your servile status is sufficient evidence that you are not among the groom's Top 6 friends. You are not a top seed.

You didn't make the cut, so the groom makes you an usher. "There, isn't that sweet? He's an usher."

Frankly, you'd rather sit in the crowd and ignore the ceremony, like every other guy at the wedding. You too could watch your watch and adjust your Walkman. To sit with the crowd is to hang with the masses, a comfortable station indeed. To be an usher, however, is to be held out alone, left dangling from the gallows, left flapping in the wind, held up for public ridicule as the groom's Seventh-Ranking Friend.

It is personal humiliation on public display. Ushership says it unequivocally: Your friendship is mediocre. Your personality is so-so. Your jokes are just OK.

And yet even in this mire of degradation, you have work to do. It is the irony of ironies: You must serve the man who disgraces you, as a serf serves the master who whips him down. "Thank you, sir! May I have another?!"

Worse still, as usher, you do the grunt work while the groomsmen get the glory: "Oh, look at the groomsmen," say the middle-aged women, smiling lustily. "So handsome, and such good friends!"

Arrrrrrgh. You overhear them as you deliver Granny Mason to her seat.

As usher, you pay the price but do not reap the rewards. You still have to rent a tux. You still have to get there on time. You still have to act happy. But you don't get that 50-yard-line seat. You don't get included in the wedding photos. You don't enjoy all the privileges of high rank. Bridesmaids, in fact, act as if you're the piss boy.

Arrrrrgh. You do the work; the groomsmen stand there looking pretty. You walk the aisle time after time, delivering cousins to their pews. You shuffle in tiny mincing steps with Granny Jones on your arm, careful she doesn't fall and break a hip. It takes 12 minutes.

Arrrrrgh. And yet, contrary to your suddenly acerbic disposition, you must act more genteel than you've ever acted in your life: "Mrs. Effington, you certainly smell nice today. Is that White Shoulders you're wearing?"

Arrrrrgh.

As you deliver Aunt Mamie to the first row, you look up to see Groomsman No. 4, Steve Meekins, giving you a haughty look, like he's better than you.

You're thinking, "Eat me, Meekins."

You stand in the aisle, seething. "I can't believe Jason picked Meekins over me," you think. "Meekins sucks. As a groomsman, Meekins can't hold my jock!"

You want to challenge Meekins to a groomsman competition—maybe see who can tie the most tin cans to the back bumper in 30 seconds.

But you can't right now. You have to deliver Aunt Agnes to the second row.

Arrrrgh.

Groomsman:

In the spirit of volunteerism, a man must occasionally give up a Saturday to don a tux and work the groomsman crew. This he would do only for a friend. Only for a friend would a man stand in one place for 20 minutes.

It's not like working the bean-bag toss at the school carnival. Anyone can tell a kid to aim at the clown's nose. But only a pal can perform the tasks necessary to effective groomsmanship. Only a pal can write "Help

Me" on the soles of the groom's shoes. Only a pal can copy door keys to the Honeymoon Suite. Only a pal can give a hoot.

There is, in fact, an unwritten but requisite relationship at work: Never would a man occupy the groomsman position for anyone but a pal; and never would a groom solicit groomsman work from anyone but a buddy. For this reason alone, one should discourage any entrepreneurial ideas of a Rent-A-Groomsman franchise. It's a friends-only racket.

Only for a friend would a man try to look comfortable in size 10 dress shoes when his feet are size 11. Or perform the precision nod-and-smile maneuver to 172 complete strangers. Or carry flowers in a public place despite the stinging ridicule of passing ruffians: "Nice carnations, penguin boy!"

More amazing still, despite the attendant hardships and woe, groomsman service comes at no charge to the groom. It's cost-free—except for the six money clips. Other than that, groomsmen are just guys working gratis. They are six cool dudes doing what they've always done—being a pal—only with better threads. The groomsmen gig is a freebie, a nice gift from six friends to one. "This one's on us, dude. Now go lay some pipe." Groomsmen do it from the goodness of their heart, terms often considered exclusive of men in general and unmarried men in particular.

Something magical happens when a guy is asked to be a groomsman. It is a process similar to when a guy meets his girlfriend's parents: Spurred by the incentive of a good impression, he mutates from a good guy to a great guy. For a few miraculous hours, he is beyond reproach. He is debonair, tactful, charming and, in many cases, can cut a rug.

Dressed in a tux, shod in shiny clods, the groomsman is in uniform. He is ready to protect and to serve.

And so it is. This is the way of the groomsman. When your time arrives, you react with appropriate reverence for the position.

You feel special, appreciated, like when the neighborhood boys chose up sides for the Summer Sandlot Classic, and you were picked third. The selection verified your status. While you were not chosen first, neither were you chosen last. You're fine with that. You were not a loser then, and you are not an usher now.

Were the selection more trifling—like choosing this cantaloupe over that cantaloupe—you might respond with a profound lack of interest punctuated by a jaw-popping yawn. But these are not fruits the groom is picking, these are groomsmen. And you are one of them. You are among the chosen few.

Via membership in this small meritocracy of men, you feel an odd connection to fraternal men of yore. In your brain you boot up images of The Knights of The Round Table and the Twelve Disciples. You envision The Last Supper. You imagine groom and groomsmen similarly engaged in the free flow of wine and ideas, a tight confederacy of friends bound by spoken jokes and unspoken love.

And like those men of yesteryear, you hew to the brotherhood of your clan. You, like they, are comrades in pursuit of a purpose. The Knights sought the serve the King. You seek to serve your buddy.

You want to get him hitched. You want it because he wants it. You're a pal.

The weeks and days preceding the big event pass like slow traffic. So numerous are the dinners, showers, roasts and toasts, you start looking around for Wink Martindale, master of ceremonies.

The protracted prologue is like a long exhibition season. With each Cuisinart opened, with each thank-you note delivered, it seems the prelude might never end. It seems the wedding might never arrive. And in some ways you are thankful, for you still have your friend, or at least a reasonable facsimile. For admittedly your friend hangs suspended in that weird netherworld between bachelorhood and marriage, an empty limbo in which he reaps the joys of neither; he doesn't sleep with lots of women but doesn't sleep with one woman, the same woman, every night. Not yet.

As friend and sidekick, you stand at his side as he navigates the unique ethic of the soon-to-be-married man. Already, at bars and restaurants, he recites the hackneyed platitudes of the veteran husband: "Hey, I can look at the menu," he says when you notice him staring at the beautiful blonde. "I just can't order from it."

You know what he is doing: He is easing into the permanent fidelity of wedlock by pretending he is married already. He is taking a few practice swings.

And then suddenly, one day, practice is over. He is playing for real and she is playing for keeps. The wedding day has come like a thief in the night.

The church bells are ringing. This is not a drill. You repeat: This is not a drill. You stand in your tux, a groomsman at last, and suddenly you realize they're not kidding around anymore. The rehearsal was yesterday. This is really happening! It's like you just snapped awake from a long dream and you really are taking an algebra test. You really are falling from a 10-story building. This is the real deal.

Everywhere you look, your field of vision is framed by the hard edge of reality. Every object, every person, every thing is irrefutable evidence that an actual wedding is about to take place. And you are an accomplice. You are an accessory to marriage.

You never thought this far ahead. You knew it would happen, but you really didn't think it would happen. Sure you want him to be happy. Sure you want him to get hitched. But not now—not yet.

You want to tell the officials, "Hey, I wasn't ready!"

You survey the lineup of fellow groomsmen. Dressed in black, each stands expressionless. The nod-and-smile routine is over. The giddiness borne of ignoring the inevitable has been replaced by the gloom of experiencing it.

Now, moments before The Wedding March begins, each groomsman seems adrift in the reflecting pool of retrospect. You too take the moment to reminisce, a moment to gaze at the past before your friend launches evermore into the future—his future. Standing silent among your best friends, the best guys on Earth, you rewind the movie of your lives, that epic saga of seven pals. It is the sweet comedy-drama unique to every group of friends but most unique to yours, definitely most unique to yours. You play it again, man:

You see the jail cell in New Orleans, a vague spinning image now as it was then, whirling, shaking, dull. You smell the odor still, harsh and terrible. You see yourself waking on that cold hard floor, a Bourbon Street hangover driving a jackhammer into your skull. You watch yourself stumble from the jail, bailed out by your pals. You see yourself: You walk into harsh sunlight, squinting against the pain. You see their faces and they yours. They are grinning and you are not. They are laughing at you, not with you. But you are a free man, free at last at 10 a.m. To celebrate, they hand you a beer. In gratitude, you puke. They give you a clean shirt. They slap you on the back. They drive you home.

Now you chuckle at the image. And you chuckle at your response. You've always poked fun at women when they say, "I love my friends. They are always there for me. They are always there when I need them." How silly, you've said. How melodramatic. How female.

But you realize now, standing in the chapel, that you also love your friends—and not just because they're cool and can shoot hoop. Not just because they're funny and clever. You love them because they're there for you. They're there when you need them. You don't need them often—no sir, not you—but when you do, they're there. The groom will soon take a wife as his companion and confidante, but as a single man, all you'll have is your friends. They are your most important people.

You've never talked about it. As a man, you've never acknowledged it, because to do so would be unmanly. But you acknowledge it now, if only to yourself. Anybody can shoot hoop. Anybody can be funny and clever, but not just anybody is your friend. Your friends are your friends. And your friends have always been there, even if it made you puke.

You stand among them now, these friends of yours, and you realize that in a corny Hollywood way, this lineup represents the past, present and future of your lives together. It symbolizes the memories, the moment, and the marriage, all tidily distilled by a single file of single guys of varying heights and varying hairlines, all clad uncharacteristically in formal wear.

Someday this wedding, too, will be a memory, one that is surely bitter-sweet.

You are not losing a friend, of course, but you are losing regular access to him. The better woman won.

Yet as difficult as the moment is, it will be a moment cherished, as surely cherished as the day 20 years ago when you told your best friend good-bye moments before your family moved away. You cherish it now because it felt bad then—because it feels good to have cared that much. There is pleasure in that pain.

And so this day too will constitute a moment to remember. You realize now that moments are small blocks of time to be enjoyed here and now, momentary interludes between the past and future to be seized in the imme-diacy of potential. Yet you realize that moments also are the fundamental materials of retrospect: They are the bricks and mortar of good memories. Great memories. And so moments are useful on two counts—they are meaningful now and meaningful later. They are like friends that way.

You will remember this moment.

With your friends by your side, The Wedding March begins. You feel a lump in your throat, and quite possibly a tear in your eye. It is a mix-ture of gladness and sadness.

Only for a friend would you feel this way.

Your friends—these guys right next to you—will help you get over it. They will be there for you, as surely as you are here for your friend on his wedding day.

Best Man:

A man's best friend is not his dog. A man's best friend is his best friend.

In a contest between man and beast, it's no contest. Man beats dog. Rover fetches the morning gazette, but a best friend hands you the sports page. Fido shakes hands, but a best friend prefers a gentlemen's agreement. Bowser supplies unconditional slobber, but a best friend has him licked. For Bowser's love is not unconditional at all. A best friend, unlike canis familiaris, does not demand free vittles and a frequent scratch behind the ears as a security deposit on loyalty.

And since he doesn't demand it, he gets it. You pat him on the back and spring for the pizza. That's the way it works. He is your best friend.

Your best friend has been your best friend since the night you fell in love with him. It wasn't the kind of love a man might have for a woman, of course. But as you talked and joked, ushering the late night into the wee hours on the Good Ship Belly Laugh, you thought, "I love this guy!"

From that moment on, you wanted to hang out with him. You could sit and talk, you could sit and not talk. It didn't matter. Laughter would prevail. Laughter was—and is—the soundtrack of your friendship.

At times it seemed you shared a cerebral cortex, so completely did you understand one another, so fully did you grasp each other's thoughts and ideas. Nobody else, you thought, would have appreciated your pithy yet subtle observation about Leonard Nimoy's eyebrows in regard to their place on the space-time continuum.

Then there was the time he finished one of your sentences, just like old Meemaw might finish a sentence for old Peepaw. Yeah, old people finish each other's sentences—

"I'll have…"

"…some prunes."

• but best friends do not. Yet despite the seeming brilliance of his linguistic achievement, he was not nearly so amazed as you.

"Actually," he told you, "I could have started the sentence for you, because I was thinking…"

"The exact same thing?"

"Exactly."

You and he were always on the same page—and frequently on the same adverbial clause.

From the start, your friendship resembled a marriage, minus the sex, the fights, the meatloaf and the in-laws. In times of trouble, you'd protect him. In good times, you'd let them roll.

Left unspoken were words to confirm the mutual devotion, but sometimes words are just empty ships, inadequate for their cargo. They are sounds signifying nothing, for words cannot describe a best friendship. Words are fabrications of the mind, not the heart, and so in description of emotion, words fail miserably. Words merely describe the benefits and byproducts of best friendship. Laughter. Fun. Support. A playing partner. A guy to ride shotgun. To describe friendship with words is to paint music.

Words, in all their insufficience, sure can't describe that spontaneous road trip to Old Mexico. You just had to be there. He just had to be there. You both had to be there. That's the way it works.

Viva los amigos.

Over the years, the depth and breadth of your fellowship has progressed not just chronologically, not just in parallel conjunction with passing days. It has developed outward and upward and deeper every day, taking on a richness inexplicable to people who don't experience it. Your initial fondness for his personality became, in time, a fondness for the person. And now he is not just entertainment, not a sitcom star you dismiss once the show's over. You care about him, even when he's dull.

Together you have gone from best friends to better.

You have shared everything—money, food, laughter, pain, the cost of cable hook-up, the crushing blows of hopes unfulfilled. You have shared responsibility. When you told him the girl was pregnant, he said he'd help; when you told him you were kidding, he said he'd kill you. You shared a laugh. You shared a six-pack. You took two beers, you gave him four.

You shared blame, too, for offenses minor and major. When you tossed a rock through that barn window, he took the rap for it. You told him, "You're the best friend a guy could have." Then he told you why he took the rap: He had played baseball with you, and he had seen you pitch, and you couldn't hit the broad side of a barn.

"Nobody would believe you hit something you were aiming at, especially the side of a barn," he said with a grin, punching you lightly on the shoulder. "I'm the prime suspect anyway. I have a better arm."

After a two-hour rock-throwing contest to determine the veracity of his allegations, you put your sorry dead arm around his shoulder and said, "You win, my friend." He tossed a stone gently to the grass, satisfied in victory.

"But," you said, "I can outrun you to the road."

You both ran and ran until you fell down laughing. You called it a tie.

You were a friend indeed when he was a friend in need. And vice versa.

For years people called you "Gas Can" because often you carried said receptacle en route to yet another best-friend out-of-gas rescue on some deserted farm road. He said he appreciated you because you gave him gas. It was funny the first time he said it.

When you broke a finger in a freak drinking accident, he helped you the best way he could. He typed your thesis paper. To show your appreciation, you sat on the couch eating Cool Ranch Doritos with your good hand and shouting periodic updates on the Bears-Vikings game. He yelled back that he couldn't hear you due to the blaring sound of typographical errors.

And then one day you took him to the airport. He was leaving for a year-long study program in the Far East. It would mark the longest time you and he had ever been apart, and already you felt a hollow you'd never felt before, as if something you'd long loved were suddenly missing. It was like your dog had died, but worse.

You had never taken him for granted, not at all, but until this moment you had not appreciated him—fully appreciated him—for what he was: your best friend in the whole wide world.

At the terminal gate you both realized the significance of the moment. You were about to be separated from a large part of your life. You were about to be severed from the man who could finish your sentences. And so until his return, your finest thoughts and funniest jokes and deepest ruminations would go unspoken and unheard. A year's time would pass in a vacuum of lost potential, the days not quite up to snuff. Life would go on, but not as well as it had.

At the gate, for the first time ever, you hugged each other. It lasted only for a moment, but that moment signified best friendship for eternity. You marked the occasion with sweet words that spoke volumes.

"How 'bout those Bears!"

This, you both knew, was true love. You were inseparable.

Now you stand together, side by side, inseparable, but on the brink of something that looks a lot like separation.

He stands content and expectant, facing the back of the chapel, awaiting the love of his life—awaiting the woman who will be his wife.

You stand confused and silent, a ring in your pocket and a thousand thoughts in your head. The jumbled thoughts are the articulation of crazy mixed emotions. If a mind is the interpreter of heart and soul, then yours is speaking in tongues. Your brain is the Tower of Babel. You are wild pyrotechnic emotion, your soul lit with big flashes of anger and sadness and gloom and madness, and yet you must endure it all in stoic silence.

Of all the actions you could take—of all the hissies you could pitch or speeches you could make—you do the one thing you'd really rather not: You stand there.

You stand there doing nothing.

This is the most important moment of your best friend's life, and as such, it might be the most important of yours. And yet despite its great import, despite all that it's cracked up to be, you stand there rubbernecking it like it's a highway disaster or a peace accord or paint drying. Whether it's bad or good or dull, you stand there like a spectator.

And yet your placid exterior does not do justice to the cauldron inside. Your best friend is getting married, and that ain't whistlin' Dixie. The flowers and tuxes and misty grannies are solid evidence: The guy means business. Your bud is getting married. WARNING: The Object In Your Future Is Closer Than It Appears. The wedding is nigh. Any moment now he will leave you for another…well, woman, which beats leaving you for another man. For the first time you chuckle softly inside. At a time like this, small jokes are prime consolation. "Yes, yes, yes," you tell yourself.

"At least he is leaving me for a woman." A good woman. A woman of substance. Standing on the smaller pulpit of slight inferiority, you bear the humble sensations of the silver medalist.

Still, for the first time, you wish your best friend were a miracle of medical science; you wish he were identical twins. That way you could go halvsies with the woman in the white dress. Instead of adhering to some goofy joint-custody arrangement—"I get him Monday, Wednesday and Friday..."—you could have one twin and she could have the other, and you'd both be happy, although you might ask to borrow her twin on softball night so your team could turn double play.

At times like this, strange thoughts are true solace against hard reality. You find it wear you can.

And so the internal infernal fireworks continue, betraying the best-man calm upon your best-man countenance: Yes, you are faking it. You are faking cool—you are Fonzie on the outside and Barney Fife on the inside. All the world's a stage when you're front and center, expected to play a best supporting role as a well-dressed caddy to your soon-to-be-married pal. How can you pretend it doesn't hurt? It does hurt—it has hurt ever since he announced the engagement. But instead of showing it, you stand silently beside him like a good sidekick should. You hold the ring that symbolizes his fine future and your lamented past; you feel like a death-row inmate told to plug in the electric chair.

Your are the Best Man, but suddenly you don't feel like such a Great Guy. You know you should be 100 percent happy, but you're 90 percent befuddled and 10 percent pissed. You pissed that you're befuddled and you're befuddled that you're pissed. You should be happy and you know it, clap your hands. But yours is the sound of no hands clapping.

You'd been a good little best man until now: You stood loyal at your buddy's side, Tonto to his Lone Ranger, as he plowed through the docket of bizarre premarital functions. You supported him through the 12-course family dinners—"a toast!"—and the Honey-Do Shower, an event so excruciatingly mawkish, you had to excuse yourself for a cigarette break when your best pal opened yet another grout remover. "Ohhhh!" cried the aunts. "A grout remover! A grout remover! You'll have to remove grout!" And you don't even smoke.

But yes indeed, until now, you've been one hell of a Kemosabe. Upon your knighting as best man, you did a quick character upgrade to match the import of your position. You went from Best Man to Better Man. You carried boxes, ran errands, picked up flowers, complimented mothers, escorted grannies, picked up cousins, crossed the Delaware, hung the moon and laughed at bad jokes by bald uncles. You even prepared a speech for the reception. It included the phrase "I love you both," and you practiced it in front of the mirror. You were the man—the best man you could be.

But now you feel like a schmo. A selfish, immature, tuxedo-wearing schmo.

You and he are inseparable—yeah, whatever—but this is looking like best-friend mitosis. There's some serious cell division going on here, and nobody's saying a word about it. A lovely ceremony is taking place to unite these two in holy matrimony, but there is no ceremony for you, the victim in all this. Yes, you see the wedding, but where, you ask, is the wake? Where is the funeral that marks the demise of a significant other—a best friend You are being put out to pasture, and nobody seems to care but you.

Your best friendship took years in construction, built on a foundation of shared everything. It was a skyscraper, tall and strong, and the view was great from the top. Now, suddenly, here comes a woman to topple it in a 20-minute ritual. Here comes the bride, a demolition crew of one. In your mind, it is Rome burning in a day.

This is no year's sabbatical. This is no share-and-share-alike arrangement. When the reverend asks her if she'll take this man, she'll say yes, and she'll mean it. She's going to keep him, and she won't be inclined to share except on Charades Night. You'll get to hang out with him when it's boys against girls. Otherwise he is hers to have and to hold.

It just isn't fair. You just want to tell someone, "Hey, I had him first!"

Yet suddenly, through the thick sludge of self-pity, you find redemption in true joy. You glance at your pal, and he is grinning. And like a benevolent cleansing rain, good emotion washes over you, sending all that sludge to the gutters.

His small grin foretells a big happiness that one finds not in friendship but in love. As he stands looking toward his bride, his face is painted in great expectations. He is a man possessed with hope. He has never looked at you this way, and if he had, you'd have popped him one right in the kisser.

But he does look at her this way. She is a better best friend—a best friend he can hug eternally with no mention of "them Bears." A best friend with whom he can share an ice cream, a bed and a lifetime. With her he is natural and free. She makes him happy.

Dum-dum-du-du!—the Wedding March begins, and contrary to prediction, it sounds to you not like a swan song but a theme song. And the theme is a new beginning for your pal. It's not "The Way We Were" but "The Way We'll Be."

In moments, the good reverend will ask if "anyone knows of any reason these two should not be joined in holy matrimony."

Earlier you might have wanted to say, "Yeah, I have a reason. A good reason. He's my best friend. Finders keepers. Him and me, we have things to do—things like hiking the Himalayas and ballooning around the world—and it is my firm belief that a wife can only get in the way."

Instead you will remain silent and still. You will forever hold your peace.

The reverend will ask, "Do you have the ring?" And you will answer, "As a matter of fact, I do."

You will answer gladly, then you will hand it over—you will hand it over like keys to a new relationship.

And soon thereafter your best friend too will say "I do." He will morph from bachelor to husband, right before your eyes.

He'll have a new roommate, but he'll still be your best friend. You will be separate but inseparable.

The Reception

As single men and official grown-ups, we show the signs of aging. The most telling sign is not crow's feet or a double chin, it is an impressive resumÇ of wedding attendance. We've been there, done that. We are hardened veterans.

The older we get, the more frequently they fall—more and more of our pals take a bite of the big red apple. We have seen it all, time and again. And thus we are privy to the unique emotions associated with every step of the way.

Perhaps no stage is as uniformly bizarre as the reception, with its weird mix of champagne glee and low melancholy.

At the reception, we see the single-to-married transformation is indeed complete. The newlyweds are, for all practical purposes, two peas in a pod. They are man and wife.

Together they cut the cake. They drink the first glasses of champagne. The bearded DJ with the skinny tie plays "Always And Forever," and the young couple shuffles across the floor in a mobile embrace. Women dab their eyes. Guys get some brisket.

We, the single men, move off to a corner to sit with the remaining members of our diminishing clan. In keeping with antithesis of the evening, we ogle hosiery and tell tall tales of trips to the happy hunting ground. Between bites of stuffed mushroom, we glance in the bride and groom's direction. Already they are in training for a lifetime together. Already they are making the rounds as husband and wife, less two individuals and more an entity: a married couple. They do a lot of nodding and smiling, and we reckon that's appropriate. Do it while you can.

In silence, we watch our formerly single friend move about as if joined at the hip. And we are stunned. He seems different, or it may be that we just want him to be the same.

We turn away and, in contradictory response to the prevailing lovey-dovey atmosphere, revert to our natural state. We knock back Molsons and scope bridesmaids for potential rendezvous, looking past the taffeta to see the "inner honor attendant." We quaff the requisite number of inhibition-blocker beers and hit the dance floor. The bearded DJ with the skinny tie is playing "Brick House," and middle-aged aunts with wedding perms are waving us to come hither and shake our booty. So we do.

We can't dance, of course. We're men. Mother Nature created a certain number of dance genes and distributed most of them to women. The others he gave to Gene Kelly.

What we men are remaindered is the attempted imitation of the only dancing we ever really witnessed: Soul Train. As kids, we watched Don Cornelius and the Soul train gang on Saturday mornings and, alone in our room, tried to mimic the loose-limbed boogie steps. We failed then, and we fail now. In the attempted facsimile of funk, we look like barnyard chickens. Play that funky music, white boy.

We retreat to our tables, loosen our bow tie, sit in a solid display of bad posture and knock back additional Molsons. Periodically our newlywed pal approaches our table to introduce us to someone we've already met. We notice he is different already, a changed man, less comfortable around us, more reserved, less natural, more married. He seems older and more mature in a bad way.

Worse, it seems as if this is a scheduled visit, a one-minute social call to say thanks for coming. We're his friends, but the way he's acting, we could be the caterers. He treats us with the same elegant politeness with which he treats everyone. We want to tell him: "We didn't start hanging out with you because you're polite." But before we can speak, he is abruptly shuttled away to meet his wife's Aunt Wanda from Kankakee. He looks back over his shoulder and nods at us, politely.

Bored and disillusioned, we go out to his car and shoe polish boyish vulgarities on the window, such as "Eat at the Y." Then we throw rocks at signs.

An hour later, the bride and groom emerge to the excited throng. Everybody smiles at everybody, as if there was a wedding going on. We stand in the background, stuck in the muck of an obvious observation: He isn't even thinking of us. We, his best buddies, are not on his mind at all. If we had left, he wouldn't even know it. He has other things to think about, and from now on, he always will. We're on the back burner now.

We watch the limo pull away, taking with it a big part of our lives. Our single friend is gone forever.

Our married friend is gone for a week.

Next time we see him, we'll be eating party mix and shouting, "First word! Sounds like...ear!"

After the Wedding

Any illusion our friend had about a simple transition into married life quickly disappears the moment he opens his wedding gifts. The crystal glasses from Aunt Eileen tell him that he has taken his last swig from the milk carton. The place settings tell him that pizza will no longer be eaten cold from the box. Parties will no longer consist of an open bag of Wavy Lay's and a televised Packers game. He'll be using his Baccarat punch bowl, by gum, and his three-way cheese slicer.

His entire haul did not include one piece of merchandise that he would ever purchase for himself. No man—well, none we know—has ever gone with his dad to pick out a china pattern. He probably thought a china pattern was an ancient trader route to Shanghai. Now he is owner of some of the finest plates that Macy's has to offer. The paper plates are gone for good. Even backyard barbecues will feature Chinette.

He is a married man.

When a friend becomes a married man, life changes—mostly for us, his unmarried friends.

Once a pal gets an official wife, we—his buddies—can only borrow him for short periods of time. Our ownership has been summarily revoked. He is now the property of someone else, and we have only visitation rights. We must seek permission to use him, and we must give the new owner a detailed account of how we plan to use him. It's like renting a car from Avis.

"We will return him, unharmed, directly after the ballgame," we tell the Mrs.

In exchange for our prospectus, we receive temporary custody of an inferior product. He is now merely the married version of our formerly single friend. It's like The Artist Formerly Known As Prince—he is The Guy Formerly Known As Single. He's the same guy, but he's not quite the same.

As we drive to the ballpark, he joins us in a chorus of Hank Williams Jr.'s "All My Rowdy Friends Have Settled Down." He sings real loud.

He doesn't think it's ironic, but we do.

Having our Baby: A Matter of Timing

For a man, there is no biological clock. At least not one so demanding as a woman's. If anything, it is more of an alarm—the dream is over. It's time to wake up and smell the formula.

Thus a single man's concern is not that the time is now. It's that the time is right. Men feel less biological pressure to beat the clock. So while Mother Nature dictates when it's natural to be a mother, men are granted a greater freedom to choose the timing of parenthood.

It is one of several advantages men have over women. And most single men take full advantage.

For we hold to a central truth: Once a man has a child, he forfeits his right to act like one.

We have witnessed it in friends and brothers. Upon the birth of Junior, a guy excises from his life a lot of stuff that makes life fun: Saturday beer, Sunday golf, fishing, hunting and sleep. The child saps from Dad any remaining tendencies toward a juvenile lifestyle.

"There's room in this family for only one kid," the new kid demands. "And it ain't you, Pops."

Thus becomes a dad. A man becomes a Man. Any impulse to youthful excess is quickly subverted by 3 a.m. cries and dirty-diaper pit stops. He has to be serious, responsible. He can't goof around anymore. It's like when a guy starts buying cereal for its nutritional value instead of the 3-D baseball card. It's a big change.

A male's life runs in uniform cycles. He is born and the world declares "Let the games begin!" He rattles his rattle and mobilizes his mobile. He bounces his ball and builds with his blocks. He hides and seeks. Kicks the can. Calls his friends: "Can you play?" He plays in the yard, plays at the playground The umpire shouts "Play ball!" and he plays ball. He plays and plays and plays.

When his own child is born the world declares, "Quit playing around!" He is expected to pull his paternal weight. Be a man. No more fun and games. Fatherhood leaves little leeway for personal amusement. Can't meet the boys for beer, gotta burp the baby. From now on, the boys will be boys without him.

For a man, awareness of parental responsibility often begins in boyhood, when 3rd-grade classmates catch a kid behind the jungle-gym comparing his innie to Suzie's outie.

A chorus of kids' voices echoes across the schoolyard.

"Timmy and Suzie sittin' in a tree

"K-I-S-S-I-N-G!

"First comes love, then comes marriage.

"Then comes Timmy in a baby carriage!"

In a span of four short lines, Timmy has gone from tree-climber to proud papa pushing a pram. Forget that he's only 81/2. He has a wife and kid and recess isn't even over yet.

The scenario plants the seed early that a guy shouldn't plant the seed too early. A guy doesn't want recess to end too soon. A lot of guys want recess to last until age 37 or so. Thus they remember that "baby carriage" line.

When we were boys, daily life issued stern cautions against premature parenthood. We learned at Sunday school that the first kid, Cain, killed the second kid, Abel. It made us realize that parenting must be a tough gig, given that Adam and Eve had little else to do but raise kids.

Life-lessons against early parenting continued well into the school years. There was the kid in grade school whose dad was younger than everybody else's older brother. The man was sloppy and crude. Each morning he'd drop off his kid real fast. Each afternoon he was late picking him up. We noticed that he always had a hard time starting his Gremlin.

This other kid's sister got pregnant. She dropped out of high school and had the baby. Months later she didn't say hi when she served us our Dilly Bars at Dairy Queen.

By high school we were fully equipped to sire children but not handle them. Unbridled hormones turned geometry-class thoughts from rhombus triangles to more immediate shapes, such as Linda McDonald's backside. Teachers knew we had the goods but not the services required for parenthood. We could sustain an erection but not a job.

Thus teachers provided sex education, which in that era consisted of telling us not to hold hands in the hall. Later we saw a film in which several salmon, reputed to be sperm, swam upstream to Loch Lomond to spawn. More effective sex education took the form of Linda McDonald's belly, which in ensuing months swelled so noticeably that she dropped out to attend an "alternative high school." She had been captain of the drill team.

In college and early adulthood, we took keen notice of child-parent relationships. At the supermarket we witnessed the young mother scolding her barefoot toddler, point emphasized by hard slaps to tiny hands: "You" SLAP! "will not" SLAP! "grab Mama's Twinkies!" SLAP!

We saw the fatigued father, bereft of patience, yelling at all five kids that it was time to leave the playground. He had a 40% to 60% range of effectiveness, successful in corralling two or three kids but never more, and never the same two or three. One kid was always on the slide, and one was always laughing at Dad's inability to remove him from it.

We saw parents grumble as they took Junior to the toilet midway through the movie. Kids at Chuck E. Cheese screaming for additional game tokens. Parents at T-ball games yelling for a catcher-interference call. Kids fighting over the blue Power Ranger. Parents putting other parents in a half-nelson for snatching the last Cabbage Patch Kid.

Not only did parenting create new people. It changed existing ones.

We also saw moms and daughters talking and giggling on the front porch. Dads and sons eating ice cream and playing catch. They looked happy, as if all those years of worrying and wondering had culminated in this simple pure moment between father and son.

We looked upon them as we passed, looked with wonder and great consideration. "Someday that will be me," we thought, satisfied by the image. "Someday."

Many of us were already uncles, and we reveled in the popularity of our position. While our brother had the unpopular role of disciplinarian, we were the messiah, the kindly uncle who wrestled and ran with our nieces and nephews—then let Dad tell them to be in bed by 9. Spot duty produced a favorable evaluation. We were their favorite. We were their uncle!

We realized, of course, that temporary custody—recreational custody—did not prepare us for parenthood or even hint at its responsibilities. For the next several years we satisfied any parental urges by playing with other people's children. When the fun wore off, we'd simply hand the kid over. We were just leasing.

As we entered our mid-20s, many of our friends were having kids. Not long before, we'd been in the back yard with them, building forts and blowing up model airplanes. Now our childhood pals were adding a baby room? Jiminy Cricket.

It made us feel strange. On the one hand, we were relieved we didn't have that kind of responsibility. We could barely manage our own lives, let alone the life of a child. But strangely, it also made us feel unproductive and somehow less important. Less needed. We couldn't escape the notion that our lives were plainly narcissistic. While our friend focused on Junior, we focused only on ourselves.

Throughout young adulthood, we remained self-centered. We had other fish to fry. Besides, we still had to meet a girl, fall in love, honeymoon in Vegas and convert our garage before we could even consider becoming a father.

More than that, we knew we weren't ready. It's not like getting a puppy. We wanted to plan for it. Prepare for it. Young men often hear the question, "When are you going to start a family?"

Our standard reply was always, "When I'm ready to start a family."

Our operative idea was always someday. Fatherhood would be the product of a personal decision, not outside influences. We didn't want to succumb to Dad's dire wish for a football-playing grandson, or Granny's desire to pinch one more cheek before she turned to dust.

More than anything, we did not want to father a child by accident. Whether by breakage, seepage, spillage, poor planning or bad timing, putting an unwanted bun in an ill-chosen oven was something we hoped to avoid.

But accidents happen. They happen to men—and women—all the time: A guy and girl have sex. Suddenly the Exxon Valdez spills its load. Then they endure the waiting period, that emotional purgatory when the guy, like the girl, anxiously awaits the onset of menstruation. It marks the one time when both guy and girl heartily welcome her period. They practically throw a party when it arrives: "For it's a jolly good period, which nobody can deny!" It's time for the Kotex Contada.

If the period still hasn't arrived, it's time for a pregnancy test. A guy awaits the results much like a defendant awaits the verdict. His future—their future—hangs in the balance of a simple fill-in-the-blank: "I'm _____," she says.

The lives of two, maybe three people hinge directly on that answer.

Depending on the verdict, a guy can go ahead and enroll at State U or start pulling overtime at the Kwik-E-Mart to buy Pampers and begin saving for someone else's college tuition.

The waiting period alone is enough to discourage some men from ever having sex again. That roiling uncertainty compels them to pledge eternal celibacy and consider any of several monastic orders. This pledge comes, of course, from the same men who in the throes of Saturday-morning hangovers pledge everlasting sobriety…at least until happy hour starts.

The waiting period with a favorable verdict often results in a nod to God: "Thank you, oh Lord. Thank you! Thank you! Thank you!

"Uh...but Lord? About that promise I made? I've decided...uh...I've decided not to become a monk. If I become a monk, I'll miss RockFest. As you know, God, I already have tickets. And God knows those are good seats. Anyway, God, I promise that next time I'll be more careful. Thanks for your cooperation, oh Lord."

Sadly, the unfavorable verdict is often followed by a pertinent question: "Are you sure it's mine?"

The lucky ones have only to grapple with the idea of unwanted fatherhood. The unlucky ones have to deal with it. What separates the two is the thinnest of margins: the breadth of latex, the timing of withdrawal, the luck of the draw.

The single man's greatest fear is not the girlfriend who gets pregnant. It's the one-night stand that becomes a lifetime deal. The one-nighter with Ann O'Nymous that produces Baby O'Nymous. And lookee there...Baby O'Nymous has our nose.

We cringe at the imagined scenario: We answer a knock at the door. Standing before us is a woman we've never seen, though she looks oddly familiar. She says something to us. Something strange.

"First of all," we say, "what was your name? And second of all, what do you mean, 'I'm pregnant with your child.'?"

It is a fear most dire: a one-night stand that smelled like bad whiskey in an old ashtray that, ironically, produced a pure innocent baby; a quickie union we hardly remember with a woman we scarcely recall that creates a lasting reminder: a child. Our child.

Single men shudder at the thought. We vow to prevent its occurrence. We pay homage to Trojan and its patented "reservoir end." We try not to behave like a sailor on a three-day liberty.

In the end, we want to choose our responsibilities, not have our responsibilities choose us. When we become a father, we want to be married to the mother. When we become a dad, it won't be by biology alone.

We don't want to be just a father. We want to be a Daddy.

THE FUTURE OF THE SINGLE MAN

Growing Old With Someone: To Have or Have Not

A commonly expressed desire is to "grow old with someone." It is an ironic wish, given the American fetish for youth and beauty.

What a lot of people probably envision is the sort of thing depicted on Dean Witter commercials: An attractive older couple snuggles on the deck of their vacation home overlooking the Royal Gorge when, impulsively, they go for a vigorous hike with their frisky retriever Thor. Indeed, in the gilded realm of TV commercials, old folks are handsome, energetic and damn good investors. They jog, they laugh, they jitterbug well past midnight.

What the commercials don't show is the likely reality: It's the second marriage for both; the guy bought the vacation home with money he embezzled; she wears Depends, he's impotent, and neither one of them does the jitterbug very well.

Likewise, the stock impression of "growing old together" is often clouded by a detached perception of comfort in old age, a shrouded idea that the happy couple will wear soft sweaters and sit on old porch swings watching pretty sunsets from now till the Great Reward.

A single man looks at it differently. In his reluctance to grow old with one person, he doesn't see porch swings and pretty sunsets. Fairly or unfairly, out of fear or ignorance, he sees something else entirely. He sees two old fogies who haven't had sex in 10 years because they forgot it's an option. He sees a musty old maid with ceramic plate collection and a grumpy old man who spends his golden years watching high school cheerleader practice. He sees an old biddy who watches The Tonight Show in the living room and an old grouch who watches Real Stories of the Highway Patrol in the den. Sometimes they cross paths in the kitchen as they fetch Ritz Crackers and spray-cheez.

It is a pessimistic view, but it strikes the core of a single man's reluctance to enter a lifetime commitment until the time is right and the woman just right.

Men like variety. They like spice. That's why men created beauty pageants, then added questions about world peace to legitimize their jollies.

The fact is, men find beautiful women beautiful. It's that simple. There is no asterisk affixed to the appreciation of feminine beauty that says: * "not valid unless man loves her deeply." To a man, beauty is beauty. It is exclusive of intimacy. Men don't have to know her to love her looks.

Nor is the woman required to be virtuous. Beauty is precisely skin deep. Give us a gorgeous ax murderess and we'll find her guilty and good-looking.

Proof of our liberal stance is that even after Princess Diana was revealed to be an adulteress, men forgave her that transgression and still considered her downright beautiful. More revealing is that men also considered her downright single. And in that tiny thing called the male brain, some men thought they might have a chance at Lady Di—if only they could meet her in some quiet coffeehouse on the Champs ElysÇes.

Additional proof of man's nondiscriminatory discriminating taste is found in the pages of Victoria's Secret. Photos reveal a variety of stunning women in a variety of stunning poses. So stunning, in fact, they don't even bother with the pretense of turn-ons and turn-offs, likes and dislikes. Their beauty alone is sufficient, and as men, we find them all equally capable of inhabiting our fantasies. We have equal-opportunity fantasies that mirror our equal-opportunity lives.

Simply put, there are a lot of beautiful women. Life is like a variety pack—you got your blondes, brunettes, redheads. You got your StairMaster hardbodies and your soft elegant flautists. Artsies and intellectuals. Urban sophisticates and rural women who bake pies. Each is beautiful in her own way. Were we Agent 007—Bond, James Bond—surely we could seduce them all, or at least impress them with a high-speed boat chase.

Alas we are not James Bond. We have not the flair and panache to woo them so effectively. So we sit and watch the passing pageant, waiting for Ms. Right to stumble and fall in our lap.

But we men have a fatal flaw: Sometimes, even when Ms. Right is sitting right on our lap, we still sneak a peek at the pageant. It's the sad truth. Men have eyes and loins that sometimes operate independent of their brains.

Were we blind eunuchs, we might be decent fellows.

In our infinite attempt at wisdom, we men grasp several important ideas: Any woman is potentially Ms. Right; most are Ms. Wrong; and the women we see are just the women we see, just participants in the pageant we're witnessing. There are thousands more we've not seen or met. And thousands of new ones entering the market each year.

It's mind-boggling, this rich pageant. In the great democracy of the heart, in a land where permitted is choice of a mate from among the masses, sometimes the burden is too great too bear. From choice comes frustration, from alternatives confusion. A girl walks by as we sip java on a patio. We think, "Was she the one? How am I to know?" In the movies the guy leaps over the railing, plucks a flower from an old woman's garden and offers it to the fair maiden. She blows him off, of course, but he keeps trying and eventually wins her heart. In real life she blows us off and there it ends. Poof!—you're gone. At least that's our fear. So we watch her until she disappears. She disappears but our curiosity does not. Was she the one? Should we have jumped the railing?

Free choice, free will. It's all so hard to handle. Sometimes we wish we were Siberian, from a frozen town called Smirkutsk; at age 17 we could marry the miner's daughter, the only female available who isn't 72 and making borscht. Olga, how we would love thee in eternal fidelity. Sometimes we wish we were from Bombay, the beneficiary of arranged marriage. Preordained nuptials would eliminate the uncertainty of the hunt, the agony of the broken heart. Men under orders, free of free will, often perform quite well in their assigned task. As an arranged husband, we'd go about our duties dutifully, never looking at another woman, just thankful we were assigned one.

But this is our reality, the Great Unknown, the eenie-meenie-minie-moe black hole of romance What keeps us cruising through the firmament is the slightest chance of meeting Miss Universe. Indeed, what often keeps a man from committing to one woman is the possibility of meeting someone better. It is the chance—between slim and none, but the chance that the lingerie model on page 16 might fall in love with us. We might be her kind of guy.

Men are loath to limit their options. It's like buying a new car. So plentiful are the good ones, how do we know which one is right? We shop, we compare, we test drive. We kick the tires and peek under the hood. Finally, after much deliberation we purchase a car. It is ours. We then spend a significant amount of time fighting the pangs of buyer's remorse. We fend regret each time we get passed by a Ford Explorer.

Likewise, how do we know when a girl is right? Old-timers say, "Oh, you'll know. You'll know." But will we? Will we?

We don't want this to happen: We're holding hands with our honey one day when a golden brown Stunning Vixen passes by. Suddenly we are struck with lover's remorse. Could she have been ours? Was she the one? Did we blow it by settling on this late-model sedan of a girlfriend?

Yes, it's sad to belong to someone else when the right one comes along.

To the single man, it is a double-edged sword that Mother Nature spawned so many pretty women. Among Mother Nature's better creations are sororities and advanced aerobics classes. Also there is aprÇs ski.

This bounty elicits both excitement and frustration in a man. While it opens a seemingly infinite variety of options, it also deals painful blows on three counts:

1) With so many candidates out there, it's particularly damaging to a guy's self-esteem when not one girl likes him. It's like when we were kids playing sandlot football and the two captains picked teams, one boy at a time, ignoring us until we were the last boy left. They chose us only because they had to.

2) At other times it's like we're a shark in bloody, fleshy waters. Life is a feeding frenzy so thick with women that we haven't the need to choose just one. We go for them all. When we're finished, they're all gone. Devoured. We have to go looking for more just to sustain ourselves. We gained nothing, met no one in particular. We only satisfied our appetite long enough to get hungry again. We fed our junkie habit.

3) There comes a time when a guy removes his gaze from the eyes of the girl he likes. It is only for a moment, but in that nanosecond of visual infidelity he sees her—the most beautiful girl in the world. Worse is when in this trice of optic adultery we make dramatic eye contact with that gorgeous Jezebel across the room. One of three things will happen, all bad, and each a metaphor for our everlasting uncertainty about women.

- We will ignore the eye contact, continue with our girl and ponder evermore whether we made the right decision.

- We will pursue the other woman only to discover she is dumber than dillweed and has the morals of Al Capone. We will spend the rest of our life knowing that in selfish pursuit of someone better, we blew it with a really great girl.

- We will meet the other woman, woo the other woman, date the other woman, only to someday look over her shoulder and see the other most beautiful girl in the world. And the process begins anew, stoking the embers of our chronic confusion about the fair sex.

In this protracted uncertainty, we envy both the married man and the ladies man. Each reaps the harvest of his circumstance. The married man is with the one he loves. The ladies man loves the one he's with.

What proves so frustratingly elusive to us ordinary single men is that often we experience neither true love nor true variety. The single man occupies a position somewhere in between, in the murky middle, where the women he'd love to love are loving someone else, and where all the lingerie models are nabbed by the ladies men with the latest mod haircut. We're left holding the bags. Often what we'd envisioned as a life of swinging singlehood is simply a life of consolation prizes, a series of encounters with women whom nobody wants to marry and nobody wants to take as a date to the Oscars. It's like being in school and making a C.

We see a man like Paul Newman, happily married to the same woman for something like 8,000 years, and we think, "Now there's a happy guy. I want to be like him." We imagine the depth of emotion necessary to sustain such a lengthy union, and we marvel at the miracle of it. For we have not yet felt it. And we may never feel it. The notion is disturbing: What if we never open the greatest gift of all—love—the gift available to all people without discrimination? Anybody can get it—millionaires to murderers, heathens to Hasidic Jews. Love. It's free. It's out there for the taking. The tricky part is that we must find it in tandem. We can't do love alone. It is not a solo endeavor. We have to have a partner. That's the deal. That's the challenge.

Meanwhile we see pro athletes and Hollywood hunks who, to attract women, do nothing more than show up. These guys wear an assortment of vixens on their arm like so many wristwatches, interchangeable and gorgeous, the babes du jour. And we think, "Now there's a happy guy. I want to be like him." We imagine the fun he must have, privy to so many beautiful faces, frolicking in the surf with a different supermodel each week, answering the phone and saying, "Which Jessica is this?" We imagine the joy of such variety minus the burden of remembering birthdays; the bliss of relationships so short they never grow stale; the ease of changing women like changing socks; the excitement of determining whether those breasts are real.

We're smart enough to know the truth: Both the happily married man and the modern Casanova have their highs, their lows and their in-betweens. We want to ask the Casanova: Do you tire of it? All the different women? So many trysts, so many conversations, but never the soft stroke of love? Do you get sick of it? The door forever opening and closing? Women coming and going? Don't you want her to stick around? Don't you like her? Do you feel like a service? A utility? Is this a game? Are you keeping score? How many points to win? Are you happy? Or do you just look happy? Is that the point? To look happy? Do you want someone special at Christmas? At Valentine's? Are you lonely when you're alone?

We want to ask the married man: Do you tire of it? The same woman, day after day? The same body? Same voice? Same aroma? What do you do when the flame flickers? Do you fight temptation? Do you stray? Do you question yourself? Are you truly thankful each morning and each night that you are married to this woman? For the rest of your life?

To "grow old with someone." It is a simple notion with diametric interpretations.

Bad Interpretation: We envision two old prunes who sleep in separate beds because one snores like a Poulan Weed Eater and the other needs a humidifier. The only time they talk is when they talk over each other's sentences. The only time they have sex is when one of them spells it in Scrabble.

Good Interpretation: We imagine two people in love so strong, it spans decades and grows stronger each day. They revel in the giddiness of having held the same hand, hugged the same body, for years and years and wonderful years.

For the single man, there is much to consider when confronted with this dual impression of growing old in tandem. The inevitable conclusion is this: When finally we marry, it has to be right. Just right. There can be no regrets, no uncertainty, no questions, no wondering, "Could it have been someone else? Should it have been someone else?" Love must occur so naturally and deeply that marriage is less an option than a necessity, an essential and natural evolution, as a chrysalis becomes a monarch. We want our marriage to produce a life, not a life sentence. We cannot enlist the possibility of divorce as a means to justify the risk of the union. We don't want to do a trade-in when we get tired of this one.

It is an idealized view, perhaps unrealistic, perhaps even utopian, that we can enter the most important phase of our life without uncertainty. We have long known of "cold feet," of course. But premarital uncertainty for the single man goes beyond the initial trepidation of the wedding day, the minor bout of butterflies that surely accompanies such a momentous occasion. We don't fear stumbling over our lines but stumbling over our life.

To marry is to enter a union that endures until death—literally the rest of our life. It is a decision that far transcends the gravity of mustard or mayonnaise with that burger. To enter it recklessly is to sabotage the one great hope: that life will get even better.

About the Author

John Paschal

John Paschal is the former editor of Aura magazine and a one-time writer for the Dallas Morning News. He is a graduate of Texas Christian University and is currently writing a book on his year-long bicycle journey throughout the state of Texas.

Mark Louis

Mark Louis is a former stand-up comedian. He currently co-hosts a top rated Dallas morning show on KSCS radio, where he is known by his on-air moniker, Hawkeye. He is a graduate of the University of North Texas and author of the book San Antonio Uncovered.